Living in the Past

Living in · the Past

An Insider's Social History of
Historic Houses

DAVID N. DURANT

AURUM · PRESS

To Diane and Louise

Contents

Introduction

The British historic house is a unique memorial to a way of life that has vanished. In no other country can be seen such a wide collection of artefacts, often of remarkable quality, reflecting a past society. Wars and revolutions in the mainland of Europe, bypassing Britain, destroyed so much of the evidence of everyday things of the past. In France, the châteaux, denuded of their contents in the Revolution of 1789–97, provide little in the way of clues to a past way of life; empty Italian villas crumble in the hot summer sun.

A journey taken through the countryside of Britain will pass any number of manor houses lording it over smaller village dwellings. In the towns the larger houses sited off the market place were built to be occupied occasionally by those same families whose houses were passed in the countryside. The contents of these houses are enormously varied; at Chastleton in Oxfordshire we can see seventeenth-century children's exercise books; at Powis Castle, Montgomeryshire, we can see a state bed in a railed-off enclosure put in for Charles II; at Felbrigg Hall, Norfolk, are pictures commissioned on a Grand Tour and still in the pattern in which they were hung in the eighteenth century; at Newby Hall, Yorkshire, there are sculpted busts and figures in the gallery designed for them by Robert Adam in the 1760s.

We look at all these artefacts and try to relate them to ourselves, and often fail. Why were seven-year-old children forced to learn Greek and Latin? Why was King Charles offered a bed railed off in an alcove? Why did William Windham of Felbrigg buy such paintings from Italy and why did William Weddell of Newby build an extravagant gallery just for sculpture? We see the evidence with a twentieth-century outlook and do not comprehend. To understand at all we have to learn something of the way our ancestors lived, thought, and how they saw themselves. We have to find out how they used the things we see, what they thought about when they looked at paintings, and what their lives were like.

From the beginning the big house in a village was not just a house, it was the centre of the community and provided the livelihood of everyone in the village: the butcher, the blacksmith, the wheelwright and the miller could hardly exist without the patronage of the family around which so much revolved. The family depended on its income from the estate surrounding the house and the income came from the rents paid by the farmers living in and around the village. It was a closely interlocked and paternal society that adapted to changing circumstances throughout the centuries. In this century it was unable to adapt, a way of life collapsed and the end came suddenly.

However, although the way of life has gone, a great deal is left. Sometimes the families remain, living in an apartment comfortably contrived so as to leave the main rooms open to the public. Saloons and great chambers filled with magnificent furniture, tapestries and paintings make it difficult for us to imagine living there ourselves. Here we face a problem, because the historic house and particularly the country house was part of the lifestyle of a very small, often very rich, section of the population who put their money into things no one would contemplate acquiring today. The grandeur of the state rooms at Blenheim Palace is overpowering and, notwithstanding the amount of space they occupy, they were never meant to be lived in. They were there for the convenience of a visiting monarch and consequently seldom used. They were apartments for very important people who did not lead ordinary lives. It was intended that the rooms should be overpowering. How much more overpowering they would have been when occupied by a monarch!

A grand house today will only impress us as being very grand. To our ancestors it would have said a great deal more; it would have told immediately of the wealth, the power and the social and political standing of the family who occupied it. Blenheim in Oxfordshire was built with apartments for monarchs because the Churchills were of the court circle; it would have been pretentious of the Yorkes at Erddig in Denbighshire to build similarly, because they were not in the court circle and no monarch might be expected to shelter beneath their roof. However, the Yorkes were related to the Earls of Hardwicke and consequently they had a state bed chamber suitable for entertaining an earl. Contemporary visitors would immediately have recognized these distinctions and, according to their own rank and place in the hierarchy, would have reflected their attitude to the family in their manners and behaviour. These subtleties are lost on the modern visitor unless the historic background of a family is understood.

Most guidebooks show a family tree, and marriage to an heiress can explain extravagant rebuilding. The Ansons at Shugborough in Staffordshire were comfortably off and married into local families, until Admiral Anson made a fortune from his naval career in the mid-eighteenth century and married the daughter of the same Earl of Hardwicke to whom the Erddig Yorkes were related. The Admiral had no children and his wealth and property went to a nephew who married a daughter of Lord Vernon and whose descendants became the Earls of Lichfield. The architectural alterations and improvements to Shugborough reflect the rising fortunes of the Anson family. The reverse is the case at Chastleton, built in the early seventeenth century by a prosperous wool merchant of Worcester who obviously had ambitions. Fortunately for us, perhaps, his descendants never realized his ambitions; they stayed buried in the Oxfordshire countryside, marrying their own kind, and the house remained unaltered. These few examples are sufficient to show how closely the buildings are connected with the fortunes of the families they sheltered. The original contents and furnishings, where they survive, also reflect the dynastic ambitions of the families who used them.

At Erddig the furniture for a small suite of state rooms, created in the 1720s, is still in the house. We cannot see what the original state rooms looked like because the ground floor was altered in 1772 to be more in keeping with contemporary social use when Philip Yorke married Elizabeth Cust, a daughter of Lord Brownlow, and the family's social aspirations rose. The green, japanned chairs, *en suite* with the state bed, the gilt pier glasses by Belchier, all ordered in the 1720s for the state rooms, are scattered throughout the house. These are extravagant pieces and indicate John Meller's ambitions for the dynasty he founded.

In more recent times American money has been spent on interiors to bring transatlantic conceptions of comfort to a large house when the owner has married an heiress from the United States. The 8th Duke of Roxburghe married May Goelet from Newport, Rhode Island, and the interior of Floors Castle, Borders, was made vastly more comfortable in the first quarter of this century. Blenheim was refurbished with Vanderbilt money after the 9th Duke of Marlborough married Consuelo Vanderbilt in 1895. This kind of expenditure on furnishings was in no way a social aspiration, but was an attempt to bring greater comfort. Again a reference to the genealogical trees of these families gives a reason for the lavish interiors.

These are tangible and material aspects of the historic house; other elements, like the people who lived in them, have vanished for ever. Vita Sackville-West, in a letter to Virginia Woolf, recalled her family home, Knole in Kent, before the First World War: 'The impression of waste and extravagance which assailed one the moment one entered the doors of the house. The crowds of servants; people's names on slits on their bedroom doors; sleepy maids waiting about after dinner in the passages.'[1] The description is immensely evocative of a vanished world. Another benefit that is lost the moment the public enters a house is one of the most valued and one which the visitor can hardly be aware of: the feeling of comfortable isolation, of having closed the doors on the bustle of outside life. To be able to look out of a window and see land to the far horizon over which the owner has complete control is an insulation against the worries beyond. Before 1800 William Cowper noted this attraction:

> *The Statesman, lawyer, merchant, man of trade,*
> *Pants for the refuge of some rural shade.*

Fortunately, although this intangible asset vanishes when a house is open to the public, it returns as soon as the last visitors have closed the front door behind them.

Cowper's and Vita Sackville-West's comments are comparatively recent; the further back we go the more difficult it becomes to understand our ancestors' lives. In medieval times they did not, for example, use rooms for the purposes for which we use them now. We may be perfectly comfortable living in smaller houses with a sitting room, a kitchen, perhaps a dining room, and bedrooms upstairs. Our medieval ancestors would find all these names incomprehensible, with the exception of 'kitchen'. Their houses had for the main room the great hall in which all living, sleeping and eating was carried on. Later they added a parlour with a chamber above for sleeping. Through the centuries the number of rooms found to be necessary multiplied. On our visits to the larger historic houses we tend to get lost in the multitude of rooms only because we are not familiar with the life that went on in them. Blenheim confuses the modern visitor with its many rooms, but these would have been perfectly understandable to Queen Anne had she ever stayed in the Palace. In trying to understand the purpose of these rooms, we shall encounter the first of only two technical terms used in this book, 'baroque'. Although this is more often applied to art and architecture, it was in fact a complete way of life. A courtier of the baroque period in Britain (1675–1714) thought of the court as being a court of the mythological gods. Consequently the whole effect was theatrical and to us it often appears ridiculous. We have to overlook this and understand that obviously they did not see themselves in that way at all.

The baroque period was immediately followed by 'Palladianism' (1714–60), the second of the technical terms. This was not a way of life, although politicians did see themselves as the equals of the senators of Imperial Rome, but was a return to simplicity after the excesses of the baroque. Andrea Palladio was an Italian architect (1508–80) who had a profound understanding of antique Roman architecture and embodied this in the villas he built for wealthy clients in the Veneto. His work was much admired and copied by Inigo Jones, but the main appreciation of his buildings came in the early eighteenth century when the Whigs, who associated baroque excesses with the Stuarts and Catholicism, turned to what they understood to be the pure architectural style of Palladio, based on the laws of harmonic proportion. Palladianism was an intellectual approach, in contrast to baroque which was emotional.

While we are discussing styles, there is one final point to bear in mind. The Renaissance, that period in the fifteenth and sixteenth centuries influenced by newly discovered classical texts and the art and architecture of ancient Rome, came later to England than it did to Italy and France. It was in the reign of Henry VIII that these influences really began to be felt in court life and in the arts in this country. Henry was hugely impressed by the French court and tried in many ways to equal his rival Francis I. However, after Henry's break with Rome and the greater isolation of England from Catholic Europe, new ideas tended to filter through to England by way of the Protestant Netherlands. In architecture and decoration the influence of German, Netherlandish and, above all, Flemish architectural wood-cut illustrations and decorative pattern-books became widespread.

Surviving Renaissance buildings are few but Longleat in Wiltshire is a good example of architecture with a strong French influence. At Burghley House in Northamptonshire, begun in the 1550s or 1560s, the early years show the French influence becoming overwhelmed by later Flemish-inspired design. From the exterior the two buildings could not be more different, but the floor plans were similar and would have been recognizable two hundred years earlier. This is due to the unchanging nature of the Tudor court following Henry's death; medieval court custom was maintained by all the Tudors. The court circle, of which the Cecils at Burghley and the Thynnes at Longleat were a part, might expect to entertain their monarch, and consequently they built their houses with an old-fashioned medieval plan to accommodate what was still a medieval court.

The change came with the accession of James I in 1603. The war with Spain ended and foreign travel was possible for a privileged few, who included Inigo Jones and the 2nd Earl of Arundel; the lifeline of Renaissance inspiration was reopened and Jones, in building the Queen's House at Greenwich in 1616 and the Banqueting House, Whitehall, in 1619, brought the first Palladian architecture to England. The only surviving interior of a domestic building of the period is at Wilton, in the state apartments. The Civil War of 1642–49 largely stifled this initiative until after the restoration of the monarchy in 1660. Indeed the Civil War was such a costly hiatus, both financially and in terms of progress, that the brilliance of Jones was all but forgotten in the enormous effort required for recovery. Recovery had been achieved by the time William III was offered the throne in the bloodless revolution of 1688, when the baroque style had already burst on England. The reaction to Puritanism must always be excess and this was achieved in the baroque. Castle Howard and Blenheim, both by Vanbrugh, are the peak of English baroque. The style, however, was never so excessive in Protestant England as it was in Catholic Italy. By 1714 baroque was being superseded by Palladianism. The great Whig houses of Holkham and Wardour Castle express Palladianism at it best. Robert Adam replaced Palladianism in the 1760s with the neo-classical style that he brought back after spending three years in Italy. The nineteenth century began with the Greek Revival, leaving us with such examples as Belsay Hall in Northumberland, built 1806–17, and Corby Castle, Cumbria, 1812. Thereafter in the nineteenth century, the earlier styles were all tried in turn and together, often in the same building.

From the sixteenth until the twentieth century inspiration for the historic house had been drawn from Italy, France and Holland. The only exceptions to this were William Kent and 'Capability' Brown who created the English park landscape much copied in France, Italy, Germany and Russia, but in doing so swept away the old formal gardens so much regretted by garden historians today.

When we visit historic houses today the majority of us are curious about the way in which people lived in the past, and when I have taken tour parties round the historic houses in Britain I have often been impressed by this fact. Indeed, a recent survey of visitors shows that fifty-five per cent gave this reason for their visit.[2] While many guidebooks give valuable facts about the building, pictures and furniture – in this respect National Trust guidebooks are particularly good and others, often produced by private owners, can be downright misleading – these facts do not interest the majority. In my experience there are many questions left unanswered by guides and guide-books. I hope this book will answer some of the questions.

CHAPTER 1

Evolution

L ittle Dean Hall in the Forest of Dean, Gloucestershire, is a remarkable house and it is probably the oldest inhabited site in the British Isles. There are stories of ghosts and indelible bloodstains on the floor, enough to satisfy the most romantic visitor. Yet the actual history of the place is sufficient without the need for imaginative invention, although it is hard not to let one's mind run riot in such a building and to take a trip back through its complicated history of 1500 years.

The sound of sudden gun-fire within its walls was almost commonplace; two brothers of the Pyrke family, which lived here from 1664 to 1896, fell in love with the same woman and foolishly fought it out in the present dining room, with fatal results for both. That may be legend, but the fighting which took place in the Civil War is hard fact. Little Dean was the headquarters of a Cavalier army under Prince Maurice who had set up a defensive line from Newnham-on-Severn to Ross-on-Wye to prevent the Roundhead army under General Waller breaking out of Wales. Cavalier officers must have waited their turn in these rooms to see Prince Maurice, while their servants held their horses outside the front door, the animals stamping the gravel as their tails swished away the buzzing, summer flies. In fact Waller outwitted Prince Maurice and marched through the line without bloodshed, although Maurice completely defeated Waller at Roundway Down in July 1643. Meanwhile Little Dean had fallen to the Roundheads. Later that same year the Cavaliers were back again at the house, by then garrisoned by twenty men under Colonel Congreve and Captain Wigmore.

The occupation was short-lived and all twenty-two were killed in a Roundhead attack; the two officers, after fierce sword-fighting, were, according to legend, killed in the present dining room. The exact spot is marked, it is said, by obstinate bloodstains on the floorboards. But all this is modern stuff for Little Dean. The present building is mainly sixteenth century, with a north wing added in *c.* 1609 and a final addition of a top storey in 1852. This stands over the remains of a Romano-British building later converted to a Saxon church. The church in its turn was, after the Norman conquest, converted into a Norman hall with an undercroft – a ground floor cellar – and known as the Manor of Dene. In the twelfth century another hall some fifty-four feet by twenty-one was added; this was again added to in the fourteenth century and, until the late nineteenth century, the Norman undercroft was used as the servants' hall.

The walls of Little Dean heard the Latin of the Romano-British farmers, the accents of the Saxon occupiers from the fifth century and the Norman French of William Fitz Norman, centuries before Colonel Congreve's dying words in the dining room after he was run through by a Roundhead sword. It also changed its name from Dene Manor to Little Dean Hall, as it is known today.

Little Dean is unique in that the story of the house tells the history of the development of the historic house in England. Successive occupations in other buildings have caused earlier constructions to be demolished; at Little Dean the earlier buildings are still there piled one on top of the other. Indeed, the only change was in its name, when, through a marriage, the manorial rights went elsewhere and the house became called no more than what is was, a hall.

In fact the names of many historic houses indicate their origins. Cranborne Manor, Dorset; Long Melford Hall, Suffolk; and Rockingham Castle, Northamptonshire, are three typical examples indicating very different origins that take us back many centuries to the Hall, the Manor and the Castle.

We are all familiar with the stereotyped picture of the typical English village – the green overlooked by a church and a manor, with cottages in picturesque groups – the 'nucleated' village. It is very likely that the manor is standing on the site of the original dwelling of the founder of the first settlement in the tenth century, and that a later successor built the church in the twelfth or thirteenth centuries. It is only due to William the Conqueror's invasion from Normandy in 1066 that the principal house of the settlement is still called by a French name, 'manoir', our manor.

Before the landing of William I, what became known as the 'feudal system' was already established in England. This created a servile society handed down from the great slave-owning races, the Romans and the north Germans. It also created the form of our 'nucleated' villages and was probably introduced and established in the eighth century by Saxon settlers from what is now north Germany. In principle the cultivated land surrounding a feudal settlement was held in common ownership by the chief farmers – the Villeins – who had rights in the two or three open fields and the common pasture of the community; in return they owed service to the lord of the manor. Lower down the social scale the labourers — the Bordars – who had no land gave labour to their lord in return for a cottage and some few strips of land to use. Centuries later an enormous amount of time and trouble was taken over dismantling the system by means of private Acts of Parliament, passed to enclose the old commonly held lands. However, until the pressure to improve yields and animal stocks caused the old ways to crumble, the waste of land was no problem; there was plenty available and the settlements surrounded by common lands became our villages and towns. The exception to the ownership of land was the tribal chief himself; he owned the manor, and the demesne land – his home farm. Technically he held it from the king and owed knight service, when called upon, as rent. The term manor meant not only the building but the administration of the settlement as well as the rights of the lordship that went with it. The lord of the manor provided leadership and protection, and in return the villagers gave service and produce. The English manor was a self-supporting enclave selling its surplus in the local market and it remained so for centuries; its wealth was in land and livestock.

Although we can find evidence of pre-conquest England in our countryside and buildings, there are only two families who can trace their ancestry back to those times. Certainly more families must be directly descended but records are lacking. Lord Sudeley of Toddington's earliest notable forebear through female lines was the Earl of Hereford, nephew of Edward the Confessor (1042–66); further back a tenuous line leads to Charlemagne. Unfortunately they have left Toddington in Gloucestershire and are no longer associated with a territorial holding. Uniquely, the Shirley family of Ettington, Warwickshire, have held on to their land through centuries of vicissitudes that disinherited all others. They trace their descent from a Saxon thane, Saswolo, who held Ettington before the Domesday survey. The Shirleys still own Ettington Park which is now a very comfortable country hotel. Norman ancestors are more easily traced; the Earl of Shrewsbury and the Earl of Derby are two among hundreds with well documented claims to descent from Anglo-Norman families.

Wealth was acquired in feudal times by conquest in battle between kings and warring factions, and by marriage to a rich bride. The last conquest was William I's, when he threw out the old Anglo-Saxon occupants and rewarded his own followers with their manors and castles. A wealthy lord of the manor held many manors, and kept a large number of armed men to defend his property and to serve under him in the king's army when required by feudal law. He therefore needed a great hall to accommodate them. Consequently the size of a feudal hall is a measure of wealth and power.

Hall, like manor, is a French word. Originally it meant the main living room. Most small cottages had no more than the one room: the hall. It was open to the rafters and had a fire burning on a central hearth, the smoke finding its own way out through the roof. Even simple cottagers called their single room the hall. Therefore any dwelling distinguished by being called The Hall would have been different from all other buildings, and that difference was size; it would have had a large hall, the largest in the settlement. But a hall was not a manor if it had no manorial rights. Confusingly, a manor house in those distant times had its hall as did all other dwellings and was sometimes known as The Hall. A hall was a convenient way to accommodate and feed a number of people; all sleeping, eating and cooking was done there. The hall survives today in the colleges of Oxford and Cambridge, more or less in its original form, a marvellously convenient way to feed a large number of hungry undergraduates.

'Castle' implies that the building is on the site of, or incorporates, a castle – a defensive building. Rockingham Castle stands on a Norman site and originally was a fortified tower on a mound surrounded by two encircling walls – a motte and double bailey – with a great hall within the enclosure. At Oakham Castle, Leicestershire, the great hall survives from the twelfth century, the earliest hall of an English castle to do so completely. However, it was not a castle but a fortified manor surrounded by a bank of earth. Nevertheless it gives a wonderfully accurate idea of the size of the establishment and a measure of the wealth of its builder, Walkerlin de Ferrers, whose family arrived in England with William I. The medieval hall was where the armed members of the household hung their arms and armour. This use is commemorated in the hall at Canon's Ashby, Northamptonshire, in a painting of *c.* 1700, showing drums, banners and weapons. Even later, Robert Adam in the hall at Osterley Park, Middlesex, put plaster trophies of arms on the walls, harking back to a medieval custom. Castles were built in the twelfth and thirteenth centuries by feudal barons who carved out territories for themselves on the Welsh and Scottish borders, and by Edward I in the late thirteenth century to control the unruly Welsh. They all had great halls.

In Scotland castles continued to be built by the warring clansmen until the failure of the 1745 Jacobite rebellion. The Disarming Act of the following year effectively brought peace to the troubled Scottish countryside. But building in the castle tradition continued and defensive features became decorative and non-functional. Even Robert Adam, the neo-classical architect, conformed to the fashion when he built Wedderburn, Culzean, Seton, and at least half a dozen other Scottish castles in the late eighteenth century. By this date the great hall was no longer necessary and none of the later castles had one, until halls were revived in the nineteenth century.

Variations of the hall-house exist in many parts of Britain. A first floor hall raised over the undercroft or ground floor cellar gave some security without the cost of an encircling wall and a large number of defenders. Two examples of this type of building are Burton Agnes Old Hall, Humberside, of 1170, and Norbury Hall, Derbyshire, dated about a hundred years later. Both are substantially built of stone or brick and must have offered considerable security against marauding gangs. A less costly defensive building was the pele tower in which a small hall was raised over an undercroft with a chamber above for sleeping in. Longthorpe Tower, near Peterborough, Northamptonshire, built *c.* 1250, is a lucky surviving example of what must once have been a more common building type. As a form of defence it was convenient, and the style continued on the borders of Scotland and in Ireland until the seventeenth century. In these defensive structures the undercroft, when trouble was expected, was where the wealth of the owner – cattle and sheep – were kept safe.

Until law and order could be maintained by the state, a defensive building was the only method by which a lord of the manor could hold on to what he considered to be his. For the more humble their only defence was to ally themselves to a strong lord who would protect them in return for some kind of service. The exceptions to this were the monasteries and abbeys. Although not entirely immune from attack, they brought a great measure of security in the areas of their influence. The church maintained law and order by the threat of eternal hell-fire in the next world for any wrongdoers. They achieved wealth by the converse: the promise of a place in heaven for benefactors. To understand the medieval outlook we have to comprehend that people saw life merely as a preparation for better things in the next world and this motivated every facet of existence – to us they appear very insecure mortals. In England this outlook only began to change in the early fifteenth century and gathered momentum under the Tudors.

The reign of the Tudor dynasty began with Henry VII's victory at the battle of Bosworth in 1485, and brought in a strong government that regarded power in other hands as a threat and was prepared to stamp out the earliest sign of opposition. The effect on building was almost immediate; for the first time since the Romans left 1,000 years before, expensive defences were no longer necessary in the greater part of England. By 1450 Ockwells Manor, Berkshire, and Thornbury Castle, Gloucestershire, both had big oriel windows in their halls only protected by a walled courtyard. By the time of Elizabeth I (1558–1603) large glass windows could be used unprotected and without fear of their being shattered by quarrelsome neighbours. Shortage of cash led Henry VIII to dissolve the monasteries (1536–40) – in effect the nationalization of monastic lands. The sale or gift of church lands by Henry resulted in the foundation of many family estates and fortunes. These historic houses, built on the old monastic lands, sited near water and low-lying – two characteristics of medieval monastic sites – are distinguished by being called Abbeys, Priories or Granges. However, the monastic buildings made very difficult homes and the adaptations were always an awkward compromise. At Newstead Abbey, Nottinghamshire, the Byron family demolished the church and lived in the domestic section of the complex. But although adapted over three centuries it was never satisfactory, even after Colonel Wildman, who bought the house from the poet Byron, had spent a fortune on it in the nineteenth century. At Buckland Abbey, Devon, the Grenville family used the buildings in the opposite way by adapting the church and demolishing the domestic quarters. Today any visitor to Buckland is conscious that it could never have made a comfortable dwelling. The real answer, given sufficient wealth, was to pull down everything and start again, as the Earls of Bedford did at Woburn Abbey, Bedfordshire.

The Dissolution was the last chance to buy large acreages of land, often below the market price, and quite a few families who took the gamble are still living off their original investment today. Land is a peculiar commodity; it cannot be made off with and it cannot be destroyed. Furthermore in Britain, an island, it is a limited commodity. For these reasons investment in land has always been attractive to the wealthy. Although, until the seventeenth century, it was the only investment available, later it continued to hold its popularity over other more profitable alternatives because of the historic association between the old landed families and social position. The wealthy landed families built their dynastic bases – their head offices in fact – on the land which supported them and, as it were, lived 'over the shop', albeit in some style. They cultivated what they termed their 'interest' – local politics – through friendship, blood relations, the influence built up through entertaining, the judicious spending of money to create local jobs and the patronage of local tradesmen and dealers. The country house was the hub of the landlord's existence; it gave his family status and a sense of permanence, of identity, and of achievement. It gave focus to the surrounding, dependent community.

Although the majority of our historic houses are country houses, the town house must not be overlooked. The town house was not in any sense a reaction from the house in the country, but an adjunct to it. Those in London were used when their owners came up for business, political, social or court duties, during a season which lasted for four months a year. The town house expressed the same message as the country base. But they regarded their estates as the prime responsibility, regarding all concerned in its running as 'part of a family' – very much a feudal outlook. By the eighteenth century, however, court life and London society were a major attraction. Typical of this is the example of the 5th Duke of Devonshire and his lively, society-loving Duchess. Both of them preferred living at Devonshire House, London, rather than Chatsworth, Derbyshire. Nevertheless the Duke did not neglect his responsibilities in Derbyshire. There were some exceptions to this rule, such as the 1st Earl of Nottingham (d. 1682), who only owned a house in rural Kensington because he never had time to look for anything else. The American Ambassador in Britain in 1819 made the point: 'they have *houses* in London . . . but their *homes* are in the country.'

The cost of acquiring a London house was high, particularly in the eighteenth century, when the great Whig landowners were enjoying a long run of political power. It was the political scene which often made their residence necessary. The Albany, Piccadilly, originally Melbourne House, was built, furnished and decorated in the 1770s by the 1st Lord Melbourne at a total cost of £100,000.[1] The Londonderrys in 1821 paid £43,000 for Holderness House, Park Lane, and spent £200,000 on altering it.[2] This was the sort of cost the very grand were incurring in acquiring houses big enough to entertain large numbers. The less grand, who had dinners for no more than twenty-four, could easily get by at much lower cost; Lord Verulam built his house in Grosvenor Square for a modest £12,902 in 1815.[3] But town houses were not always a good investment. The Dukes of Leeds made a loss after they built their house in St James's Square in 1725 for £38,000, selling it in 1803 for only £11,000.[4] In 1800 a perfectly adequate property in the West End could be rented for £1,000 a year. Although nearly all these properties have been demolished, or turned into offices or clubs, some idea of the splendour of their interiors can be gleaned from three still left: Ashburnham House, Westminster, built in the 1660s; Apsley House, built for Lord Apsley in the

1770s and altered for the 1st Duke of Wellington in 1828; and Lancaster House, built for the Duke of York in 1825 and later altered for the Earls of Strafford and the Dukes of Sutherland.

Not all, however, made bad investments like the Dukes of Leeds. At the turn of this century, Piccadilly and Park Lane were lined with family town houses standing unused for half the year. With the high cost of land in the area it is not surprising that they were sold off and their high capital value realized, indicating the dynastic priority: to preserve the main estate. The 10th Duke of Devonshire sold Devonshire House in Piccadilly, facing Green Park, in 1920 for the then astonishing sum of £1,000,000. At present there are twenty-nine surviving once great aristocratic town houses in London, not one of them now privately occupied. The last to be so was 44 Grosvenor Square, the home of Lady Illingworth, which was disgracefully demolished in 1967, to make way for the new Britannia Hotel.

County towns too have town houses built for the local county families who found it necessary to be in town for local functions, the assizes and elections. Although the custom goes back to the fifteenth century, the old properties were rebuilt and they are now mainly Georgian. Their elegant façades can still be found in Norwich, York, Winchester and other county towns. The creation in the eighteenth century of turnpike roads, together with sprung carriages, led to faster and more convenient travel and made the county town house superfluous. By the early nineteenth century a journey of twenty-five miles was no longer laborious. Rather different in nature are the town houses of Bath, built in the eighteenth century specifically for renting. Some, fitted out with imposing interiors equal to many country houses, were intended for wealthy visitors going to Bath for the water-cure and taking a grand house for three months or so. The lesser spa towns had apartments for visitors rather than a complete house. Families which saw themselves as grand would rent a grand house.

Today we visit a historic house to see the building and its contents. However, we are only seeing a part of the complete picture and the house was not a particularly significant part – buildings were demolished, altered and rebuilt as finance allowed and social change required. The house was a minor part of the organization composed of the dynasty and the estate that supported it, and it represented the power and wealth of the dynasty. Now we have completely lost the notion of the continuation of a dynasty, yet it was a very real thing to our ancestors who lived half our lifespan and who hoped to provide a male heir to continue in the same way after them. We are conditioned to rapid change, but until communications became fast and widespread the world altered little in one lifespan and ideas changed slowly. Apart from sheltering the family and providing a 'head office', the function of the building was to display the political influence and power, as well as the real or imagined wealth, of the dynasty.

Who can fail to be impressed by the entrance hall at Holkham Hall as an example of an architectural display of power and wealth? Yet this was built in remotest Norfolk by plain Mr Coke – he became Earl of Leicester after the house was begun. Thomas Coke was making a clear statement that he was expecting a great future for his dynasty; Holkham Hall takes a lot of living up to, but it could never have been built without the wealth Coke created by improving his estate and, as a result, increasing the rents. In fact when he began the house in 1734 he had lost a great sum of money in the scandal of the South Sea Bubble (1720). By the time he died in 1759 he had spent nearly £90,000 on the building and it was still incomplete. Furthermore he had spent £5,500 on furnishing the place, and Lady Leicester, up to 1771, spent another £3,000 on furnishings; for the saloon and drawing room alone velvet and damask ran to a cost of £3,000. Although Coke spent more than the estate could afford and died in debt, his expenditure on building reflects current values rather than eccentric extravagance.

Yet the country house as an investment showed no tangible return, while the building of it, and the subsequent modernization and repair, often consumed a large slice of estate income, or even swallowed up capital when land was sold to pay for the extravagance. Wollaton Hall, Nottinghamshire, completed in 1588, cost its builder, Sir Francis Willoughby, £5,000 that he could not afford;[5] this outlay and the cost of marrying off his five daughters put the estate in the red for a considerable period. The Countess of Shrewsbury, after completing one power-base at Chatsworth for an unknown sum, went on to build another, Hardwick Old and New Halls, Derbyshire, in 1590 for about £6,000.[6] A hundred years later her direct descendant, the 1st Duke of Devonshire, demolished the old Chatsworth house piecemeal and rebuilt on the same foundations at a cost of over £40,000. Chatsworth was expensive to rebuild because the Duke never knew what he wanted until it was finished. If he disliked it he would have it taken down and remade. The Duke of Kingston rebuilt Thoresby Hall, Nottinghamshire, in 1745, at a cost of £30,000,[7] after a fire had destroyed an earlier house. In the following century Thoresby, inherited from the Duke of Kingston's family by the 3rd Earl Manvers, was again rebuilt at a total cost of £250,000 in the 1870s.[8] Eaton Hall, Cheshire, was completed for Lord Grosvenor at a cost of £40,000 in 1804–12[9] and transformed by the 1st Duke of Westminster in the 1870s for £600,000.[10] This gives some idea of the kind of cost of building which the wealthy landowner might incur.

Methods of financing the building work were varied; the cautious husbanded the estate income, often carefully accruing a capital sum in advance. The incautious went right ahead whether the estate could afford it or not. The 1st Earl of Leicester left his estate embarrassed. Having borrowed from his heir, a nephew, he never troubled to repay the loan, on the principle that his heir would eventually have the property anyway and he might as well help to pay for it! Whereas the converse was the case with Gregory Gregory, who prudently spent some twenty years building Harlaxton Manor, Lincolnshire, all out of income; started in 1831, it was unfinished by the time he died in 1852. When building Thoresby Hall, Nottinghamshire, in the 1870s, Earl Manvers allowed his French wife's ambition to run ahead of his own; the sum he had calculated the estate could stand was exceeded and he had to sell land and take out a mortgage to pay for the unforeseen charges.

By the nineteenth century the great landlords were no longer so dependent on estate income – the industrial revolution created families whose wealth was generated in industry. Somerleyton Hall, Suffolk, was built by Sir Morton Peto in 1844 and once had the biggest winter garden, or conservatory, of any house in Britain. Peto had made a fortune as a railway contractor. By 1866 he was bankrupt and the house, with 3,000 acres, was sold to the Crossley family from Halifax. The Crossleys had made their money in carpet manufacturing and were financially sounder than Sir Morton Peto, but were unusual in moving far away from the centre of their wealth to set themselves up as landed proprietors. Eventually, raised to the peerage, they took the title of Somerleyton and the family still inhabits the house and owns the estate. Some landowners were able to profit from new forms of transport and raw materials. The Duke of Bridgewater at Ashridge, Hertfordshire, made a fortune from canals. Other landowners, lucky enough to have minerals beneath their land, developed coal mines, exploited lead, copper or tin. The Marquis of Bute's family enjoyed a very high return from their investment in Cardiff docks and in coal mining, enabling the 3rd Marquis to spend a great deal of money on restoring Cardiff Castle in the 1870s. Scarisbrick Hall in Lancashire, built in the 1840s by Charles Scarisbrick, was entirely financed by the high rents from land he bought in expanding Southport.

A new wing or a new front to a house, a range of spacious entertaining rooms or even a complete new building were often financed by the land-owner's marriage to an heiress. Her elevated rank would be the cause of the expenditure and a suite of rooms or an impressive front would reflect the improved fortunes of the dynasty. The service wings were always the very last to be altered.

To find the money for building on an estate was one thing; to find an estate to build on was another matter. Thomas Coke, 1st Earl of Leicester, is classified among the great landlords, the four hundred eighteenth-century families whose income ranged from £5,000 to £50,000; the average of this top class was £10,000. Below them came the wealthy gentry and squires whose income ranged from £1,000 to £5,000. Between them they owned some eighty per cent of cultivable land. Great houses surrounded by profitable acres seldom came on the market.

Consequently, for the newly rich with soaring ambition, buying a ready-made estate was something of a problem. What were available were the smaller properties of minor gentry; an old-fashioned house would eventually be demolished, then rebuilt to reflect the owner's vision of his dynasty, and the estate steadily enlarged as land came up for sale. It was only the very successful and affluent newcomer who could start from scratch with a brand-new house by the current fashionable architect and be prepared to pay over the odds for land in order to get it. The 2nd Earl of Nottingham, Daniel Finch, did exactly this. His father, a very successful lawyer and Lord Chancellor to Charles II, was made 1st Earl in 1681, the year before he died.

The only house he owned was in Kensington and consequently the 2nd Earl, who married a wealthy bride, felt the need for the establishment of a country seat. Eventually he found what he needed at Burley-on-the-Hill, in what was then Rutland, and it cost him £50,000 with a rental income of £2,500. Unfortunately there was no house and it set him back a further £30,000[11] to build one – more than most were prepared to spend on buying an estate.

In the eighteenth century an estate of 2,000 acres producing an annual income of £1,000 would need a capital outlay of £20,000, whereas a great landlord of 10,000 acres bringing in £5,000 required capital of £100,000 – a return of five per cent, about the same as the return on Government bonds. The cost of a country house and estate was high because they were difficult to get. And that remained so until the last quarter of the nineteenth century.

On very rare occasions it was necessary for the state to equip a new, landless, peer with the capital to set himself up with a suitable country house and estate. An eminent historian, Sir Nicholas Nicholas, stated in 1830 that the only group whose ennoblement was unobjectionable was the landed gentry because their estates assured them the means of supporting their rank. Clearly a peer without land was nobody. Charles II's illegitimate sons were made dukes and fitted up with estates to carry the dignity of the title. In 1919 Haig was given £100,000 with his earldom; earlier Wellington had been given the means to buy Stratfield Saye. If a peer fell on hard times the Establishment saw to it that he was rescued; the 9th Viscount Falkland, who died in a duel in 1809 and whose title dated from 1620, came of a long line of destitute predecessors who had all been found sinecures to keep them afloat. In this case a government pension of £200 a year was provided and continued with his son who was conveniently married off to an illegitimate daughter of William IV. This act of self-sacrifice rescued the family fortunes and he died leaving an estate of 3,000 acres. It was unthinkable that a peer in the House of Lords should be seen to be penniless. Today there are generous allowances amounting to a maximum of around £46 for any peer putting in a day's appearance in the House. The allowance is the modern equivalent of Viscount Falkland's pension.

Similarly leading politicians were sometimes helped by other party members. Disraeli, who might appear to us as the last type of man to lead the Tories, was landless, and the sons of the Duke of Portland advanced £25,000 towards the cost of buying him Hughenden Manor and 1,000 acres.[12]

Having acquired a country house, the owner then had to take into account the cost of running it. The attractions of life in London or the spa towns did not detract from the amusements of the country house. In both summer and winter they were magnets of social life. Some visitors came on business, some canvassing political or other forms of patronage, as well as those who were there for purely social reasons; but all had to be catered for. Consequently the consumption of food and wines and the necessity of keeping large numbers of servants resulted in considerable expenditure in most country houses. In 1600 at Hardwick the Countess of Shrewsbury was entertaining something like a hundred guests every dinner time, which cost her an average of £2,000 annually. But then she was the richest woman in England with an income in excess of £10,000.[13] Nearly a hundred years later the Earl of Bedford was paying out an annual £1,500 at Woburn but he was in somewhat straitened circumstances and charging his relations £2 each per month for living with him;[14] he was not typical of his class. More typical of the prodigality expected of the very grand is the 2nd Duke of Kingston at Thoresby in Sherwood Forest; in twelve weeks in 1736 his household consumed £300 in meat, and the total household bill for the three months came to £1,477.

The wealth to support the grand life was generally carefully built up over generations, and a typical example of a steady climb is that of the Ashburn-hams, a Sussex family. Their situation remained unremarkable from medieval to Tudor times; they advanced slowly from being small farmers to the middle rank of county gentry. During the reign of Elizabeth I they suffered a set-back and sold their estates. No more might have been heard of the family had it not been for John Ashburnham who prospered in the first half of the seventeenth century and bought back the family lands. John himself suffered a set-back in the Civil War when, as a Royalist, he was heavily fined, by the Puritans, a sum totalling half the value of his estate. At the Restoration of 1660 he was handsomely rewarded by Charles II with grants of lands and the gift of a house at Chiswick. His son continued on the path set out by his father and was made Lord Ashburnham in 1689 for his support of William of Orange against the Catholic James II.

The 1st Lord Ashburnham, restlessly ambitious, was the easily recogniz-able prototype of the present day tycoon. When it came to marrying off his son he, in typical fashion, asked his lawyers what settlement he would have to make on a bride bringing £5,000 in cash as her dowry. Marriage among this class of people was always a business matter – money married money – until very recently. The 2nd Lord Ashburnham married money, and sadly both he and his new wife died of smallpox five months later. This, dynastically speaking, didn't matter as his brother inherited all the lands and the title. He married three times, each wife bringing £10,000 with her. By the time of his death he had become an earl. His son dutifully married a wealthy girl who contributed something in excess of £20,000 to the dynastic coffers.[15]

The Ashburnhams' material success was achieved in the space of a hundred years and was due to each generation single-mindedly following policies set by their predecessors. Also, they had few children and consequently did not have to find a number of expensive dowries for daughters or commit capital in setting up a number of sons. This scarcity of progeny eventually worked against the Ashburnhams; the title is now extinct and their house, Ashburnham Place, Sussex, was demolished in 1959.

Like many other families the Ashburnhams owed their success to the astuteness of one ancestor who consistently got his gambles right and to succeeding generations building on that first advantage by means of the accepted 'business-marriage'. On marriage a woman's wealth became her husband's and this was not changed until the second Married Woman's Property Act of 1882. Until then a woman had no wealth until she became a widow – in all things she was merely the chattel of her husband. Happiness in marriage was not expected; if it was found then it was a bonus, otherwise it was sought for elsewhere. It was expected that personal contentment and romantic inclination should be sublimated to the demands of dynasty. Moreover, until the 'Act to amend the law relating to Divorce . . .' of 1857, divorce was all but impossible. Lord Ross was the first to achieve the difficult legal manoeuvre in 1670 and he needed an act of Parliament to do it. Before that date no one in England had ever obtained a divorce in the fullest sense; not even Henry VIII. From 1670 to 1857 only four wives were successful in divorce proceedings. Marriage really was for better or worse and, if the latter, both parties were stuck with it. We should remember these points when we admire the magnificent backgrounds against which the dramas of the lives of the wealthy were played.

CHAPTER 2

Provisioning

A coachman standing by his horses, one among many early arrivals who ranged their vehicles tidily in the large gravelled court on the north front of Hatfield House in Hertfordshire, watched the patient line of later carriages waiting to drop their passengers at the front door for a ball in the winter of 1886. One footman opened the carriage doors, unfolding two steps, while another helped the guests descend from the carriage, to mount the flight of eleven stone stairs out of the chilly night air into the warmth of the entrance hall. Through the open door came the distant melody of a Strauss waltz playing in the great hall, against the background of the clink of harness as horses nuzzled into their nosebags, the creak of polished leather and the clip-clop of latecomers' horses. The observant coachman would have noticed with wonder that the entire house was incandescent, with nearly every window alight – Lord Salisbury was a pioneer in this matter and, in 1881, only beaten by one year to be the first to light his house by electricity. Cragside, Northumberland, owned by Lord Armstrong, may have been the first, in the winter of 1880.

In 1886 Hatfield was the home of the talented and eccentric 3rd Marquis of Salisbury, Conservative Prime Minister of one year's standing. A few of the guests who wandered upstairs into the long gallery might have encountered the Salisburys' seven children. The 3rd Marquis believed that children should develop their own ideas and opinions and some ten years before, Hugh, the youngest son, then only five, startled the Liberal Minister, William Gladstone, with the firm opinion, 'You are a very wicked man.' Dismayed by the young Salisbury's precocity the great man remonstrated, 'Dear boy, what would your father think if he heard you say that?' The honest Hugh answered, 'He thinks you are too,' then added brightly, 'And he is coming to kill you.'[1] It is easy to understand why many acquaintances had the opinion that the Salisburys' children were out of hand.

This particular evening at Hatfield demonstrates that the country house could, with little trouble, entertain two hundred and fifty guests. They were fed, warmed, transported, and the rooms illuminated – all with minimal interruption to the regular routine of the house.

The evening was also noteworthy for the narrow avoidance of a social gaffe. The Marchioness was abashed to find that there were only ices and jellies for the final course of supper, although it was unheard-of not to serve pudding. The cook and the housekeeper were immediately called to order and by dint of a great deal of impromptu baking the omission was remedied without any of the guests being aware.

The logistical problems in supplying any great house were considerable and required precise organization if they were to be surmounted. At an establishment like Hatfield there was a large family and an indoor staff of thirty to be fed and kept warm, their clothes washed, and so on. Hatfield had the advantage of being within easy reach of London and, from the nineteenth century, of a railway line. A house in the mountains of Cumbria or the Wolds of Yorkshire had none of these advantages, yet grand entertainments, sometimes in the presence of royalty, were undertaken without mishap, even in remotest Scotland.

Without the convenience of a public transport system, the grand houses had been supplying themselves for centuries. In the main they were self-supporting, but for such items as coal, wine and luxuries they had to go far afield. In the 1590s the Countess of Shrewsbury at Hardwick Hall, Derbyshire, bought her wines in London. Claret, malmsey, Rhenish white wines and sweet Muscatel were shipped in giant hogsheads holding fifty gallons to Hull and thence by barge up the Trent to Stockwith. From there they were carted by ox-drawn wain overland for thirty-five miles and finally dragged up an amazingly steep drive to the house. It was a journey that could only be undertaken in summer and there was, therefore, no question of getting it wrong; consumption had to be accurately gauged six months in advance. Occasionally wine was bought in Nottingham, but even that required a twenty-five mile overland journey before it reached Hardwick's cellar.

In the nineteenth century, when the family drank wine the servants drank beer. This was routinely supplied at the servants' midday dinner and evening supper, to be drawn by the butler only. Tradition died hard below stairs and beer had always been supplied in the servants' hall. In Tudor times it was kept by the botelier in charge of the buttery – a word derived from the butts of ale, although he was also responsible for eggs, cheese and butter. Even today in the Oxford and Cambridge dining halls drinks are served from the buttery bar. Earlier, in c. 1500, the 5th Earl of Northumberland and his Countess breakfasted off bread, salt fish, a quart of wine and the same of beer. But by the end of that century beer was the drink of the yeoman class and wine that of the wealthy.

At the country house beer was brewed on the premises from October to March because it was not possible to cool the fermentation in summer, but the hops and malt to brew it, unless barley was grown on the home farm, had to be bought. The brewery was usually in the stable-block to the north-east of the house so that the prevailing south-west wind blew away all smells.

Charlecote Park in Warwickshire, home of the Lucy family, has a completely equipped brew-house; when George Lucy died in 1845 there were 4,650 gallons in the cellars. Traquair House, Borders, Scotland, still brews beer and, more to the point, sells it to visitors. At Thoresby Hall, Nottinghamshire, the brewery was in the stable-block and connected to the servants' hall by a cast-iron pipe passing through the carpenter's shop. It was often noticed that the estate carpenter, while not quite the worse for drink, was certainly the better for it. After he retired it was discovered that he had drilled the beer pipe and fitted a tap in his workshop.

While drink had to be carried, meat was usually driven on the hoof to the house. At Woburn, Bedfordshire, in the second half of the seventeenth century, the 1st Duke of Bedford had sheep and cattle regularly driven for four days from his estate at Thorney, Cambridgeshire. Usually the country house would have its own slaughter house, but the Duke preferred to use the one in the village – it belonged to him anyway.[2] In 1681 his family and household of forty servants got through an average of seven fat bullocks each summer month. Not all of these would have been eaten at once; some of the meat would have been salted down for keeping and large amounts of salt were needed for the process. At Haddon Hall, Derbyshire, the salting troughs are still there in the butchery along with the chopping blocks for dismembering the slaughtered beasts.

Salt, therefore, was very important, and always had been. The brine springs of Worcestershire and Cheshire had yielded salt from Roman times; the salt mines of Droitwich were another source, and more was produced on the coast by evaporating sea-water in heated pans. By the fifteenth century demand for salt exceeded production in England and it was imported from France. Called 'Bay salt', it was first produced in the Bay of Bourgneuf by natural evaporation. Eventually it was imported from the entire Atlantic coast and still called 'Bay salt'. The sharp, sweet taste of coarse-grained 'Bay salt' was preferred for preserving, and the fine white salt from mineral springs and mines for the table. Both came into the house in either bricks or sacks.

For a supply of fresh meat through the winter it was often more convenient for large estates to keep a deer park; the animals foraged for themselves through the worst of the winter and gave a good supply of fresh meat. Moreover they provided sport. The drawback was the difficulty of keeping them inside the park; in the eighteenth century costly brick and stone walls six feet in height replaced less permanent, high wooden paling. Aukland Castle, County Durham, has a deer house of 1767 for sheltering deer in severe weather; Sudbury Hall, Derbyshire, has a castellated deercote serving the same purpose, built in the mid-eighteenth century. And Farnborough Hall, Warwickshire, is provided with a deer larder in a brick-walled garden and a wheel from which to hang the game. Pork was not generally eaten in the grand house although pigs' trotters and whole roasted piglets were prized dishes. Pork became a lower-class food. Commonly peasants kept pigs, as they were no trouble and found for themselves. The staple peasant diet was pork and beans, and to them we owe our breakfast of bacon and eggs.

Yet another source of fresh winter meat was the dovecote. To keep pigeons was the right of the lord of the manor and the birds were allowed to scavenge for food on any neighbouring fields; tenants' crops suffered in proportion to the population of the dovecote. There are many houses where dovecotes survive, sometimes with the potence, a rotating ladder giving access to the nesting boxes in the wall, still intact. What must be the oldest dovecote in any house open to the public is at Athelhampton, Dorset, which dates from the early sixteenth century. The earliest may be at Kinwarton, Warwickshire, complete with its potence, built in the mid-fourteenth century, but it is unconnected with any historic house.

Fish, likewise, were easily raised on the estate in fish ponds. Hardwick Hall in the late sixteenth century had its own part-time 'fisherman' responsible for stocking the ponds as well as catching the fish. At Woburn in the late seventeenth century, the ponds were restocked by bringing perch and pike alive in water from Thorney, taking fourteen days on the journey.[3]

The home farm, with fields near the house but out of sight of the main living rooms, supplied milk, butter, cheese, eggs, corn for bread, sometimes barley for making beer, potatoes and root vegetables. The home farm was not expected to show a profit but to supply the household, and it grew out of the medieval land surrounding the manor house. One drawback to the common feudal farming method was the impossibility of improving crops and breeds by careful selection – when all the cows of the village ran with the village bull in the open pasture no selective breeding was possible. For the lord of the manor, with his demesne farm fenced off, such experiments to improve yield were possible and the home farm could become a centre of agricultural innovation for those with a mind for such matters. Gradually, the feudal custom of free labour provided in return for land was replaced by wages and rent, thus providing the lord with a cash income. The home farm was usually the only acreage on an estate not let, but was 'kept in hand' by the owner. That is not to say he managed it himself; traditionally this duty was left to the steward who managed the whole of the estate, leaving the family free to pursue other interests. For a landowner to run the home farm himself was considered eccentric. As late as 1931, at Long Melford in Suffolk, Sir William Hyde Parker ran the home farm, but only after a struggle with his father who thought the occupation 'ungentlemanly'.

The kitchen garden was the direct descendant of the medieval monastic herb garden. Initially the medieval herb garden grew four types of herbs: medicinal, culinary, plants for dyeing, and sweet-smelling 'strewing herbs' for fumigating the house – our pot-pourri comes from this practice. Fruit trees and vines were always grown.

By Elizabethan times salads were grown with the culinary herbs and, as the apothecary became more skilled in dispensing, the medicinal herbs were phased out of the garden. Boughs and garlands were used to decorate rooms until as late as the seventeenth century and the carved limewood swags of leaves, pea-pods and wheat ears, so loved by Grinling Gibbons, may be an echo of the earlier boughs and garlands brought in from the countryside to use for decoration. By the late seventeenth century the kitchen garden, under the care of a head gardener and with many under-gardeners in a large establishment, provided vegetables, salads, hard and soft fruit, grapes, peaches, even oranges and lemons, and house plants from hothouses and south-facing heated walls. In general vegetables were used in potages and not eaten as a dish until the mid-eighteenth century; they were not popular because they generated stomach wind which was thought to be unhealthy. The exception was the globe artichoke, which was believed to be an aphrodisiac and which John Evelyn christened 'the noble thistle'.

Much of the food needed to feed the household in winter had to be stored and many of today's recipes reflect the necessity to preserve it in an age before refrigeration. Fruit was preserved in jams and marmalades – the latter came from Portugal and was originally a jelly made from quinces; the Portuguese for quince is *marmelo*. Pickling preserved vegetables and fish, such as roll-mop herrings; meat and fish were dried or salted; bacon, hams and salmon were smoked in a smoke house. Potted meat, sealed with a layer of fat, was the last culinary preservation discovery, made in the late eighteenth century, before the invention of canning. The prudent housekeeper stocked up with all these provisions and by the end of summer her shelves and cupboards were weighed down with pots, jars and boxes to see the household through the winter. Canned food only became generally available in the 1830s.

Although refrigerators are a recent invention, by the mid-eighteenth century most large country houses had an ice-house, sometimes called an ice-well, built conveniently near a lake or pond, with a north-facing door, usually vaulted in brick or stone over a pit thirty feet deep. The first was made in St James's Park in 1660 and like so much else the idea was imported from France, where chilled wine was fashionable. In hard frosts ice, sawn from the surface of a frozen lake, was stored between layers of straw. It would keep for up to three years and was used for ice-boxes and for making ice cream. At Linley Hall, Staffordshire, there is an ice-house built in the form of a Roman temple. Holkham Hall has a well preserved ice-house, out of sight of the house and consequently not near the lake. Probably the best preserved specimen of an ice-house is at Heveningham Hall in Suffolk. J. C. Loudon gave detailed directions for their construction in his *Encyclopaedia of Gardening*, published in 1834, but this was near the end of their practical use because they were superseded by ice-making machines in the 1870s and from then onwards ice-houses fell into decay. Anyone interested in the provisioning of a great house should visit Erddig, Clwyd. There the gardens, home farm, buildings and equipment needed to keep a remote country house supplied are all displayed. The visitor to this National Trust property enters the house not through the front door as a privileged visitor but by the back door. After going through the timber yard, farm yard, stables and coach house, one passes through the laundry into the kitchens and finally into the servants' hall and butler's pantry before being allowed 'above stairs'. This brilliant presentation of a historic house allows the visitor to appreciate the enormous industry needed to keep a moderate sized country house running.

In the past the country house could never be entirely self-sufficient. Home-produced honey could be a very acceptable substitute for sugar, but sugar loaves, salt, spices, tea, cloth and paper were commodities that no estate could produce and such things were, from medieval times, bought at traditional fairs and local markets. In London almost anything from the known world was available and in the 1550s, when Bess of Hardwick was living in the shadow of old St Paul's, she was able to buy figs, raisins, currants, saffron, almonds and rice, as well as luxuries like sugar candies and cracknel for her young children. For those unable to visit London the traditional fairs were the only sources for unusual goods. Sturbridge fair, held on Sturbridge Common on the River Cam, about two miles from the centre of Cambridge, was the largest, stretching for half a mile from the Cam to the main road. It ran for twenty-eight days from 24 August and a complete township was established for its duration. Here anything could be bought. It was a great centre for fabrics, including West Country cantaloons, shalloons and druggets – the first two being woollen cloths and the last a cheap floor covering – hosiery from Leicester and Nottingham and vast quantities of woven cloth from Leeds and Wakefield. Defoe saw one warehouse with £20,000 of cloth in stock. Also on sale were metalwork, leather goods, pottery, china, comfits or sweetmeats, prunes from Damascus, salt cod from Newfoundland and precious stones which came from the East by way of Russia. It was here, in 1661, that Isaac Newton bought a prism and books on astronomy. Considering the difficulties of transport, it is remarkable that such huge quantities of goods were gathered together from the four corners of the world.

Although the big annual fairs were the main source of supply for the unusual, local markets and stalls provided the means of buying more common items such as needles, nails, wire, spades, knives and such things that could not be made on the estate. In sixteenth-century London one was able to send out for supplies at any time of day or night, including Sundays, from stalls, open-fronted shops, markets and the forerunner of the snack bar, cookshops. Cookshops provided hot foods because few town houses had room for a kitchen. Although Bess of Hardwick, a wealthy woman, had a kitchen, she had no baking oven and sent out for her bread. In the 1590s, when she was the richest woman in England and staying at her house in the countryside of Chelsea, she had herds of cattle and sheep driven up from her Leicestershire estate to supply her household for a nine month stay.[4].

The eighteenth century saw inevitable changes in London, and shops with opening and closing hours replaced stalls and markets. Dairies in London changed little and even in the late nineteenth century the sight of a cow in dairy shops was still usual. By the mid-nineteenth century London town houses were supplied from the larger shops rather than markets such as Smithfield and Covent Garden. In 1841 Mr Gladstone, at 13 Carlton House Terrace, London, instructed his housekeeper that anything ordered on credit must have written authorization from himself and be bought from clearly specified tradesmen, the grocer being Fortnum and Mason[5] – the only one of Gladstone's suppliers still in business.

The gradual change in methods of supply came about because of major improvements in communications in the eighteenth century. Well maintained turnpike roads carrying the stage and mail coaches meant quicker and easier transport for small parcels of goods, while the bulkier loads went by canal. This spelled the end for many fairs, and local shops in market towns took their place. The housekeeper no longer needed to send to London for tea, coffee, pepper, or to Droitwich for salt; the grocer in Hereford, York or Berwick could supply what was needed. Indeed, the eighteenth century saw more changes in country house administration than any previous century; nearby towns had butchers and, except in remote houses, the butchery became redundant; local newspapers provided local news, London newspapers and books could be delivered to Manchester within four days. Banks opened in many county towns, making the payment of wages easier; no longer was it necessary to send to London for cash. The greatest changes came in agriculture, with new crops and methods of husbandry giving increasing yields. Consequently higher rents gave greater income to landowners.

Feeding the household, although a major operation, was only one facet of supplying the country house through the winter; the essential provision of heating and lighting began in a small way and eventually became an industry in its own right. We all know of the problems of heating large rooms – with our modern central heating we wear fewer clothes than our ancestors and are more aware of a drop in temperature. The medieval household burnt wood and turf exclusively: it was convenient, plentiful and came from the estate. Wood was commonly burnt in flat hearths until the sixteenth century when it became scarce, although the custom continued in Kent. Wood fires were still common in the 1780s. Good timber was reserved for building houses and warships. Thereafter coal, which will only burn with a draught under it, was burnt in basket grates. Many a historic house open to the public shows the coal grates quite wrongly filled with logs. The portable charcoal brazier supplemented the open hearth and was used as we use electric fires to warm a room quickly. Charcoal was also used in the kitchen from the late seventeenth century in stewing ranges, the forerunner of the cast-iron range; it gave a more controlled heat than was possible with an open fire and could be built where needed without a chimney. Llanfihangel Court, near Abergavenny, has a stewing hearth dated 1679; Hardwick Hall has a range of six eighteenth-century stewing hearths. All kinds of fuel had to be transported to the house, unless the estate had the good fortune to have open-cast coal, drift mines or pits. Usually coal was transported by sea to the nearest coastal port and then hauled overland. It was known as 'sea-cole' to distinguish it from 'cole', which was charcoal. The exception to the burning of these fuels was in Scotland and parts of Yorkshire where limitless peat bogs supplied a traditional slow-burning fire.

Nowadays we are so accustomed to central heating that we never spare a thought for all those tons of fuel carried into houses for winter heating in the past. Similarly we all take the convenience of electric light very much for granted and overlook the countless centuries when our ancestors groped around after sunset, often preferring to go to bed from sunset to sunrise. Rushlight and candle were the standard forms of illumination and, until the eighteenth century, both were made on the premises. A rushlight was a cheaper form of lighting used in kitchens and service rooms and was, as the name suggests, made from rushes, washed, bleached, dried, peeled and dipped in mutton suet or grease with a little beeswax. A two-foot rushlight would burn for an hour and was held in a wrought-iron clasp. It needs little imagination to see that as the rushlight burned down the stem easily bent under the softening grease. In almost any timbered house the burn marks on the uprights are clearly visible where a conflagration was stopped in time; the kitchens at Haddon Hall, Derbyshire, have a considerable number of such marks, but the kitchens at Hampton Court show so many burn marks on the serving hatch that it is surprising the rooms are still standing. Wax candles were used in the finer rooms of houses; although more costly they made less smell and left no messy pools of grease. Tallow candles, made from animal fat, were a cheaper alternative to wax; they burnt with a smell and were used often in combined holders with rushlights. Traditionally, chamber candle-sticks, with tallow candles or part-used wax candles, were set out each night on a table near the foot of the stairs, for guests to light themselves to bed. The candle tax of 1709, only repealed in 1831, made it illegal to use other means of lighting, even outlawing the private making of them. Only candles on which tax had been paid by the maker were permitted. This effectively stopped the development of oil lamps in Britain, then burning fish oil, which was very smelly. It took a Swiss, Ami Argand, to invent in 1783 a better lamp, burning Colza oil made from rape-seed, which gave a brilliant light. Illegal or not, the illicit making of candles and rushlights went on during this 120-year period and many museums have candle moulds and rushlight-holders dating from the eighteenth century.

Lighting, therefore, was an important matter and we overlook the inconvenience of cheerful gloom in a large room, the family grouped around a single source of light, the far corners out of sight in the pitch darkness. Nor do we consider the decorative effect of such rooms which came to life when parties were held by the light of a hundred candles – gold leaf, in these circumstances, glints and glows on carvings and plasterwork, making the decoration come alive. Our imagination has to provide the characteristic smell made by these various forms of illumination, wax, tallow, rushlight, oil and finally gas, smells that were banished only by the introduction of electricity.

Electric lighting, as we have seen, was introduced in 1880 at Cragside, where it was generated by water power, and this was followed by its installation at Hatfield the next year. The family of the Marquis of Salisbury, sitting in the garish brightness of this novelty, threw cushions at the wires strung across the ceilings when they caught alight! Cragside has its original electric fittings, so has Arundel Castle, Sussex, where they were installed in 1903 and today are barely adequate. Generally electric lighting was considered vulgar by the upper classes and some houses were still lit by oil in 1939; the principal rooms at Claydon House, Buckinghamshire, and Erddig, Clwyd, have no electricity to this day.

Another element we take very much for granted is water; it flows into our baths, basins and mouths from convenient taps without our giving it a thought. Plenty of servants in the house to carry water was only half the story; it had to be got out of the ground in the first place, unless by good fortune there was a natural spring and the supply could be piped from it into the house, as in the grotto at Woburn. Chatsworth, Derbyshire, had such an abundant source that it serviced a grotto, a bathroom and, unusually for the 1690s, at least ten water-closets. A pump over a well in the kitchen or yard worked by manpower was the most frequent method of raising water, followed by a treadwheel or a horse-powered pump in the yard. Thereafter, for a household needing large quantities of water, some ingenious machines were devised to perform this task. At Chicheley Hall, Buckinghamshire, a tank in a water tower was installed in 1729, served by the water from a stream which filled two buckets, one large and one small; the weight of the larger hauled up the smaller to the height of the tank. At Houghton, Norfolk, there is a very elegant water-house of about 1730 which might be taken for a gazebo or garden house; this held a tank filled by a horse-wheel from which the water was fed by gravity through pipes to the house. At Cobham Hall, Kent, there is an engine house of 1804 that once contained a steam pump. By far the most ingenious means was the ram pump, widely used from the mid-nineteenth century. Needing no fuel, ram pumps still run almost forever under their own power, using the force generated by that disagreeable 'thump' we get in the pipe when a tap is turned off suddenly. The power behind the thump caused by percussive force is sufficient to raise one third of the water flow.

When supplies and water are brought into the house it becomes necessary to get rid of the waste. The disposal of human waste was never taken very seriously until the nineteenth century, when it was realized that it was unhealthy to have a casual attitude to such things. Medieval monks were the first to solve the problem, if only because they had to. Large numbers living in a community left no room for compromise. At Fountains Abbey, North Yorkshire, and Roche Abbey, South Yorkshire, two typical examples, the rere-dorters – latrines behind the dormitories – were built over rivers flowing through the sites; a copious supply of water was essential for all monasteries. Domestic medieval garderobe turrets – the equivalent of the modern lavatory — have survived on many early buildings. Haddon Hall has two turrets, one a two-seater, projecting from the second storey to ground level making a shaft about twenty feet high – the minimum if smell is to be avoided – with hatches at the base for clearing out. At Stokesay Castle, Shropshire, there are some on the top floor in a half-timbered addition of the late sixteenth century. These project over the moat and, on a day with no wind, may have been quite efficient. At Audley End, Essex, a massive complex built by the 1st Earl of Suffolk in 1603 on the site of a Benedictine abbey, the old monastic drains were utilized and the interior garderobes discharged into culverts with running water. At Wollaton Hall, Nottinghamshire, completed by the eccentric Sir Francis Willoughby in the year of the Armada, 1588, the interior garderobes discharged into dry culverts. As the house is on top of a hill there was not the advantage of running water as at Audley End and they were only flushed out in rainstorms by downpipes from the roofs.

By 1600 garderobes were replaced by the close-stool – a pot inside a box with a hinged lid and a padded seat – kept where they would be needed and emptied by servants when required. Although Sir John Harrington demonstrated a flushing WC to Queen Elizabeth I, she was not impressed and preferred her close-stool. Without royal patronage Harrington's invention languished. In the seventeenth century, although a few houses did have flushing WCs, like those at Chatsworth, close-stools were almost universal; after all they could be used where most needed. At Ham House, Surrey, there is a ducal example of a japanned lacquer close-stool made in *c.* 1679 for the Lauderdales, but this is outdone by the Sackville's close-stool at Knole, Kent, of about the same date; covered in cut velvet and embellished with chased silver, the lid is fitted with a lock! As late as the nineteenth century it was customary in many British country houses to have a chamber pot in the dining room for the gentlemen to use after the ladies had left the room. Not so in France; Bartolomé Faujas de Saint Fond, visiting the Duke of Argyll at Inverary Castle, Strathclyde, in 1784, commented with wonder on the custom: 'If the lively champagne should make its diuretic influence felt, the case is foreseen, and in the pretty corners of the room the necessary convenience is to be found. This is applied to with so little ceremoney, that the person who has occasion to use it, does not even interrupt his talk during the operation. I suppose this is one of the reasons why the English ladies, who are exceedingly modest and reserved, always leave the company before the toasts begin.'[6] At Flintham Hall, Nottinghamshire, built in the last half of the nineteenth century, there is a small cupboard behind the library shutters which modestly conceals a chamber pot!

The casual attitude to the disposal of human waste was severely shaken in 1861 when Prince Albert died, it was believed of typhoid – now thought to be a mistaken diagnosis – caused by the evil state of the royal drains. Thereafter the water-closet came into its own. But not so bathrooms; bathing and washing, a favourite medieval occupation, became infrequent for six hundred years until this century, the exception being the essential washing of hands before a meal eaten with fingers. Although Prince Albert had a shower bath at Osborne, a contraption like a modern car-wash, and Bear Wood, Berkshire, completed in 1870, had five bathrooms as well as twenty-four WCs, the old rich considered bathrooms, like electricity, to be vulgar. That Prince Albert was a foreigner, and the builder of Bear Wood, a man named John Walter, was a newspaper owner, might have explained their eccentricity. It also explains why Carlton Towers, Humberside, built in the 1870s, had no bathrooms at all; everyone used a hip bath in front of a hot fire in the bedrooms. But then Carlton Towers belonged to a family who had been there since the early seventeenth century.

Soap, historically speaking, was not much used. At Hardwick Hall in 1600 it was bought at eighteen shillings the firkin – a cask holding eight gallons – from Sturbridge fair in September and 'sweet soap' was bought in February from Hull at the same price. Three firkins – about twenty-four gallons – seemed to have served the whole household for a year.[7] However, for economy it was used with lye – a mixture of vegetable ash and water which, being alkaline, causes grease to emulsify. Account books from 1666 to 1753 at Chirk Castle, Powys, show frequent payments for soap, wash balls and fern ash, for making lye. In fact soap could only be made on large estates with a surplus animal fat and someone prepared to undertake the long, tedious process of boiling the lyes and fat. Most found it far easier to buy soap. In 1643 a high tax was put on soap, which was not removed until 1853. However, after 1750 and notwithstanding the tax, the rich stopped washing themselves with lye and began to use soap, mainly because lye could not be made from coal ash – another effect of the wood shortage. But it was not until the mid-nineteenth century that toilet soap came into its own and brands, a Victorian marketing invention, proliferated.

The Victorians also had a great love of ingenious invention; at Batchwood House, near St Albans, Sir Edmund Beckett had self-locking WCs and the doors were only released after the apparatus was flushed! Quite a few houses had their own railways running from the kitchens to the dining rooms, small scale affairs pushed along by the hall boy. At Welbeck Abbey, in Sherwood Forest, the 5th Duke of Portland had a complicated layout under ground. Conversely, Gregory Gregory at Harlaxton Manor, Lincolnshire, using the natural feature of a hill behind his house, had a two mile railway track that entered the house on the top floor and discharged the supplies down chutes. But these were not labour-saving gadgets for the servants. Gregory did not want the disagreeable sight of carts rumbling up his mile-long drive, while the Duke of Portland was concerned about his unemployed coal miners and put them to work doing what they knew best: making tunnels. He had quite enough house anyway and ended up with a vast complex of underground entertaining rooms he did not need.

The nineteenth-century love of gadgetry extended to house planning, and the space necessary to run the historic country house reached a peak with the amazing Victorian passion for functional classification and separation; there were rooms for every domestic activity. The services were carefully sited on the north side away from the prevailing wind. What is now done by the deep-freeze and refrigerator was encompassed by the game larder, the cold meat store, the salting house, the larder, the pastry larder, the dairy and the vegetable store – there is a well restored range of such rooms, dating from 1881, at Lanhydrock, Cornwall. The work done by the modern dish-washer was done by the scullery maids in the scullery for pots, pans and dishes, while the silver and glasses were washed up in the butler's pantry. Castle Drogo,

Devon; Cragside, County Durham; and, inevitably, Erddig, Clwyd, all have butlers' pantries. The washing machine and spin-dryer have taken the place of up to five laundry maids under a head laundress working in a wet-laundry, a dry-laundry with drying racks for winter and a drying ground for summer. The full range of laundry rooms and equipment are restored at Barrington Court, Somerset; at Kingston Lacey, Dorset; and at Erddig, Clwyd; while at Beningborough, Yorkshire, there is a fully equipped dry-laundry. The oil boiler and oil storage tank for central heating take the place of the coal-yard and coal cellars, the kitchen coal house, the house coal house and a stick room. We no longer need cleaning rooms for brushing mud off clothes, lamp rooms and candle stores, a bake-house and bread room, a still room, a pastry, a room for ice-making, a servery, a knife room, a shoe room, a linen room, a soiled linen room, the odd-man's room, a pot room, a china store and, a late nineteenth-century addition, a bicycle room. We can dispense with a cellar for white wines and another for red – Kingston Lacey, Dorset, has a fully stocked wine cellar – a beer cellar, a storeroom for ashes, a carpenter's shop and saw pit, a kennel yard or smithy; neither do we need a porter at the gate to check in all the multiplicity of supplies. The list of purpose-designed rooms seems endless, and to it must be added the housekeeper's room with her storeroom, housemaids' room and pantry, cook's room, servants' hall, steward's office and deed room. Although many houses have these rooms they are not shown to the public, and once more Erddig is almost the only house showing the full range. Belle Isle, Cumbria, has restored an entertaining service basement showing some of these rooms, complete with running mice and sound effects! It is almost as if there were a type of domestic Parkinson's law proving that the space needed for service multiplied threefold with the number of servants.

Is it a paradox that the large historic house took nearly a thousand years to reach its peak as a complicated piece of domestic planning at the end of the nineteenth century, just as its quick decline was about to set in? Possibly the greatest domestic luxury was achieved in the Edwardian age, 1901 to 1911. At the time it was unbelievable that all would have gone in the space of one lifetime.

CHAPTER 3

Eating

Probably not one visitor in a thousand to the kitchens at Haddon Hall, Derbyshire, will have noticed the lack of an essential feature: there is nowhere to wash up the pots and pans, there is no scullery. In the late sixteenth century, the Manners family, Earls of Rutland, acquired the property by marriage (and still own it), but chose to stay on living in the greater splendours of Belvoir Castle, Leicestershire. The kitchens, which were built around 1370, remained as they had been left. By the beginning of the present century the buildings were in urgent need of repair, and this task was skilfully carried out under the direction of the 9th Duke of Rutland. When the house was restored the Duke also made some alterations and it is these which confuse the observant visitor.

Behind the screen in the great hall at Haddon there are three doors. The central door leads along a dark passage into the kitchen; those on either side lead to the buttery and pantry. The kitchen's low ceiling was possibly inserted in the sixteenth century when its only window was introduced, and this would have made the space unbearably hot in summer when two open fires were alight. Originally the kitchen ceiling was higher and the window would have been placed higher up than the present one. Immediately to the left as you go into the room is what the guidebook calls, incorrectly, a log-box. An open fire, also on the left, was converted to coal burning some time in the seventeenth century and the log-box was probably a bed for the kitchen boy who made up the fires. Ahead is the curving arch of another open fire which was destroyed when the 9th Duke made a tunnel to connect this room with new kitchens on the top floor of the stables, thus preserving the old kitchen. Beneath the window to the right of this hearth is a stone trough to store water and in the corner next to it is a small baking oven. A half-timber partition wall divides the kitchen from the next room, which is known as the bakery. A preparation table runs along this wall and the posts of the partition are marked with burns from rushlights sagging in their holders. An upright post, inconveniently in the middle of the floor, also carries burn marks which indicate that a table once stood by it. Immediately to the right of the door into the kitchen is another preparation table, made in the shape of a U and fixed to the floor. As well as lacking a scullery for washing up, these kitchens also have no servery: the essential place where the kitchen staff handed over a cooked meal to the servers. These kitchens are in fact only the remnants of the service rooms. If you go through the door to the right into the narrow room called the bakery, you can see the second of two small baking ovens in the outer wall. But this room could not have been the bakery because the ovens are not nearly large enough to cater for a household that must have numbered over a hundred at times. It was probably the pastry, the room used for baking pies and cakes. The two oak meal arks for storing flour must date from the fifteenth century. The real bakery is in the upper court at the bottom of the eleventh-century Peveril Tower and is not open to the public. To the right of the pastry is a door leading into what may have been a larder, but the early oak furniture is the important feature here. There are several fifteenth-century 'dole cupboards', or bread cupboards, their doors pierced with gothic designs to let in air. 'Dole cupboards' were filled with unwanted food and placed by the main entrance for poor folk to help themselves. Haddon would have used two or three at most and the survival of so many suggest that some or all were bought by the 6th Duke, or brought over from Belvoir. Ahead is the last service room you can see here. This is called the butchery, although it is more likely that this room was the scullery. However, it contains an oak salting trough for salting down meat, and a chopping block. The interest of these service rooms lies in their contents and in the fact that much remains structurally from the fourteenth century. But anyone going round Haddon should be aware that the way they are presented simply does not make historical sense.

Nevertheless, the rooms do give a good impression of what facilities were like. The layout of kitchens did not change appreciably for centuries and what was used at Haddon in the thirteenth century would have been just as convenient in the seventeenth century. Old kitchens can also be seen at Raby Castle, County Durham, where the kitchen was built in 1370, modernized in the nineteenth century and used until 1952, or at Gainsborough Old Hall, Lincolnshire, where there are kitchens with enormous open hearths dating from the mid-fifteenth century. Stanton Harcourt, Oxfordshire, has one of the most spectacular and complete medieval kitchens in Britain, dating from the late fourteenth century. A splendid monastery kitchen is the Abbot's kitchen at Glastonbury, dating from c.1350, which has a fireplace at each of the four corners. Today kitchens such as these are usually presented as orderly gleaming places with shining copper pans. Undoubtedly this was not always so, although the scullery boys used a great deal of sand for scouring copper pans and the cook would have seen to it that their job was well done. But a busy kitchen filled with smoke and the smell of cooking must have appeared chaotic, with half-prepared meals on the tables and people rushing about. Unfortunately, early eyewitness accounts of kitchens simply don't exist, but there is a telling description from the late eighteenth century by François de la Rochefoucauld. While staying at houses in Norfolk and Suffolk he noticed that in the rooms of entertainment, 'cleanliness . . . pervades everything', but in the kitchen he was disillusioned; the women who worked there were as black as coal and the dirt was 'indescribable'.

Very early kitchens had fires in the middle of the room. Medieval monks were the first to move the fireplace to a side wall, an important change which had the effect of throwing all the heat forward. The open fire for cooking always presented problems of heat control, which is why kitchens in large houses had more than one hearth; one would be for a hot fire while the other would be kept at a lower temperature; both would have turning spits in front of them. At first the spit was operated by hand or by a small dog on a caged wheel – as in the kitchens of St Fagan's Castle, South Glamorgan; later technology produced a fan in the flue that turned on the convected air in the chimney and, by cogs and shafts, controlled the spit. Other spits were powered by clockwork. Apart from food being roasted in this way, it was also boiled, or stewed, or baked in the bread oven, but in every case the major problem was controlling the heat. Enormous pies were baked occasionally, which were so big that they had to be cooked in specially constructed, outdoor, temporary ovens. The introduction of charcoal ranges in the late seventeenth century was a big innovation, although not everyone appreciated them. In the 1780s Mrs Raffald, whom we shall meet later in the chapter, did not hold with them because she found them expensive, adding as an after-thought, 'as well as pernicious to the cooks'.[1] She promoted a coal range of her own design. No doubt she also displayed over her apparatus the words so often painted in the kitchen: 'Waste not, want not.' Since well over half the food sent up from the kitchen usually came back again, the instruction might appear pointless.

Mrs Raffald's range was eclipsed by the much more scientific approach of Count Rumford, an American-born Englishman with a Holy Roman Empire title given by the Elector of Bavaria. He put his mind to the problems of smoking hearths and the efficient burning of fuel. At the end of the eighteenth century he invented the first true cook-stove giving a controlled heat – the forerunner of cast-iron ranges with ovens. By the mid-nineteenth century the old open kitchen hearths were being filled with smart new cast-iron ranges, which had to be black-leaded and lit early every morning before the cook came into the kitchen; those faced with these tasks may have cursed the new invention as the fire in the open hearth would have stayed in all night. Although more efficient for cooking, using only one and a half tons of fuel per month, the range gave a great deal more work to the kitchen maid, who would have been lucky to be paid £20 a year in the mid-century. By comparison, the monster open range would have consumed £30 of coal yearly. Good nineteenth-century kitchens with cast-iron ranges can be seen at Lanhydrock in Cornwall; Longleat, Wiltshire; Brodie Castle, Grampian; Castle Drogo, County Durham; and Croxteth Hall, Merseyside.

Preparing and cooking food is only the prelude to the equally important business of eating. A wonderfully detailed description of a dinner in 1770 has been left to us by Parson Woodforde, who was one of life's compulsive diary keepers. He was then curate of Castle Cary and Ansford in Somerset and living at Lower House, Ansford. His entry for 12 October reads:

> Mrs Carr, Miss Chamber, Mr Hindley, Mr Carr, and Sister Jane dined, supped and spent the evening with me, and we were very merry. I gave them for dinner a dish of fine Tench which I caught out of my brother's pond in Pond Close this morning, Ham, 3 Fowls boiled, a Plumb Pudding; a couple of Ducks roasted, a roasted neck of Pork, a Plumb Tart, an Apple Tart, Pears, Apples, and Nutts after dinner; White Wine and red, Beer and Cyder. Coffee and tea in the evening at six o'clock. Hashed Fowl and Duck Eggs and Potatoes etc. for supper. We did not dine till four o'clock – nor supped till ten. Mr Rice, a Welshman who is lately come to Cary and plays very well on the Triple Harp, played to us after coffee for an hour or two . . . the Company did not go away till near twelve o'clock . . . [2]

There are several things about this entry that strike us as strange: dinner at four o'clock, which Woodforde felt was late; the large amount of food for only six people to eat; and the fact the food is either roasted or boiled. In fact the usual hour for dinner in the late eighteenth century was 3 pm. This was the biggest and longest meal and had traditionally always been eaten in daylight and served formally. The lesser meal of supper would have been candlelit and may not have been served in a formal eating room – Woodforde used his parlour. The explanation for the staggering amount of food is that, although it was all put on the table at once and the host and five guests helped themselves, they did not have something of everything but only took what they wanted, and large quantities would have gone back to the kitchen. The open fire in Woodforde's kitchen could only be used for roasting on a spit or boiling in a pot; the tarts would have been baked in a bread oven. There was no means of controlling the heat for ambitious recipes. Although we would probably have enjoyed the basic cooking of the very fresh food we should have found ourselves puzzled and perplexed many times that evening. Guests would have used the same glass for both red and white wines and may even have added water to the red; anyone who decided to try the pork after the splendid tench would probably have found it was cold; the absence of vegetables at dinner and having to wait until supper at ten for potatoes would have seemed strange to us. It is doubtful if the room in which Woodforde and his friends ate was called a dining room in remotest Somerset; more probably it was the eating room.

'Dining room' is in fact a comparatively modern term; it did not come into general use until after the mid-eighteenth century and even then the preference was to call it an eating room – borrowed, like so much else in Britain, from France, where *salle à manger* is still used today. However, a dining room was only for dining in; breakfasting and supping were done elsewhere, in whatever room was convenient. Dr Johnson recognized the expression dining room in his dictionary, published in 1755, but others thought the use of the term vulgar. Samuel Pepys had a room he called his dining room in the 1660s, and a hundred years earlier William Sharington had a dining room at

Lacock, Wiltshire, with furniture plainly meant for a room set aside for the purpose of eating. Great Chalfield Manor in Wiltshire, built in the 1570s, had a similar arrangement, which shows how unwise it is to generalize! Nevertheless, Lacock and Great Chalfield seem to have been exceptions. In the sixteenth and seventeenth centuries, the rich generally dined in the great chamber, sometimes called the great dining chamber. From the mid-seventeenth century meals were eaten in the saloon, but more often in the parlour. People did not eat in a room set aside for the purpose until the mid-eighteenth century. Before that the room used for eating was a dual-purpose space, and when it was not in use for a meal the tables were put away and the chairs placed against the walls, to make it a room for parade and reception. While the fronts of Chippendale or Hepplewhite chairs display restrained and inventive carving, the backs are plain; the chairs were decorated in the knowledge that they would be made to stand against the wall when not in use. Where dining rooms pre-dating the nineteenth century are shown with chairs placed round a dining table not set for a meal, this is historically wrong. This practice would have been deplored by Robert Adam, Hepplewhite and Chippendale, whose chairs are not seen to advantage in such circumstances.

One of the best presented houses is Newby Hall, Yorkshire, the home of Mr and Mrs Robin Compton. They spent a great deal of trouble, time and money on the house before it was opened to the public. Visitors leave Newby with the impression that they would like to live there, if they could accommodate themselves to rather more space than they are used to. In a word, it is comfortable. Some of the rooms are undeniably grand but Newby has been lived in by Compton ancestors since 1748 and is very much the Comptons' home, not in any sense a museum. The library at Newby is now used by the family as a living room and the visitor feels at home here. Yet this room existed in the 1690s and was nothing like it is today. The furniture in this south-facing room is arranged in a modern fashion owing nothing to historical precedent; no piece is placed where our ancestors would have put it. Everything is set where it can be conveniently used with minimum effort. Yet our predecessors of two hundred years ago would have found the arrangement cluttered, while one hundred years ago the room would have been thought to be rather bare.

In the 1760s there would, for example, have been no tables placed in the windows, as at present, and the two splendid pieces of furniture in Louis XV rococo style on either side of the fireplace would have been used very differently. The French *bureau plat* of c.1750 would have been freestanding, for it is decorated on every side. The English commode of the same date, which must have been one of a pair, was out of fashion and would, if used, have stood between windows beneath pier glasses in a balanced arrangement. The decoration of the room is neo-classical and would have been the latest thing when it was done in 1767; this would have clashed with the old-fashioned Louis XV piece. If used at all, rugs would not have been laid over a grey carpet, but placed directly on the bare floorboards. The sofa now positioned before the fire would have been consigned to a wall. Today the room has only two chairs and a sofa of the same date as the decoration, but the festoon curtains are completely in period for the 1760s. The air of grandeur about this living room/library gives a clue as to what the room was used for in the past. It is altogether too grand for a living room, although the comfortable furnishings soften the effect, and it was in fact designed by Robert Adam in 1767 to be an eating room. Following the advice of another architect a hundred years earlier, a Swede called Daniel Cronstrom, Adam recommended that eating rooms should not have fabric on the walls as this tended to retain the odour of food, so the walls of this room were painted in the colour scheme of buff, black and French grey, which has happily been restored. Paintings, concerned with food and drink, are set into the walls, and there are also plaster panels decorated with classical designs. Because this is one of the few south-facing, warm rooms in the house, the family built another dining room only forty years after it was completed and the old room became a library and then a living room.

Even so the story does not finish there. If we go back even further, to the 1690s when the house was built, the space now occupied by the library consisted of several rooms, one of which was a bed chamber. Newby is just one example of the fact that when we are shown a dining room in a historic house it is very likely to have been designed for some other purpose. Similarly, meals are now usually eaten in the company of many fewer people than was once the case.

Our early medieval ancestors always ate in a great hall with the fire burning on a central hearth. A fine example of such a hall exists at Penshurst Place, Kent. There was a real fire hazard from the rushes strewn on the floor, which partly explains why so few timber-framed, early medieval halls have survived. At the Weald and Downland Open Air Museum near Chichester, a re-erected, half-timbered hall-house of the mid-fifteenth century has been restored to its late-medieval state. Visit this on a cold, wet day when the wind blows smoke from the central hearth into your eyes and it is possible to understand fully the discomfort endured by our ancestors.

The great hall was ideally suited to accommodating and feeding large numbers of people. It had a raised dais at one end for the lord's family and important visitors, and at the other were the buttery and pantry. Such halls have survived unchanged at the Universities of Oxford and Cambridge, even to the high table on a raised dais, with screens hiding the service doors, pantry and buttery. In contrast to the wet goods kept in the buttery – butter, cheese, milk and beer – the pantry was the store for dry goods such as flour, bread and, oddly, wine, under the charge of the pantler. Both offices are always situated at the entrance end of the hall and behind a screen deliberately placed to keep the draught, caused by the opening and closing of the entrance, buttery, pantry and kitchen doors, out of the body of the hall. The medieval house plan is always predictable.

The Norman great hall of Oakham Castle, Leicestershire, mentioned in Chapter 1, dates from the late twelfth century. It is all that is left of a complex of buildings and even though now seen on its own gives a clear impression of a medieval great hall where all the life of the castle went on: eating, drinking and sleeping. The kitchen at Oakham was a separate building, a wise precaution in view of their habit of catching fire. The hall at Stokesay Castle, Shropshire was built about one hundred years later, around 1280. The earth floor and unglazed windows present another impression of the discomfort of medieval life, even for the well-off. Both Oakham and Stokesay have central hearths; the hearth in the great hall at Pembroke Castle became a talking point when it was moved to a side wall with a chimney in the mid-fourteenth century. Haddon Hall, Derbyshire, has a hall built in c.1380 which was modernized for the last time one hundred years later when the central hearth was moved to a side wall. These are all examples of halls that were abandoned, and have remained unaltered. Because halls became, in time, outdated, there are many that have been modernized, floored over or otherwise altered so as to be all but unrecognizable. It is perhaps surprising that any have survived over the centuries, since they were undoubtedly very draughty, cold and ill-lit rooms. Moreover, they were also crowded, noisy and, with unwashed bodies, smelly. Household orders of the Duke of Clarence, dated 1469, lay down that the hall fire should not be lit until 1 November and never be alight after Easter. Household orders of the same date from *The Boke of Curtasye* forbid a hall fire after 2 February![3]

Even before the arrival of the Normans in 1066 the hall was the place of eating. It continued so for six hundred years, the longest time a space has been used for one purpose continuously. In remote parts of the country, and in farmhouses where the farmhands ate with the family, this was still so into the eighteenth century, although conditions became more comfortable by, for example, the insertion of glazed windows in the sixteenth century. Imagine yourself in one of these great halls with no ceiling overhead and the rafters lost in the darkness, smoke billowing from a central hearth, blown by winds from windows protected only by wooden shutters and lattice to keep out birds. Above you the smoke collects until it escapes through a central lantern in the roof, through vents at either end of the roof ridge, or simply finds its own way out through gaps in the tiles or thatch, gaps through which birds creep to roost on the rafters at night.

Birds on the rafters were a problem to everyone, but particularly to the proud lord of the manor as he sat at his high table. A canopy suspended over his chair provided some protection against this hazard. However, this cover was late in coming to England and probably was not used until the fifteenth century.[4] The origin of the canopy, or 'cloth of estate', is religious: the splendid ceremonies of Corpus Christi and Easter carried the host beneath a canopy. It was only a small matter to transfer the idea to the sovereign who was exhibited to his people in solemn rituals of coronations and funerals, washing the feet of the poor in imitation of Christ on Maundy Thursday and touching for the king's evil. The earliest record of a royal canopy was that carried over the French monarch in the late fourteenth century. Whatever its origins, the canopy was undeniably useful. Placed over the chair of state, it not only protected the persons beneath but served to set them apart and to advertize their power in the days before photography and television made political figures instantly recognizable to everyone. Mary Queen of Scots carried a folding canopy around with her during the nineteen years she was a prisoner of her cousin Elizabeth I. When she was sentenced to death at Fotheringhay Castle in the winter of 1586 her canopy was taken away because from that moment she was legally dead. There is a canopy made from sixteenth-century needlework in the Burrell Collection, Glasgow, and a splendid coved, wooden canopy at Adlington Hall, Cheshire, a unique survivor of the late fifteenth century. Hampton Court has two restored royal canopies of the late eighteenth and early nineteenth centuries. A more modern canopy exists in the House of Lords over the throne used by Elizabeth II when she opens Parliament. Made of oak, it was designed by Pugin in the 1840s, and must be the last to have been made and certainly the last to be used.

Owners have a tendency to call the great hall a banqueting hall, which it never was; a banquet was not always a feast, but also marked the end of the meal when the party left the room to allow the tables to be cleared away. This final course of sweetmeats and cordials, similar to the liqueurs and choco-late mints we serve at the conclusion of dinner today, was later called the dessert because it was the point at which the room was vacated. In the sixteenth century there was even a fashion for retiring to small banqueting houses where the cordials and sweetmeats would be served. Montacute House, Somerset, has two such houses in the garden, while Longleat has several on the roof, and Wollaton Hall, Nottinghamshire, has one in a roof turret.

But by the fifteenth century the hall was no place for the family to eat, except on special occasions. A long and detailed 'Orders of service belonging to the degree of a duke, a marquess and an erle'[5] of the fifteenth century makes this perfectly clear. A nobleman would take breakfast in the great chamber, as the room where he slept was known. While he was attending mass, the grooms of the chamber set up a trestle with a 'breakfast board' on a small carpet at the foot of the bed. Although the meal itself was simple, the vastly complicated ritual surrounding it called for the services of no less than thirteen servants, including a gentleman cupbearer, a carver and a server. The food and drink was 'saied', or tasted, first before being put before 'the estate' to prevent the mischance of poison. Anything the nobleman would perso-nally use, such as napkins, was kissed before being laid out, except for the spoon and breakfast knife. He was never allowed to serve himself but called for bread, meat and soup as he wanted them. Drink – beer or wine – was offered by his kneeling cupbearer, and each fresh draught would be 'saied' before the nobleman drank. A noble visitor to the household would breakfast in the great chamber with 'the estate' but would be placed at a separate 'long board'. Gentleman servants – the officers of the household hierarchy – breakfasted in the outer chamber. Yeoman servants – the ordinary ranks – breakfasted downstairs in the great hall when the nobleman and his party had finished. A typical breakfast served in the great chamber would consist of mutton and chickens boiled in gruel, with boiled beef and a chine, and on fish days ling or cod and buttered eggs.

Dinner was likewise served in the nobleman's great chamber, after high mass between 10 am and 11am. As this was the main meal of the day it was served with incredible pomp. Like breakfast, it was initially eaten at the foot of the bed, but by the sixteenth century the bed had been moved out of the great chamber into a separate bed chamber, where it developed its own particular ceremonial.

In keeping with the discomfort of medieval living, medieval eating was literally a mess. Food was sometimes eaten with knives and spoons, but mainly with the fingers of the left hand. Everything was put on the table at once in bowls and dishes, and diners helped themselves to whatever they fancied with their left hands. Here again, as in so many other aspects of life, rank was taken into account. The more important had dishes to themselves, but those of lesser rank shared two to a dish and, further down, four and even six to a dish; these were called messes and the name still lives on in our armed forces.

There were no plates and food was piled on to trenchers – two or four slices of stale bread with a further slice over the centre join. 'Trencher' comes from the Norman-French *tranchier*, to slice. A hungry person could eat his trencher, but it was more frequently scraped into a bucket with all other leavings and given to the poor as dole. Because the foundation off which the diner ate was so insecure – it is impossible to cut anything up on soggy bread – all food had to be chopped into manageable pieces before it came to the table; conversely food could not be too mushy. These limitations inevitably restricted recipes. However, although there were no plates, there were bowls and a great deal of soup was eaten. The cauldron over the fire, into which almost everything edible was thrown, was the mainstay of most households and almost the only way in which vegetables were used, apart from in salads. A Latin diet sheet of the fifteenth century says firmly, 'Don't eat cabbages; they make your belly ache.'[6] Everyone had to wash his or her hands before any meal; those at the high table were served with their own elaborate and costly ewer and basin, the rest made do with a basin and jug in the hall. 'Don't spit in the basin . . . especially when a prelate is present,' was another injunction.[7]

Dinner was the main meal of the day and the occasion for exotic dishes when important guests were present. The first course of a mid-fifteenth-century dinner from John Russell's *Boke of Nurture* included brawn, made from wild boar, with mustard; a potage of herbs, spice and wine; stewed pheasant; swan; capons; pork; baked venison; leche lombard (a kind of haggis made from pork, eggs, pepper, cloves, currants, dates and sugar, served with a hot rich sauce) and meat fritters. The swan, with its feathers replaced, would have been the centrepiece; John Russell recommended that web-footed birds took precedence over others. There was also a 'device' or 'subtlety' – a scene modelled in sugar or marzipan – to add an intellectual slant to the meal, in this case a portrayal of Gabriel greeting Mary. Often it would take the form of a flattering reference to the chief guest. The device is the direct ancestor of our decorated wedding cakes.

The second course consisted of two soups, a meat blancmange, bustard, partridge, plover, egret and rabbit, with a centrepiece of a peacock with its tail feathers displayed and in its pride, with the beak and head gilded. It is very doubtful if this bird would have been eaten and its purpose was probably purely decorative. In addition there were small birds roasted on a skewer, sweet cakes, amber jelly and poached fritters, with a 'device' of an angel appearing to three shepherds. The dishes of the third course were almond cream, roast curlew, snipe, quail and sparrows, crayfish, baked quinces and sage fritters, with a device of the Virgin Mary presented by the King of Cologne.[8] With the exception of the fritters, eggs do not feature on this menu, although many were eaten in omelettes and pancakes, or scrambled. Fifteenth-century eggs were smaller than they are today, so households used what appear to be vast quantities.

All the dishes would have been very decorative. Some would have been set in tinted jellies; others would have been coloured with saffron or powdered sandalwood or striped with spinach or parsley to give a marbled effect. The final dessert, which the guests ate standing while the tables were cleared away or in banqueting houses, was white apples, caraway cakes and a kind of spiced wine called hippocras. All the dishes for each course were put on the table at once and the whole meal would have been rather like a modern buffet with all the guests helping themselves. The grandest would have eaten with their host in the great chamber while their servants ate in the hall with the household. As with the serving of food, rank was observed in how the guests were seated both in the chamber and in the hall. People eating in the latter were usually put at three tables. The highest was the steward's table where the gentleman servants and visitors sat. Servers, waiters and carvers and those of similar status ate at the clerk of the kitchen's table, which was second in rank. The remaining staff sat at the lowest table. The kitchen staff always ate in the kitchen. It is not quite clear where young children fitted into this picture, but it is very likely they were fed in a nursery. Hardwick Hall had one on the ground floor for the grandchildren in 1601 and there was also a nursery at Knole in 1613. The four women who staffed the nursery at Knole ate at their own table in the hall,[9] presumably after their charges had been fed. When the meal was finished the tables and benches were all pushed to the sides of the room. The sixteenth-century hall benches at Hardwick Hall have had their feet cut off on one side so that they now fit snugly against the walls.

Trenchers made out of bread were replaced by plate-like wooden trenchers in the fifteenth century. By the mid-sixteenth century yeoman families were using pewter and copper plates, and the wealthy plates of silver and silver-gilt, the best being ostentatiously displayed on the shelves of a buffet or 'cup board' – the Tudor equivalent of a display cabinet. Pottery plates first appeared in the late sixteenth century. The first examples came from Delft, but a pottery was soon established at Lambeth, copying the distinctive Delft designs. The earliest surviving English pottery plate can be seen in the

Museum of London. Dated 1602, it is painted in tin-enamel in blue, green, orange and yellow, outlined in dark purple. Forks came to England from France about fifty years later. Although commonly used in the Low Countries and France, both plates and forks took a long time to be accepted. The problem was England's innate conservatism. Even Queen Anne, who died in 1714, preferred to eat with her fingers. When plates had been universally adopted, the same plate would be used throughout the meal. A trencher was not removed, so why remove a plate? As late as 1752 Horace Walpole was amazed to see the 6th Duke of Hamilton and his Duchess eating their entire meal off the same plate. But Walpole was very much abreast of London fashion, which the Duke plainly wasn't! While the mighty drank out of silver-gilt cups, those of lesser rank used horn until the mid-sixteenth century, when glasses became available. Even so everyone drank out of the same vessel. By 1600 Delft mugs and jugs were becoming commonplace.

In the mid-fifteenth century some guidance on behaviour was clearly felt to be necessary; either people were behaving worse or, more likely, they were becoming fastidious about what was acceptable. As adults should already know how to conduct themselves at meals, or were beyond help, the strictures were directed at children. *The Babees Book* of 1475 tells the young man not to stuff his mouth so full that he cannot speak, not to dirty the cup with his hands (surely very difficult in the circumstances?) and (another impossibility) not to dirty the table cloth. It also instructs him not to scratch, although the rush-strewn floor, like the diners, would have been harbouring fleas. Twice he is told not to recite naughty stories and not to pick his nose, teeth or nails at meal times. 'Don't bring a cat in to dinner as a companion' is another instruction; presumably a dog was acceptable since they are not mentioned. However, the *Babees Book* is restrained by comparison with earlier instructions – perhaps standards of behaviour were improving. In his *Boke of Nurture* John Russell is sensitive to the 'firing of stern guns' during dinner. Ten years earlier an anonymous improver was very concerned that young men should not wipe their noses on the table cloth. All these sources of advice are in full agreement that no one should spit at meals; and if they must, that they should grind the result into the rushes with their heels. If these habits were felt to be disagreeable to their contemporaries, and the rules necessary, it is obvious that behaviour at meal times must have been, by our standards, somewhat disgusting.

Queen Elizabeth I, three times a visitor to Loseley Park, Surrey, demanded when she first went there that the house be kept cleaner and sweeter for a future visit; no doubt it was the hall that was giving the trouble. Elizabethan letters often complain of the noise and smell of great halls; no wonder families preferred to eat elsewhere. By 1500 they had migrated from the parlour, a room off the hall situated behind the high table, upstairs to the great chamber. As we have seen, this was the principal bed chamber, but the bed was moved out into a state bed chamber when the great chamber became an eating and reception room. Here, members of the family dined and lived in what was definitely a warmer and more private setting, only 'holding state' in the hall on feast days such as Christmas.

When a meal was to be set up in the great chamber, those within the room withdrew into an annex, called the withdrawing room, while servants set up trestles for serving what was still a medieval meal, with a variety of dishes all placed on the tables at the same time.

It is unfortunate that many guidebooks refer to the great chamber as the 'solar'. This is a legacy of the romantic movement of the early nineteenth century; the heroines in Walter Scott's Waverley Novels, for example, tended to inhabit solars. The term 'solar' was originally dog-latin, but is also of French derivation from the same Latin source. It meant no more than an upper room, which might even be in the attic. The good Anglo-Norman term, great chamber, is more precise and unambiguous.

Although the Victorians are credited with creating rooms for every purpose, the trend began when the family moved out of the great hall into the parlour in the fourteenth century and into the great chamber by 1500, and continued with the development of a range of state apartments.

The family's gradual retreat into a system of apartments had the effect of underlining the rank of those in positions of power. The apartments acted as a filter system which kept out the less worthy. However, it is debatable whether the initial impetus was a desire to retreat from the noise and smell of the crowded hall, or a desire for greater privacy. Privacy is a comparatively modern concept which would not have been understood before the eighteenth century. In the medieval household servants were everywhere. Although the family had retreated to their own rooms in the Tudor period, they were still surrounded by servants and their life was far from private.

The multitude of available servants explains why furniture was kept against the walls for so many centuries; if a chair was wanted in the middle of the great chamber a servant was there to make it instantly available. And likewise he would take it away when it was finished with so that the centre of the stage was left clear.

Maintaining a household run in medieval fashion, staffed by an army of servants who dined in an archaic great hall, was, by Elizabeth I's reign, a costly operation. The practice of keeping a large household had been abandoned in France over fifty years earlier. Change came slowly in England, partly because of the active opposition of the Tudors. Henry VIII issued an order in 1526 which forbade his courtiers to 'dyne in corners and secret places' and ordered them to eat communally in hall or, if of high rank, in the king's outer chamber.[10] Clearly Henry's courtiers were attempting to adopt the French custom of eating in their own chambers. Henry was in fact repeating a similar order made by his father, Henry VII. Both monarchs also went to great lengths to emphasize their ancient ancestry; the Tudor claim to the throne was weak, and propaganda was aimed at making their roots appear more substantial than fact warranted. Cadwallader, the ancient Briton, and Julius Caesar were claimed as their forefathers. Busts of both were displayed in royal palaces to remind the court of the fact. Henry VII believed that what was good enough for his ancestors was certainly good enough for him and deliberately maintained a medieval court on that basis. Although Henry VIII continued his father's practices, he was clearly planning changes toward the end of his reign. Nonsuch Palace, begun in 1538, had no great hall and patently intended to compete with Francis I's French palaces. It was unfinished when Henry died in 1547, and his heirs never completed it. Edward VI only reigned for seven years, Mary had other things on her mind, while Elizabeth I was a born reactionary and never changed anything if she could help it. The fact that the monarch maintained a medieval household accommodated in great halls meant that courtiers had to do likewise or chaos would result in the event of a royal visit.

The accession of James I to the throne in 1603 marked the end of the great hall in large houses. Inheriting an expensive and ramshackle medieval household from Elizabeth I, James soon rid himself of archaic officers and superfluous servants, leaving the halls empty. Those servants that remained ate out on board wages or in the service rooms. His Queen, Anne of Denmark, quickly found another use for the wasted space in her husband's palaces and used it for court masques, written by Ben Jonson and designed by Inigo Jones. Jones introduced the proscenium arch and perspective scenery, the beginning of modern theatre architecture.

These developments had a far-reaching effect on the plan of the historic house. The old great hall gradually became redundant and in new buildings was no more than an entrance hall where the visitor gave up his cloak before proceeding to the principal reception room. Holland House, London, destroyed in the Second World War, was in the forefront of fashion when it was built in 1607, and here the hall was merely an entrance hall. Aston Hall, Birmingham, begun in 1618, is another good example of how houses were beginning to reflect new lifestyles. Altered to its present form in the 1650s, the hall is magnificently decorated but is no more than an entrance vestibule. The great chamber on the first floor now came into its own as the principal reception and eating room. After the mid-seventeenth century it was moved down to the ground floor and tended to be called the saloon – a French term brought to England with the Restoration of 1660. Ham House, modernized in the 1670s, has a good example of a saloon, and there are later ones at Ragley Hall in Warwickshire, built in 1680, and at Clandon Park, Surrey, built in 1713. The large number of surviving oval gate-leg tables of the Restoration period reflect the fashion for eating at smaller tables in the saloon. By 1700 the modern practice of seating men and women alternately at the table was standard. The saloon had ceased to be used as an eating room by 1730 and another room, known as the eating room and, occasionally, the dining room, was devoted to this activity.

In the seventeenth century children were looked after by a nurse and nursery maid who brought their food up from the kitchens. They did not mix with the rest of the household and by the eighteenth century were confined to the school room and taught by a governess, living in nurseries on the top floor of the house. The windows of these rooms are distinguished by their iron bars which prevented anyone climbing out on to the sill. In the nineteenth century children who had reached a civilized age and were unlikely to misbehave were allowed to eat dinner in the dining room, in the company of their governess at a separate table. The late 7th Earl Spencer remembered how, in the early years of this century when he was about twelve years old, Winston Churchill dined at Althorp and, as a special treat, he and his older sister were allowed to eat in the dining room at a separate table with their governess.

If the eating habits of the nursery remained unchanged over many centuries, this was paralleled by the reluctance of the British to change generally. There were always exciting examples from France to stimulate the fashionable, which worked against national conservatism. Over many centuries recipes hardly altered and what was served at a medieval dinner would have seemed appropriate at any time up to the mid-seventeenth century. But from that point cooking techniques were gradually transformed. Innovations included the introduction of the fork, which meant that dishes could be more ambitious and were not restricted to the small morsels that could be picked up in the fingers, and the use of French recipes at court following the Restoration in 1660. Although French dishes were slow to gain popularity and were not really fashionable until the late seventeenth century, the techniques and ingredients on which they were based were to have a profound influence. Recipes involved fewer spices than was traditional in England and sauces were based on meat dripping combined with vinegar or lemon juice. The globe artichoke, stuffed mushrooms and snails are all examples of French delicacies introduced at this time.

Although the room where meals were eaten changed over the centuries and the recipes altered, the method of serving meals remained the same until the early nineteenth century. At a medieval dinner a large number of dishes were placed on the table at the same time; this was called a course, but it bore no relation to what we think of today as a course. Elizabeth Raffald, the eighteenth-century equivalent of Mrs Beeton, who published *The Experienced English Housekeeper* in 1782, included 'Directions for a GRAND TABLE' of two courses. Each of her two courses has twenty-five dishes. The centrepiece of the first was a large bowl of mock turtle soup. The other dishes included hare and veal soups placed at either end of the oval table, veal, ham, turkey, pork, chicken, pigeons, rabbit and beef olives. There were also some very small dishes of vegetables – broccoli, peas, kidney beans and a salad. Her second course offered pheasant, woodcock, chicken and hare on large dishes at each side of the table. These would not strike us as particularly unusual. However, the centrepiece was 'Transparent Pudding', a sort of nutmeg custard, which was surrounded by small dishes of snipe in jelly, potted lamphreys, stewed mushrooms, pickled smelts, marbled veal, macaroni and pork. The course also included a fish jelly, a shaped fruit jelly and two cheese cakes. Elizabeth Raffald concludes the feast with a dessert, which is effectively a third course; twenty-five dishes (the same number as the first two courses) of nuts, fruit, ices and sweetmeats were served in china dishes and fruit baskets.

What seems strange to us is the way that the dishes for each course do not go together, and could include both savoury and sweet recipes. This approach is the same as it would have been at a medieval dinner. Everything was put on the table at once and each guest would take a little of what he fancied and so build up his own menu. Apart from the principal guests, people were not told where to sit at table and guests moved themselves around to be near a favourite dish or fellow guest. The timid had a hard time of it, for it was bad form to ask a fellow guest to pass a dish and the servants would have been busy serving wine. At Mrs Raffald's first course a timorous guest might have sat down before the boiled turkey and got nothing else until it was cleared away, and then been stuck with chick peas in asparagus.

The whole method of service appears to us to be chaotic, but in fact there was some rationale behind the dishes for each course. The heavier recipes were served first, and although the table was covered with a wide choice of food, often presented in small dishes, high ranking guests at a formal dinner had the right to the best on offer. There was, therefore, no question of every guest getting a helping of everything – lower ranks had to make do with the less elevated preparations. What is missing from the menu is any indication of what everything looked like. Nearly all the dishes were designed to catch the eye with both colour and shape. One had hidden mottoes in it – the ancestor of our Christmas pudding. In the seventeenth century the table would also have been decorated with sculpted sugar figures, and in time these were made more permanently in porcelain. The delightful Meissen figures made by Kändler from 1731 to 1756, which now fetch such high prices, were initially table decorations and typical of what would have decorated Mrs Raffald's table. Her feast is modest in comparison with what would have been provided a hundred years earlier, but meals in both periods would have produced spectacular waste. This was to some extent true in the twentieth century, as is shown in Vita Sackville-West's recollection of Knole in her father's time (see page 3).

An interesting commentary on British eating habits seen through French eyes has been left to us by Bartolomé Faujus de Saint Fond, who visited Inverary Castle in 1784. He recorded that:

At ten o'clock a bell gives warning that it is breakfast-time: we then repair to a large room, ornamented with historical pictures of the family; among which there are some Battoni, Reynolds and other eminent Italian and English painters. Here we find several tables, covered with tea-kettles, fresh cream, excellent butter, rolls of several kinds, and in the midst of all bouquets of flowers, newspapers and books. There are besides, in this room, a billiard table, pianos and other musical instruments.

After breakfast, some walk in the parks, others employ themselves in reading or in music, or return to their rooms until half-past four, when the bell makes itself heard to announce that dinner is ready; we all go to the dining-room, where the table is usually laid for twenty-five or thirty covers. When everyone is seated, the chaplain, according to custom, makes a short prayer, and blesses the food, which is eaten with pleasure, for the dishes are prepared after the manner of an excellent French cook, every thing is served here as in Paris, except some courses in the English style, for which a certain predeliction is preserved; but this makes a variety, and thus gives the epicures of every country an opportunity of pleasing their palates.

The entrees, the roti, the entrements are all served as in France with the same variety and abundance. If the poultry be not so juicy as in Paris, one eats here in compensation hazel-hens, and above all moorfowl, delicious fish, and vegetables, the quality of which maintains the reputation of the Scottish gardeners who grow them.

At the dessert, the scene changes; the cloth, the napkins, and everything vanish. The mahogany table appears in all its lustre; but it is soon covered with brilliant decanters, filled with the best wines; comfits [sweetmeats], in fine porcelain or crystal vases; and fruits of different kinds in elegant baskets. Plates are distributed together with many glasses; and in every object elegance and convenience seem to rival each other. [11]

He then goes on to express surprise that fresh grapes, melons, apricots, figs and cherries should be served as late as September in a climate so far north.

Today we eat less but more often. Dinner has always been the main meal of the day, with more modest fare at breakfast and supper, but the time at which these meals are eaten has changed radically. Dinner in the fifteenth century was served around 10 am, breakfast at 6 or 7 am and supper at 5 pm. Gradually the time of serving dinner became later; Mrs Raffold's dinner was served at four in the afternoon, her breakfast at 8 or 9 am and her supper at ten in the evening. By the early nineteenth century breakfast was served at 9.30 am and dinner at 7 pm. This left a huge gap in the middle of the day and so another light meal, luncheon, was invented to be eaten around noon. The time of luncheon has remained relatively unchanged, but with the advent of good artificial lighting, dinner moved ever later and the vacuum between luncheon and dinner was filled in the mid-nineteenth century by tea, with dainty sandwiches and cakes (a meal at first eaten only by the ladies). Below stairs the old customs died hard; dinner in the servants' hall was at midday to the very end, with supper in the evening.

Above stairs fashionable society was led by London and the court. In 1776 Admiral Boscawen's widow, who lived at Hatchlands, Surrey, had dinner in the country at her usual hour of 2 pm before setting out for a rare visit to London and she was amazed to find she could have another dinner in town at 5 pm the same day! [12] In the country, even a mere two hours' drive from London, habits had not caught up with the latest fashion. One of the reasons why dinner was eaten later and later is that Parliament had begun to sit later. Until the mid-eighteenth century, the House rose before 4 pm, but a century later it was likely to be 7 or 8 pm. As speeches became longer so dinner became later. Moreover, the Prince of Wales, who liked late hours, encouraged the fashion for eating late in the early nineteenth century.

Neither Mrs Raffald nor Mrs Boscawen would have been surprised to find some of the dishes from the far end of the table quite cold by the time they tasted them. However, they would have been astonished could they see how food is served today. A revolution took place in the early nineteenth century which enabled hot food to be served to all the guests at once, no matter where they were sitting. This was the fashion for serving meals *à la Russe*, which came from France and which meant that food was served to each guest by footmen from dishes placed on serving tables; at grand dinners one footman stood behind each chair. This innovation caused a drastic reduction in the number of dishes on the menu but it also meant that recipes could be more complicated because the food would be eaten as soon as served. This left the table less cluttered and the centre could be used for flower arrangements rather than for the display of perilous pyramids of sweetmeats and fruit.

By Mrs Raffald's time guests were provided with a wine glass each. When changing wines, the glasses were washed by the footmen – a tap and sink for this purpose can be seen outside the family eating room at Chatsworth. Robert Adam, who invented the sideboard in the 1760s, often provided it with two vases. One was a container for cutlery, while the other was lined with lead to hold water and provided with a tap so that servants could wash glasses. The cutlery vases were often confusingly given matching taps which had no real function. The water used to wash glasses was held in the sort of container frequently referred to as a wine cooler. There is a pair of water-holding vases in the eating room at Osterley, designed by Robert Adam in the 1770s. At Harewood, Yorkshire, there is a magnificent sideboard set with two water-holding vases and a 'wine cooler' to catch the water, designed by Adam and made by Chippendale in 1769-71. However, this system was not always effective; Horace Walpole complained that the footmen didn't bother to wash the glasses and that guests were getting them back dirty. The alternative to having the footmen wash the glasses was to provide guests with their own 'washing glasses' and let them get on with the job themselves. These glasses, with a small lip to hold the stem of an inverted wine glass, are often called 'wine glass coolers', although they were more usually used to rinse glasses once the brief fashion for chilling wine glasses in ice had run its course.

The practice of washing glasses in the eating room did not last, although the evidence for it is still there balanced at either end of many sideboards. It was, in fact, a late fashion. The watershed in eating customs was at the Restoration, and this was mirrored in other areas of life. As Chapter 4 will show, where and how people slept followed a similar pattern up to 1720, when it diverged.

CHAPTER 4

Sleeping

When Horace Walpole saw the state bedroom in Osterley Park for the first time in 1778, he commented: 'The next [room] is a light plain green velvet bed-chamber. The bed is of green satin richly embroidered with colours, and with eight columns; too theatric, and too like a modern head-dress, for round the outside of the dome are festoons of artificial flowers. What would Vitruvius [an ancient Roman writer on architecture] think of a dome decorated by a milliner?'[1]

Fortunately this bed chamber still contains the same furniture as in Walpole's time and the fabrics have been restored or replaced in their original green colours. As a result we can have the rare privilege of sharing his experience. The bed is the main feature of the room, with an overpowering mass of festoons, tassels and fringing, and with brightly coloured embroidered flowers on a background of green velvet. Robert Adam, who redesigned the interior of Osterley in the 1770s, was the first architect to give his patrons complete decorative schemes, even down to the door knobs. The bed was designed by Adam in 1775-6 and was conceived as a Temple of Venus, based on an engraving of the Temple of the Sun at Baalbeck, published in 1757 by Robert Wood. The headboard shows a medallion of Venus, the goddess of love and fertility, with her attributes of cupids on dolphins. The whole confection referred to Arcadia (the ideal region of rural happiness) and the four gilded sphinxes at the corners of the bed were the guardians of the garden of Arcadia. The matching carpet surrounding the bed was also designed by Adam. It looks as though it runs beneath the bed, but it is U-shaped and only surrounds the edge. The rest of the furniture is completely overshadowed by the bed, but the set of gilt chairs in the Louis XVI style repeat the sphinx detail and in any other room would stand out in their own right. Between the windows is a large pier glass topped by a small medallion of Venus and Cupid with two more sphinxes at the corners. Beneath the mirror is a fine English commode (another name for a chest of drawers), made from the panels of a Chinese lacquer screen and attributed to Thomas Chippendale. The cupid motif is repeated on the mantelpiece and is also carved on the crest of the overmantel mirror. The painting in the centre of the ceiling is of Aglaia, one of Venus's attendants, being enslaved by love. The walls are covered with pleated velvet in a restful shade of green. All in all few people would feel up to spending a night in this bed alone. To us the decoration seems excessive and most people would be inclined to agree with Walpole. Yet earlier beds were even more magnificent, and bedrooms were once viewed very differently from how they are now.

In his diary for 4 October 1683, John Evelyn gives a curious view of a bedroom: 'Following his Majesty [Charles II] thro' the gallerie, I went, with the few who attended him, into the Dutchesse of Portsmouth's *dressing roome* within her bedchamber, where she was in her morning loose garment, her maids combing her, newly out of her bed, his Majesty and the gallants standing about her . . . '[2] As the Duchess of Portsmouth was the king's mistress, this description seems even more extraordinary. But Evelyn was simply witnessing the Duchess's *levée*, when she received friends in her bedroom, or, in this case, in her dressing room, off the bedroom. It was customary for people to entertain and to be entertained during their toilet.

The occasion we are seeing through Evelyn's eyes was a reflection of the ceremonial connected with very grand bed chambers, which reached its peak at the court of Louis XIV; by 1720 society had become more relaxed and the *levée* and *coucher* (a similar ceremony when grand people went to bed) were losing their importance. From then onwards the bed chamber lost more and more of its significance. Today a bedroom is where we expect to find a bed or beds in which to pass the night. Unfortunately there are very few references to the use of bedrooms way back in the past, and none earlier than the fifteenth century. In the Bayeux Tapestry Edward the Confessor is shown dying in an upper chamber of his palace of Westminster on 5 January 1066. The bed's foot has a post carved in the form of a fearsome beast, while a pair of curtains above the bed are tied back to show the king dying with his crown on, supported by Queen Edith. The episode is illustrated with heavy use of symbolic convention and tells us little of how a Norman king slept in 1070-80, when the tapestry was made. We know nothing of how a Norman baron slept and only a little more of how a medieval nobleman went to bed. As is the case today, what was taken for granted was seldom noted – only the extraordinary and curious were recorded. However, we are better informed about fifteenth-century sleeping customs.

Putting a nobleman to bed in the fifteenth century was a complicated matter which required the attendance of no fewer than nine servants before he even put a toe into the great chamber where his state bed was set up. The very detailed set of household orders given in the fifteenth-century *Orders of Service*, quoted in the previous chapter, gives the essential procedure. A nobleman was expected to pass the night equipped with a chair placed at the foot of this bed (with a cushion and a foot stool); a wax torch, lit in winter but unlit in summer; a basin; a ewer of water for washing and a towel; two kinds of bread in a napkin; a great silver jug of beer with a drinking cup; two large pots of wine with another cup; and a good fire in winter. All emergencies that might overtake the nobleman in the night were catered for. The only item missing from this list is his pot, but he would have had a garderobe off his great chamber and so would not have needed one – just the wax torch to light his way across the room.

The night equipment of the nobleman in the fiteenth century does not seem particularly unusual, with the exception of the quantity of alcohol provided. Even allowing for the fact that weak beer was then commonly drunk when we would now drink water, the provision of two great pots of wine as well seems unnecessary. But what would seem unusual is the ceremony that was involved in preparing the chamber, which gives an insight into what it was like to be a fifteenth-century nobleman. As at meal times, the bread and drink were tasted, or 'saied', by the yeoman of the chamber, or by all nine servants in the case of the beer. The practice of tasting had become largely ceremonial by this date but it was still to some extent a safety measure and protection against poisoning. The bread, the pots, the jugs and the cups were all covered by napkins. As the great chamber had no ceiling and was open to the rafters this was a practical measure. The chair placed at the foot of the bed was covered by a sheet for the same reason. But these coverings also had a ceremonial significance. The napkins, the bread and the cloth covering the cup board on which all was set out, in fact everything the nobleman would use, was kissed by the yeoman of the chamber before it was set in place. This was an example of the ceremonial of the church being carried over into the domestic life of the great and powerful – 'the estate' was to be revered. The *Orders of Service* also gives instructions on the order in which the items are to be brought into the chamber; the procession of servants was headed by one carrying the bread, followed by others with the beer and the wine. The yeoman carrying the ewer, basin and torch entered last in summer but first in winter. This is exactly the kind of ceremony that would have been played out before Ralph Lord Cromwell (d.1456) at Tattershall Castle, Lincolnshire, in the great room on the second floor of the Great Tower that was built 1434-45. The now bare brick walls would then have been plastered, with rich tapestries covering them.

When the nobleman got up in the morning, there were more formalities to be observed. The yeoman of the wardrobe appeared in the outer chamber carrying the nobleman's clothes folded in a sheet. These were taken by one of the grooms who passed them to the gentleman usher of the chamber to dress his master (only gentleman servants were allowed close intimacy with 'the estate'). Once dressed, the nobleman went to the closet off his chamber for seven o'clock mass which would be said by the dean of his chapel or the almoner of the household. A gentleman servant kissed a cushion before placing it for 'the estate' to kneel on, and the other attending gentleman servants would also crowd into the closet to hear mass.

In the meantime servants were stripping linen off the state bed and taking it away. At this time meals were taken in the great chamber and breakfast would be set up at the foot of the bed. By the following century the bed had been moved out of the great chamber into its own bed chamber where it developed its particular ceremonial.

To imagine these rooms as they would have looked, we have to conjure up a background of brightly coloured bed hangings, the equally colourful tapestries worked with gold and silver thread which covered the plastered walls, the brilliant liveries of the servants, the gold and silver of the plates and cups, and the rich hues of the foot carpet and cushions. The servants would perform their customary pageant like clockwork, both gentlemen and yeomen genuflecting and kneeling with absent-minded precision. This daily ritual resembled something between modern church Communion and a royal function in Westminster Abbey, and it was a less complicated version of what would have taken place at court, as is shown clearly by the 'Articles Ordained by King Henry VI for the Regulation of his Household', dated 1494.[3] These include instructions for the formalities to be used when the queen had a child. After the heavily pregnant queen had observed some minor rituals, including having spiced wine beneath a canopy of state in the great chamber, she was taken by her courtiers to the chamber, which had been hung with 'rich arras' on both ceiling and walls, leaving only one window to give light. The state bed was quite unsuitably covered with cloth of gold and ermine for the event. A pallet to receive the baby was placed alongside the bed, magnificently decked out with matching coverings and with a canopy suspended from the ceiling above it. Once the queen was brought into the chamber the courtiers withdrew, leaving her to 'her ladies and gentlewomen', some of whom then assumed the male posts of butler, pantler, server, carver and cup bearer.

It is interesting to note that the state bed and the child's pallet were 'en suite' at that early date, because the earliest reference to a state bed and 'en suite' seat furniture is from an inventory for Chatsworth of about 1566.[4] The 'Noblemans Bedde Chamber', at that time, had a bed with curtains of black and white damask and was covered with a black velvet quilt embroidered with silver and pearls. This matched a great chair and stool which were covered in black cloth of gold, and there was a long cushion of black velvet which was presumably on a window seat. The overall impact can only be imagined, but the richness of these costly coverings must have been very striking. Decorative effect was obtained solely by the use of bright colour in tapestries and with fabrics of ostentatious richness. The faded Flemish tapestries with tarnished metal thread that we see today have a definite charm, but their muted colours do not do justice to the original colour schemes.

Surprisingly, some beds have survived, although their fragile hangings have perished. There are no state beds with their original fabrics dating from before the 1670s, and no authentic English beds have survived from a date earlier than the sixteenth century. Moreover, there are no illustrations of early English interiors either. Tantalizingly, inventories of possessions taken at death record what beds were worth in the fourteenth and fifteenth centuries, but what these beds looked like can only be surmised on the basis of foreign medieval illustrations showing bed chambers.

The grandest of several beds belonging to Sir Baldwin de Fryville was valued at £5 with its curtains in 1355.[5] As the average farm labourer, who slept on the floor, would have taken two years to earn that sum, it must have been a very grand bed indeed. Shakespeare's second-best bed, the one that he notoriously left to his wife, was not valued highly. The surviving beds from the late sixteenth century are heavy affairs made of oak, with bulbous bedposts, deeply carved headboards and a completely wooden tester or canopy. In every case the original curtains have perished, and there are only fragments of material from which to gain an impression of their appearance. It is undoubtedly true that these beds have survived simply because they are so massive and it would be wrong to assume that all state beds of those times were similar.

Although no richly embroidered curtains and covers now exist, there are a surprising number of Elizabethan clothes. These are covered with fine needlework, which is the reason they have survived – they were too splendid to throw away. The clothes of a wealthy medieval nobleman were kept in a department (or office) of his household known as 'the wardrobe' under the care of a yeoman of the wardrobe. The wardrobe itself might simply be a small cupboard-like room off the bed chamber, or something larger. In Elizabethan houses, there would be a brushing room as well for cleaning clothes. Where a family was not grand enough to have a wardrobe, clothes would be kept in chests and presses. The modern hanging wardrobe only came in during the nineteenth century.

Other changes came more quickly. Window curtains were rarely used in Tudor times and, when mentioned by Elizabethans, were only to keep draughts out of principal rooms or to reduce sunlight, rather than to prevent those outside seeing in. Where they were used, there would only be one draw curtain to a window. The fashion for decorative curtains on either side of a window dates from the Restoration, with the use of a pelmet board to hide the rods and rings. Those who had spent the years of the Commonwealth in exile had been influenced by what they had seen in France. However, by about 1690 draw curtains were eclipsed by the festoon curtain, which could be raised or lowered by five cords on pullies. These were very elegant indeed, but also extravagant as they took five times more material than the old draw curtains. The festoon curtain remained in vogue until the 1770s and can still be seen in the grand rooms of many houses. Where window shutters have high decorative carving or detail they were plainly meant to be seen when festoon curtains were hoisted up, as in the library at Clandon Park, Surrey, which still has the original mechanism. Likewise, both Osterley Park and Uppark have many examples of festoon curtains with their original machinery. After 1770 the French draw curtain became fashionable once again, and from this date window shutters, hidden behind the curtains, were no longer decorated. Thereafter, curtain styles proliferated and variations carried on throughout the nineteenth century.

By 1550 a succession of state reception rooms had evolved, one following off the other and culminating in the bed chamber, the heart of the system;

great chamber, withdrawing chamber, state bed chamber, and off that, a closet. These were used for important occasions and were far too grand for everyday family use, so a second set of rooms, using the same sequence but smaller and more intimate, came to be provided for the family. These can be found in many grand houses; Hardwick Hall has the two sets; likewise Hatfield House, Hertfordshire. Montacute House in Somerset, built by the courtier Edward Phelips, also had two. But Chastleton House in Oxfordshire, built around 1602 and not so distinguished, has no apartments set aside for important state occasions. Here the family would have used the great chamber themselves for formal events, otherwise using their parlour for everyday living, and the state bed chamber – the term bed chamber dates from the mid-sixteenth century – would certainly have been reserved for important visitors. But grand or not, at Chastleton the house would have been filled with servants and there were apparently no bedrooms for them.

Even in the reign of Elizabeth I servants never had bedrooms to themselves, with the exception of the most senior, such as the steward, who ran the staff. Servants would sleep in passages and outside chamber doors, on folding beds which looked like chests when folded up, or they slept on the floor of the hall. Servants were always within earshot should they be needed and it must have been difficult to move about the Elizabethan house without falling over a sleeping servant. Obviously privacy was an unknown luxury.

Personal servants, such as man servants and ladies' maids, slept near their masters and mistresses. All adult members of a family had bed chambers to themselves. There is no record of what the form was when they needed privacy for lovemaking, but presumably servants were dismissed. When servants had the privilege of a room to sleep in, the rule was 'two to a bed and only gentlemen with gentlemen'. Servants had to wait many, many years before the sleeping accommodation provided for them improved. From the time of the Restoration they slept in dormitories and continued to in some houses until this century. At Mamhead in Devon, built in 1828, the maids' dormitory contained six double beds for twelve maids. There was a shelf over the head of each bed and another at the foot for their clothes, with small cupboards for other possessions. This dormitory was in use until 1939!

Children were treated more generously than servants. Elizabethan children slept in a room with whoever was their nurse until they were old enough to have a room of their own. Nurseries first appeared in the late eighteenth century and by the nineteenth century had evolved into a suite consisting of night nursery, day nursery and adjacent governess's room. These were usually situated directly above the rooms occupied by their parents. Lanhydrock in Devon, built in 1881, has a complete nursery suite with its own bathroom, scullery and even a spare nursery for small guests, but unfortunately this is not shown to visitors to the house. The nursery at Dalemain, Cumbria, has been restored, and Arreton Manor, Isle of Wight, has a very interesting childhood museum on the top floor; Sudbury Hall, Derbyshire, has a nineteenth-century wing converted to a museum of childhood.

Penshurst, Kent, has a toy museum, while Sudeley Castle, Gloucestershire, has the biggest collection of toys and dolls on view in Europe.

With children banished from view and cared for by servants, in the high society to which the majority of the rich belonged, parents could devote themselves entirely to court life where preferment was to be found. Although the principle of Divine Right of Kings had been exploded in the Civil War, and Parliament exercised the authority to rule, there was still a considerable influence vested in the sovereign and consequently the court led fashion. After the Restoration in 1660, French influence was the most apparent. In France the state bed chamber was used for the most important occasions. When the 1st Earl of Portland, William III's special Ambassador to Louis XIV in 1698, had his first public audience with the king, Louis received the Earl in the state bed chamber, standing by the bed with his hat off – a particular mark of respect. A low balustrade in front of Louis, rather like an altar rail, marked off the significant ritual area around the bed that was denied to all except the highest in rank. The Earl reported back to William: 'There can be nothing so ridiculous as the behaviour of the Court of France.' Clearly formality in the king's bed chamber was out of fashion in London by 1698, but this was not the case forty years earlier. John Evelyn, the diarist whose account of a visit to the Duchess of Portsmouth was noted in the last chapter, was very honoured to be received by Charles II in his bed chamber, by Princess Henrietta in her bed chamber in 1660 and four years later by the Duke of York. However, Evelyn had the status of a modern junior minister and was considered worthy of this honour. The state bed and en suite seat furniture at Powys Castle, prepared for a visit of Charles II, has the only surviving balustrade in Britain.

The list of state beds surviving from the period 1670-1740 is too long to give, but notable examples are at Burghley, Belvoir, Knole, Hampton Court, Hardwick, Warwick Castle, Belton, Beningborough, Erddig, Dyrham, Clandon, Wingfield Castle, Houghton and Holkham, with possibly the earliest at Dalemain, Cumbria. This was made in about 1670, and although not entirely in its original condition, it still has a complete tester.

Descriptions of state beds actually being used in England are very few indeed. A rare report is of the Duke of Lorraine sleeping in a state bed at Houghton, Norfolk, during a visit in 1731.[6] An early guidebook to Stowe, produced in 1817, reports that the state bed there was used at a christening which must have taken place a hundred years earlier.[7] However, by 1660 the state bed chamber had become a status symbol and was used only when visitors of the very highest rank deserved the honour, perhaps once in twenty years. For most of the time the chamber would remain shut up, the furniture shrouded in covers and protective curtains closely drawn round the bed – the state bed at Dyrham Park, Gloucestershire, is fitted with extra curtains. Where state bed chambers are on view today, they get far more wear and tear in one year than they ever did in a hundred. It remains to be seen how long these ageing survivors can last.

A state bed from 1629, restored in 1852, when its original embroidery was remounted on new blue silk damask copying the original, stands in the Blue

Room at Hardwick Hall, and is the one example of a countess's state bed of that time. This same room also contains the remnants of two 'triads', which were essential in any bed chamber of the post-Restoration period.

A triad was composed of three pieces of furniture – a wall mirror, a table beneath it and two candle stands. These were placed between the window piers and the idea came from the Low Countries. The set could be used as a dressing table or a writing table. But it was found that the candles tended to set fire to window curtains, so the candle stands were gradually abandoned. By the end of the seventeenth century, the triad consisted of two pieces only: the mirror and the table. This arrangement became fashionable in eighteenth-century living rooms, where it was transformed into a pier glass and table and placed between windows. A candelabrum placed on the table was enhanced by reflected light from the mirror. Bed chambers were also distinguished by the foot carpets placed by the bed; because carpets were costly, this was often the only place where a carpet would be used. We saw that the fifteenth-century nobleman had a carpet at the foot of his bed, but many bed chambers at that time would have had rush matting as a floor covering. Where there was no covering at all the boards would have been scrubbed, a practice that continued into the late eighteenth century. The dangerous habit of polishing floors to a high state of slipperiness was a nineteenth-century innovation; before then most floors were of oak and scrubbed with dry-sand, such as those at Clandon Park in Surrey.

A recent and unexpected discovery of a possible royal state bed was made at Calke Abbey in Derbyshire. The bed, believed to have been made for George I's daughter Princess Anne when she married the Prince of Orange in 1734, was discovered still in its contemporary packing case, with the Chinese silk hangings and cover as fresh today as when they were new. It is not known why the princess never received this splendid gift, but this surprising addition to the list of state beds goes some way to make up for those lost through wear and tear or careless and incompetent conservation.

The term 'four-poster' is a modern name given to the type of bed our ancestors slept in. Few of them, in fact, had four posts. They were made more often with two posts at the foot and a massive headboard rising to the full height of the tester, but many had no posts at all and the tester appears to float over the bed. Beds of this type have the French name of *lits à la duchesse*, or more explicably 'angel beds', because the tester gave the happy impression of being supported by angels. However, unromantic chains from the ceiling were the means of suspension, whatever the sleeping figure on the piled mattresses below may have believed.

Before 1688 state beds were comparatively simple. Ham House has several restored examples of beds dating from the 1670s. The Queen's bed chamber has been altered and the bed no longer exists, but a model of the chamber shows how simple an important bed was at that time. Three beds at Knole date from the same period, two of which, including the remarkable spangle bed, are thought to be from royal palaces. The spangle bed still has many of the original sequins, now completely tarnished, from which the bed takes its name; when the breeze stirred through an open window, the hangings must have given the impression of rippling sparks as they glinted in the candlelight.

The beds themselves were considerably less comfortable than today's. Until the invention of the sprung mattress in the present century, most of the population slept on a straw mattress, while the wealthy might have a flock-filled bed (i.e. a mattress stuffed with wool), a bed filled with feathers, or a bed of down. Both flock and down tended to form humps and valleys that had to be shaken out. Horsehair mattresses were introduced in the late seventeenth century but, like most novelties, were slow to catch on because they were thought to be unhealthy. Sarah, Duchess of Marlborough, agreed. As part of her orders for the furnishing of the newly built Blenheim in 1724, she said, 'I shall want a vast number of Feather Beds and quilts. I would have some of the Feather Beds swansdown, all good sweet Feathers, even for the servants.'[8]

Until recently beds were built up on the layer principle. A straw palliasse was laid on a base of laced canvas, followed by two or three hair or wool mattresses which were then topped off with a feather mattress. This construction reached to such a height that people needed steps to get into bed. A bed designed for several mattresses that has been modernized and fitted with one comfortable sprung mattress will look ridiculous and the proportions will be thrown out unless the bolsters and pillows are brought up to the bottom of the headboard. If sheets were used as well as blankets they would have been made of a scratchy hemp for lower ranks and of fine linen for the better-off. Heavy curtains round the bed kept out the piercing winter draughts blowing through ill-fitting doors and windows, or between the timbers and infilling of half-timbered houses.

Although many beds survive, it is less easy to reconstruct the rooms in which they were placed. Many have been removed from their original chamber or the decoration of the room has been altered. This is particularly unfortunate because the bed had become part of the complete design of the chamber by the late seventeenth century.

From the Restoration in 1660, the emphasis in interior design had been moving from a horizontal to a vertical focus, as is seen particularly well at Clandon Park, Surrey. This is most evident on the backs of chairs, which were comfortably low in 1660 but became higher and more uncomfortable as the century progressed. By about 1700 chairs, beds, rooms and even clothes all had a vertical emphasis. Doorways, cornices around rooms and fireplaces were perilously adorned with oriental porcelain pots and vases. Beds became vastly higher and at this point English fashions diverged from those of the French, who never achieved the same towering loftiness in bed design. English styles were based on the designs of Daniel Marot, a Huguenot who left France before the Revocation of the Edict of Nantes in 1685 and joined the Protestant court of William of Orange. When William came to England in 1688 Marot came too, bringing with him French ideas from earlier in the decade but developing them in a different direction.

1. Penshurst Place, Kent: the Great Hall, built in the mid-fourteenth century out of 'new money'. The central hearth can clearly be seen and the doors to the buttery and pantry are visible behind the screen.

2. RIGHT: The royal state bed of
c. 1734 at Calke Abbey was found
still unpacked and so has retained its
original colours unfaded. The silk
hangings depict scenes from Chinese
life and the walls of the room in
which it should have stood would
have had matching hangings (see
page 55).

3. FAR RIGHT: The State Bedroom,
Powis Castle: the only surviving
example of a state bed protected by a
balustrade, from the late seventeenth
century. This was once a common
feature in the houses of the court
circle who expected to entertain the
monarch. Only the most privileged
would have been allowed beyond
the balustrade.

4. *The Countess's morning levée* from
'Marriage à la Mode' by William
Hogarth. By 1743, when this was
painted, levées in a state bedroom
were sufficiently old-fashioned for
Hogarth to satirize the event. The
state bed in the alcove and the
dressing-table set are some thirty
years out of fashion (see page 57).

1ˢᵗ Course — Fish Remove

Transparent Soup

Pigeons Comport · Soria · Fricad Chickens

Lambs Easy Hand · Pork Griskins · Calebram bla Little Cattle

French Pye · Kidney Beans · Broccoli &c. · Fricando Veal

Boild Turkey · Minced Larks · Small Ham

Cattle Veat

Mushrooms in Rampfront · House Saint · Another Otto & repast · Sallat

Lardis Option · is fulled

Beef Olives

Florendine of Rabbits · Duchs Alamode

Hare Soup

Remove hanch of Venison

5. A table layout from *The Experienced English Housekeeper* by Elizabeth Raffald, 1782. At this date meals were still served as they had been in the Middle Ages, with many dishes being placed on the table at the same time, seemingly haphazardly. This shows one of two courses, each of twenty-five dishes (see pages 44-5).

6. RIGHT: The first of the Chatsworth state rooms intended by the 1st Duke of Devonshire to accommodate William III should he have visited Chatsworth. The painting on the ceiling by Verrio, 1692, is *The Virtues and the Vices* and, like all baroque ceiling paintings, it reflects the purpose of the room. In this case the gods and goddesses assembled represent the Royal court (see page 66).

7. BELOW: A sketch recording the visit of King Edward VII and Queen Alexandra to Chatsworth. By the early nineteenth century a new way of serving meals was established, *à la Russe*: footmen brought the food to the guests and the centre of the table was used for displays of flowers and plate (see page 47).

8. A painting by Charles Leslie showing the axis of honour in the state rooms at Petworth. The more important courtiers were allowed further into the succession of rooms; the axis allowed this filtering system to be clearly visible to the more humble left behind in the first of the rooms.

9. ABOVE: *The Throne Room, Hampton Court* by James Stephanoff, *c.* 1820, showing the canopy of state which is still in place (see pages 37-8). Although described as the Throne Room by W.H. Pyne, in whose book the painting first appeared, this is in fact the First Presence Chamber.

10. BELOW: The library at Newby Hall was designed by Robert Adam as an eating room in 1767. The furniture is here arranged in a comfortable modern fashion; the sofa, for example, would originally have been placed against a wall. The festoon curtains are correct for the date (see pages 35-6).

11. ABOVE: *The Dance* by Hogarth, *c.* 1745. By this date society was becoming more relaxed, and Hogarth was the first to portray people actively enjoying themselves in movement.

12. ABOVE RIGHT: *A Kill at Ashdown Park* by James Seymour, 1743. Foxhunting was not established as a pure sport until the early eighteenth century; before that hounds hunted wild boar or deer (see pages 106-7).

13. RIGHT: The plan of the principal floor at Blenheim Palace shows two baroque apartments of state radiating from a central saloon intended to be occupied by a king and a queen. The saloon would have been used for state dinners.

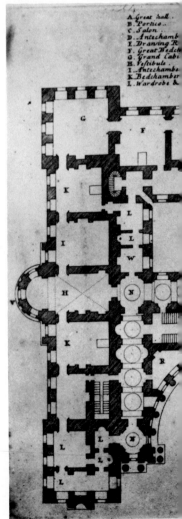

A. Great hall.
B. Portico.
C. Salon.
D. Antechamb.
E. Drawing R.
F. Great Bedch.
G. Grand Cabi.
H. Vestibule.
I. Antechambe.
K. Bedchamber.
L. Wardrobe &.

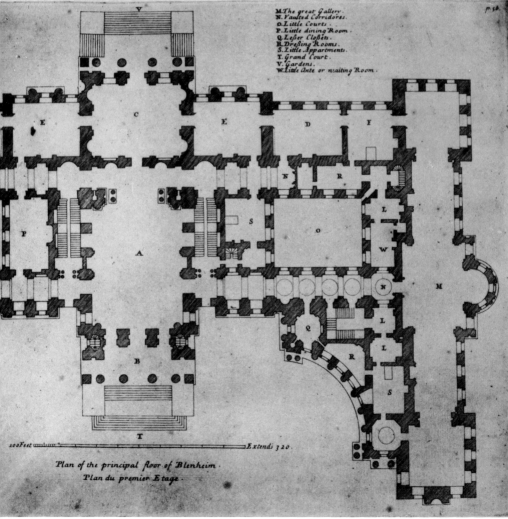

M. The great Gallery.
N. Vaulted Corridores.
O. Little Courts.
P. Little dining Room.
Q. Lesser Closets.
R. Dressing Rooms.
S. Little Appartments.
T. Grand Court.
V. Gardens.
W. Little Ante or waiting Room.

p. 56

100 Feet   Extends 320

Plan of the principal floor of Blenheim.
Plan du premier Etage.

14. This French shower is similar to the many fitted in British houses at the turn of the century. One still in existence at Castle Drogo is a massive piece of plumbing assuring total drenching from every side.

15. ABOVE: The butler's pantry at Erddig. The butler was responsible for wines, the silver and glasses. Here many items of equipment may be seen, including an automatic corkscrew, a knife cleaner, a bottle-holder for decanting port and a bottle basket.

16. BELOW: The kitchen at St James's Palace painted by James Stephanoff, c. 1820. Kitchens were rarely the subject of paintings before the nineteenth century; here the painter Stephanoff has caught something of the frenzied activity which attended the preparation of dinner, but shows none of the dirt which must have characterized most kitchens.

17. Lord Guilford's London servants, *c.* 1895. The butler sits at the back wearing a winged collar, next to a footman; the housekeeper stands on the right, dressed in black, and the housemaids wear white with caps; the kitchen maid holds the house-dog.

18. ABOVE RIGHT: A posed scene in a Victorian kitchen showing the cook rolling pastry, with two kitchen maids. A butler is shown on the right, although it is unlikely that he would have been allowed into the kitchen of a large household – the hall boy collected the cooked food and took it to the butler to serve in the dining room.

19. RIGHT: The dry laundry at Petworth in the 1880s. The laundress, in black, is shown with six laundry maids – a large staff. Traditionally the laundry was a separate department, independent of the housekeeper. The aged male figure in the foreground has nothing to do with the laundry: men were not usually allowed near the laundry maids.

20. ABOVE: Two details from *The Family of Henry VIII* by an unknown artist, showing the royal garden with heraldic beasts on poles and the beds lined with coloured rails. The lack of colour in flowers lasting through the summer was made up for with such garden 'props' (see page 118).

21. RIGHT: The baroque gardens at Chatsworth in 1707 from Kip's *Britannia Illustrated*, based on a drawing by Knyff. Like so much else of the baroque period, this garden appears to us to offer far too much. Despite the profusion, nature was seen as needing to be strictly controlled and contained.

Chattsworth

180 foot Front

22. ABOVE: The terraced gardens at Powis Castle are based on the Renaissance gardens of Tuscany. Designed in the late seventeenth century, they have survived only because it is difficult to alter the terraces on such a steep site as this.

23. ABOVE: An open carriage outside Goodwood House, c. 1905. No car has ever approached the elegance of the carriage, which reached its peak in design and efficiency just as the motor car was invented.

24. BELOW: The demolition of Devonshire House in Piccadilly, 1920. In the nineteenth century Park Lane and Piccadilly had been lined with private houses, but by this date they were becoming too expensive to maintain and the value of the land was high; Devonshire House was sold for £1,000,000 (see page 13).

Apart from their vertical emphasis, Daniel Marot's designs were also distinguished by a wealth of decoration. His beds are covered with tassels, fringes, bells, ruches and festoons, in a riotous display of the upholsterer's art. The Melville bed at the Victoria and Albert Museum, made about 1690 for a courtier of William III, the Earl of Melville, includes two startling festoons flying out diagonally from the tester. The greatest part of the cost of a bed of this kind was the upholstery – the framework was merely to support the rich fabrics. One of the most famous of these flamboyant beds was made by Francis Lapierre for the 1st Duke of Devonshire in 1697 for Chatsworth. The woodwork cost a mere £15 but the upholstery bill was £470. The only parts surviving today are the head and canopy. These are fixed to the wall mid-way down the long gallery at Hardwick Hall, where the 6th Duke of Devonshire put them in the early nineteenth century. Although only these remain, they are enough to show the extraordinary richness of the upholstery: crimson silk covering every inch of woodwork is worked to imitate feathers, scrolls, strapwork and even a ducal coronet, the detail delicately picked out in gold and silver embroidery. The Lapierre bed is the earliest surviving example of a *lit à la duchesse* or 'angel bed'.

Inevitably the fashion did not last and although the beds continued to be extremely high, a reaction to excessive decoration had set in by the second decade of the new century. This is evident in Queen Anne's bed at Hampton Court Palace, made in 1714. The design of this bed, apart from the curves of the cornice, consists entirely of straight lines and rectangles. A sumptuous effect is achieved simply by the richness of the fabric used to make the curtains, covers and tester: crimson silk velvet made at Spitalfields, with an imposed design in cut and uncut pile, was mounted on satin silk with a white design on gold. The cost of this astonishing fabric must have been enormous.

Although we do not know the cost of Queen Anne's bed we do know how much money was spent at Houghton, Norfolk, in 1732, when Sir Robert Walpole's bill for gold lace for the Green Velvet Bed alone came to £1,200[9] – at a time when a farm labourer earned forty pence a week! This bed was designed by William Kent and, like all his furniture, is architectural in inspiration. The headboard consists of a huge shell (almost a trademark for Kent) mounted on a pediment. Everything is covered in green cut velvet and the detail is picked out with gold braid, now tarnished, which was used as if it were gilding on a plaster cornice.

By 1743 state bedrooms in Britain were sufficiently *passé* for Hogarth cleverly to satirize their use in his fourth illustration in the series 'Marriage à la Mode': *The Countess's morning levée*. The arranged marriage between the Earl and Countess of Squander has gone rapidly downhill and the countess, seated with her hair in curling papers, is shown in the intimacy of her bed chamber entertaining her lover, who reclines on a sofa, and others of her raffish friends. She has just risen from a state bed set, in French fashion, in an alcove and upholstered in pink velvet. The decorative effect of the bed is achieved by the silhouette of the tester in a style some thirty years out of date by 1743, as is the superb silver dressing set and mirror. The countess is the daughter of a *nouveau riche* merchant and does not realize that her equipment is out of fashion amongst the aristocracy.

A man would have had a much more official *levée*, when favours were asked and patronage was given, but for both men and women a *levée* was an occasion when they were not 'on parade' and they could talk without being interrupted or overheard. *Levées* were very much a feature of the fashionable world and were almost exclusively confined to London. In the early 1700s the 1st Duke of Newcastle's were particularly well patronized. Lord Chesterfield in the 1760s wrote of him: 'He loved to have them crowded and consequently they were so. There he generally made people of business wait two or three hours in the ante-chamber, while he trifled away that time with some insignificant favourite in his closet. When at last he came into his levée-room, he accosted, hugged, embraced and promised everybody, with a seeming cordiality . . . with degrading familiarity.'[10]

By the time Kedleston, Derbyshire, was completed for Sir Nathaniel Curzon by Robert Adam in the 1760s, the grand style was out of fashion. Nevertheless Kedleston has a state bedroom and a state bed with posts made of cedar of Lebanon fashioned to look like palm trees, a symbol of peace. But in general life among those in the top ranks of society was becoming more informal. When the Earl of Guilford went to visit the Duke of Portland at Bulstrode Park, Buckinghamshire, in the 1760s, it was hinted beforehand that 'the good Earl would find himself more comfortable if he were not honoured with the great apartment'. The bedroom never again assumed a formal significance and gradually evolved into the room we know today.

Curiously there is almost no information on how long people thought they ought to sleep, apart from Dr Johnson's dictum: 'eight hours for a man, nine hours for a woman and ten hours for a fool'. At the lower end of the social scale those who could not afford candles and rushlights went to bed at sundown and rose at sunrise. A fifteenth-century nobleman's day began with mass at seven in the morning and he went to bed by candlelight in winter, which could have been at any hour after supper at five in the afternoon. If Dr Johnson were correct, then the fifteenth-century nobleman would have gone to bed around ten in the evening and risen at six in the morning.

References to bed chambers are few, but there are almost none to bathing. As we have seen, the household orders for a fifteenth-century nobleman included the provision of a ewer and basin for washing, but they say nothing about the act of bathing. However, John Russell's *Boke of Nurture* is rather more informative. He tells us that sheets full of sweet herbs were hung over the place in the bed chamber where the bathing was to be done. Five or six sponges 'to sit or lean on' were put in place with a large one to sit on. The bather was then covered with a sheet and the servant sponged him from a basin of hot water and herbs. Finally the servant threw rose water over his master before drying him and putting him to bed. Since John Russell does not make any mention of a tub, this procedure seems to have been carried out on the floor, which must have been very messy. An occasional bath of this kind was probably all most people had. Most houses obtained their water supply from a well, with the water brought into the house by hand – few medieval noblemen could afford the cost of piping it. The bathroom installed in Chatsworth by 1697 was sufficiently unusual for Celia Fiennes to describe it in detail: 'There is a fine grottoe all stone pavement roofe and sides, this is design'd to supply all the house with water besides severall fancyes to make diversion; within this is a batheing roome, the walls all with blew and white marble the pavement mix'd one stone white another black another of the red rance [veined] marble; the bath is one entire marble all white finely pollish'd as some, it was as deep as ones middle on the outside and you went down steps into the bath big enough for two people; at the upper end are two Cocks to let in one hott the other cold water to attemper it as persons please; the windows are all private [ground] glass . . . ' Water was never a problem at Chatsworth, but unfortunately the bathroom disappeared long ago.

A massive bath house, in the classical style, was built in 1719-20 at Carshalton House, Surrey, the home of one of the wealthy directors of the South Sea Company. The bath house still exists, with a water tower rising from the middle of it and an engine room in the basement powered by a water-wheel. By the time Ashridge, Hertfordshire, was built for the 2nd Duke of Bridgewater by James Wyatt in 1808-13, bathrooms were often included in the family wing; the Earl's was put in between his study and his dressing room. Bathrooms for the family were normal in the nineteenth century, but guests were left to have their tubs filled in front of their bedroom fires. Occasionally houses were provided with primitive pillar showers, as at Erddig, Calke Abbey and Wimpole, where the tank which held the water had to be filled each time the shower was used. Dunham Massey, Cheshire, and Lanhydrock, Cornwall, both have good Victorian bathrooms with massive fittings and baths. Croxteth, Cheshire, has two substantial Edwardian bathrooms, while Lord Curzon's bath at Montacute, Somerset, is cunningly installed inside a Jacobean-style cupboard; Curzon rented the house in 1915-25. Castle Drogo, Devon, has a splendid marble bathroom in Julius Drewe's own private suite; the bath is a late version of apparatus patented in the 1860s and must have been installed after the First World War. It has a shower and a control panel of five taps at the business end of the bath.

By now we can appreciate what a complicated piece of domestic machinery the houses of the very rich had become by the nineteenth century. Their running depended entirely on trusted servants. It was a way of life for a small and powerful minority with the leisure and money to follow any course they chose. Some took the way of least resistance and did nothing but marry wealthy heiresses, such as the Drydens at Canon's Ashby and the Harpurs at Calke Abbey; other families followed an ambitious path of public duty, such as the Cecils at Hatfield and the Cavendishes at Chatsworth. But whatever course a family chose to follow, they displayed their wealth according to how they saw their place in society. The ostentatious display of riches reached its peak in the baroque period, 1675-1715. Baroque was far more than an architectural and decorative style; it was a philosophy which penetrated everything: theatre, painting, politics and dress. How the baroque way of life affected the historic house and those who lived in it is outlined in the next chapter.

CHAPTER 5

The Grand Life

Anyone walking into the two-storey entrance hall of Beningborough Hall, Yorkshire, will share the experience of an eighteenth-century visitor; it has been restored, with other rooms in the house, to the original colour scheme by the National Trust. The Hall is one of the finest of English late baroque interiors.

Against the walls are placed a few hard hall chairs, for waiting servants, and two plain marble-topped tables; in general the interior is arranged in a way that the eighteenth-century visitor would have expected. The colour scheme in the hall is in different tones of grey – in the early eighteenth century, when the house was built, pale colours were the most expensive.

When Beningborough Hall was completed in 1716, it was, with Castle Howard, the latest in baroque architecture in the north of England, and had the most fashionable interiors. John Bourchier, who created the house, had married the daughter of a rich lawyer and Beningborough represents an expression of his wealth. The plan remains virtually unaltered. Today we can sense something of the impact that a contemporary visitor would have experienced. Unfortunately the furniture has no association with the house and has been installed by the National Trust from their own collection, together with borrowed pieces; the paintings are on permanent loan from the National Portrait Gallery. The Bourchier family died out in 1827 and the contents were sold in 1917 when the house was bought by the 10th Earl of Chesterfield. On the death of his countess in 1957 only a few of the contents went with the house to the National Trust; the remainder were sold to pay death duties.

From the hall a contemporary visitor would have been taken through the huge double doors opposite the front door into a dining room, which was probably called the eating room. Today the visitor does not follow this route. The pine panelling of this room was covered with many layers of paint, of which the earliest was a grey-green colour which has been restored. Chairs of *c*.1715 with splat backs and cabriole legs are placed against the walls and, an authentic touch, there is an oak gate-leg table in the centre of the room. The table is far too small to accommodate more than ten at a time and would have been used for family eating; when more were to be catered for other gate-leg tables would have been brought into the room. The walls are double banked with portraits of members of the Kit-Cat Club. Again the arrangement of this room is what an eighteenth-century visitor would expect.

From this eating room the contemporary visitor went into a bed chamber, indicating the dual nature of the dining room; it could be used for eating or as an ante-room to the bed chamber. Today this room is called the state bedroom. The original state bed chamber, however, was at the other end of the house in what is now the drawing room, then half its present size. In the present state bed chamber is a magnificent state bed of *c*.1710 from Holme Lacy in Herefordshire. Covered and curtained in crimson damask and of immense height, it is one of the finest of baroque state beds. The pelmets over the windows, made for festoon curtains, are *en suite* with the sides of the bed tester. The remainder of the furniture is good late seventeenth-century walnut. Off the bed chamber is a dressing room and closet with a corner fireplace and stepped overmantel, made to exhibit oriental and Delft blue and white porcelain. Porcelain from the Ashmolean Museum and the Bushell Collection have been placed on the overmantel shelves, and the visitor will get an impression of the late baroque fashion for verticality. Conveniently near the fireplace is a cupboard set into the wall where the close-stool and chamber pot were kept. The dressing room was not only used for dressing but for entertaining close friends and taking tea or chocolate; it was where small and valued pictures would have hung. It is the final room in a progression of apartments originally comprising ante-room, bed chamber and dressing room: a typical baroque plan.

The Bouchiers, although wealthy, were not connected with the court circle and the plan of the house shows this – there is no state bed chamber grand enough to receive a royal visitor. The state rooms, when they existed, would have been given to high-ranking visitors. Ragley Hall, Warwickshire, built in 1679 for the 1st Earl of Conway, Secretary of State to Charles II, had four complete sets of such apartments on the ground floor. It is a far grander house than Beningborough and the state rooms here could have been used for Charles II.[1] Clandon Park, Surrey, built for the 2nd Lord Onslow in the 1730s, is also far grander than Beningborough, and although it is very unlikely that Onslow thought of entertaining royalty, the state rooms are there for the use of high-ranking visitors.

These suites of apartments are nothing like as grand as those in the houses of the inner court circle, such as the more or less untouched magnificence of apartments at Boughton, Northamptonshire, created by the 1st Duke of

Montagu in the 1690s. At Burghley, Northamptonshire, an even more magnificent range was created, also in the 1690s. Although drastically altered for a visit by George IV when Prince of Wales, the ceilings and walls by Verrio remain. As so many of these apartments which became outdated after the mid-eighteenth century have been altered to another use, it is sometimes difficult to recognize the original purpose. At Ragley they have been converted into two drawing rooms and two dining rooms, which is confusing for any visitor; at Blenheim the two drawing rooms following in succession are the remains of very grand apartments. An understanding of the evolution of these apartments is the only way that we can now comprehend their significance.

In Britain since the reign of Henry VIII the upper classes have expressed their power in buildings. Cardinal Wolsey's Hampton Court of 1515 is a typical example, built to entertain his king but so splendid that Henry coveted the great palace. Wolsey was forced to give Hampton to the king, who later engineered his downfall. Burghley House, Northamptonshire, was begun in the 1550s or 1560s by William Cecil, 1st Lord Burghley and treasurer to Queen Elizabeth. His motive was to build a house large enough to entertain his queen. Hatfield House, Hertfordshire, was built in 1611 by Cecil's second son to entertain James I. Wilton House in Wiltshire was enlarged in 1636 by the 4th Earl of Pembroke to entertain Charles I. All these houses were expressly created to accommodate sovereigns, with whom all power rested and who governed with the assistance of a Privy Council. When the sovereign travelled, the Privy Council travelled with him. Consequently considerable accommodation was needed by any of the court circle who might expect to receive the sovereign. By the time the Civil War ended and the monarchy was restored in 1660, the attitude towards the monarchy had understandably changed; the Crown had lost its absolute power, which had been transferred to Parliament, and government eventually became centralized on London. For the ambitious there was no longer any need to build for the sovereign; they could build for themselves and express their own political power and influence through their houses.

However, the habit died hard and Chatsworth was rebuilt by the 1st Duke of Devonshire, starting in 1686, with state rooms in which to entertain William III. Likewise Boughton House in Northamptonshire, built by the 1st Duke of Montagu in 1695; Castle Howard, Yorkshire, built by the 3rd Earl of Carlisle in 1699; Kiveton Park, Yorkshire, built by the 1st Duke of Leeds in 1694; Wentworth Castle, Yorkshire, completed in the 1720s but planned as early as 1709; and Canons Park, Middlesex, begun in 1713 for the 1st Duke of Chandos and demolished in 1744, all had state apartments which could be used to entertain a sovereign. Others, not prepared to face the cost of demolishing a perfectly good building and erecting a new one, contented themselves by modernizing old apartments of state; at Burghley House the 5th Earl of Exeter employed Verrio to paint the walls and ceilings of a magnificent range of state apartments. Petworth House, Sussex, in 1688;

Kimbolton Castle, Cambridgeshire, in 1691; Drayton House, Northamptonshire, in 1702; and Grimsthorpe Castle, Lincolnshire, in 1722, were all
brought into a suitably grand state to receive a royal personage. Castle
Howard and Wentworth each had two sets of state apartments. Blenheim
Palace, begun in 1705, also had two sets of state apartments, one for a king
and the other for his queen.

The sequence of the apartments was based on those of the royal palaces in
London. Of these royal apartments of state, those at Whitehall have been
destroyed and others at Windsor and St James's Palace completely altered. At
Hampton Court the state apartments designed for William III and Queen
Mary survive, with minor changes, in the Wren wings. As the state apartments at Hampton Court were being built at the same time as the state
apartments at Chatsworth, Boughton and Burghley, the decoration of the
latter can have been little influenced by the Hampton Court interiors.
However, the layout and appearance of the Hampton Court range of apartments would have been similar to those at Windsor, designed by the architect
Hugh May, which did have great influence, and in order to understand the
purpose of state apartments it is useful to know how they were used at court.

At Hampton Court the names of the rooms in the state apartments have
been altered from those by which they were originally known, owing to a
later change of use. After climbing the grand staircase one enters what is now
called the King's Guard Chamber, because the Yeomen of the Guard were
stationed here, but which was first called the Great Chamber. This was the
most public room of the suite, and here gathered those who waited to be
introduced to the king in the next room, now called the King's First Presence
Chamber. The Great Chamber was also used for dining on special occasions
when the privacy of the inner rooms was not desired. In the King's First
Presence Chamber (the Presence Chamber, to give it its original name),
William III sat in a chair of state beneath a high canopy to receive ambassadors, to create peers and to watch court entertainments. Beyond this is the
room now called the Second Presence Chamber, which now has another state
chair and canopy though originally it had neither; it was called the Privy
Chamber and was used by William for private dining. This was the furthest
that peers were permitted to penetrate into the system. The next room, the
King's Audience Chamber, was the Withdrawing Room, which is why it
occupies the centre of the wing: important visitors waited here and had the
benefit of an axial view of the gardens (the Queen's apartments still have a
central Withdrawing Room). Only privy councillors were received in this
room, although later, when protocol relaxed, senior members of the Navy
and Army and others of rank had the privilege of being received here. The
final rooms of this enfilade, the King's Drawing Room, the State Bedchamber
and the King's Dressing Room, have only suffered a change of name in the
case of the first, which was known as the Ante-Room and was where the
exalted few who had access to the bed chamber waited. In 1683 this was
limited to the king's brother, the king's ministers and secretaries of state.

When away from London and staying at the house of a subject, the sovereign would not have needed the seven state rooms that comprised the royal state apartments; ambassadors would not be received, peers would not be created and the full protocol of the royal court would be unnecessary. The Privy Chamber and the Ante-Room were therefore dispensed with and the complex reduced to a suite of five rooms.

These are the suites we see surviving in the houses of the court circle of the period which lasted until 1720. By the time the Blenheim state apartments were completed in 1725, the building was old fashioned; the Whig aristocracy had moved on to a new kind of house – the simpler and less cluttered Palladian style. Although kings and queens continued to stay in the houses belonging to their circle and apartments of state continued to be built, it is doubtful if, after 1722, any were designed specially for royal accommodation. They were more commonly used to honour high rank on formal occasions. The period from 1688 to 1705, a brief seventeen years, marked the apogee of state apartments; nothing like them had been seen before in England and never would be again. Indeed the period was so short that their purpose was quickly forgotten; in 1830 the 6th Duke of Devonshire had no idea what function the great apartments at Chatsworth had been designed to serve.

The rebuilding of Chatsworth was begun by the 1st Duke of Devonshire in 1686, using Talman as his architect, Verrio, Laguerre and Ricard as decorators and Tijou as a smith. These were the most talented artists and craftsmen in England; all had worked, or were still working, for William III at Windsor and Hampton Court. Verrio, Laguerre and Tijou had all worked at Versailles. The Chatsworth state apartment was completed in the 1690s and designed with the intention of accommodating William and Mary, as the subject matter of the painted ceilings confirms. Exactly how these aristocrats saw themselves is difficult for us to grasp, but the Earl of Carlisle, when planning Castle Howard, claimed that he was building a 'Palace of Apollo' and obviously considered himself the equal of the classical gods. Certainly they saw themselves as no ordinary mortals. Indeed William Cavendish, 1st Duke of Newcastle, did not think he was going too far in the 1670s when he advised Charles II to show himself 'Gloriuslye to your People Like a God, for the holye writt sayes wee have Calde you Godds'.

It should come as no surprise to us now, when we look up at the ceiling in the Painted Hall at Chatsworth and see Julius Caesar being carried up to heaven, to realize that for Caesar we should substitute William III – for that was the compliment the 1st Duke of Devonshire was paying his sovereign. One can easily read the message on the walls, for they trace Caesar's life in relation to William's. After all, William had crossed the Channel as Caesar had crossed the Rubicon and for both there was no turning back. Caesar was offered the Emperor's crown and William accepted the crown of England. The Duke who was closely involved in these events was rewarded with his dukedom in 1694. The only problem encountered by the use of this comparison was that Caesar was stabbed by Brutus – and this is clearly shown on one of the walls. The problem was happily answered by the apotheosis of

Caesar in the main painting of the sequence, whereby the Duke hints that William will be similarly transmogrified. The figures in this series were painted by Laguerre, and Ricard painted the backgrounds. Both were Frenchmen, the former a godson of Louis XIV, and both came to England in 1684 and worked with Verrio at Windsor. The subject of the painting would have been chosen by the patron, the 1st Duke.

The stairway, with handrails by Tijou, leading to the state apartments above, as at Hampton Court, continues the compliments on the ceiling of the stairwell. This time the paintings are by Verrio and show the *Triumph of Cybele*. Cybele was the Phrygian 'earth mother', bringer of fruits, and symbolized Queen Mary.

On climbing the stairs and entering the great chamber, now called the State Dining Room, one finds that the compliments cease, to be replaced by a multitude of near-naked figures floating above in a tranquil heaven, as if the room had no ceiling but merely a painted architectural balustrade to contain the throng of deities. This is the second ceiling at Chatsworth by Verrio, and when considering his work we must remember that the painted ceilings were subjected to the smoke of candles for over two hundred years – electricity was only installed at Chatsworth in 1909 – and to restorations often by unskilled hands. This particular ceiling has already been restored three times and is about to be restored again; there will not be much of Verrio's original work left. Consequently the ceiling appears dull; moreover Verrio only took one year, 1692, to complete the work and it is not one of his best. The subject is *The Virtues and the Vices*; the eternal moral conflict in which virtue has to be victorious. It is more than this, however; it represents the 'gods' of the royal court who would have been moving about on the floor beneath, for the great chamber was a room of assembly – the first of the apartments of state – as well as a room for formal dining. Atropos, one of the three Fates, leans forward on the right of the chimney breast, to cut the thread of life. Her hooked and witch-like features are those of the unrelenting Mrs Hackett, housekeeper to the 1st Duke, with whom Verrio had fallen out. All painted ceilings have a focal point from which they are best viewed, which is where the principal visitor would have been placed. In the case of this room it is before the fireplace; in the hall – a room of movement – the ceiling is viewed as one enters.

The subjects painted in the great chamber, like the subjects of the four rooms which follow it, reflect what would have taken place in them had William and Mary ever visited Chatsworth. The ceiling of the withdrawing room, still so called, by Laguerre again, takes for its subject *The Assembly of the Gods on Mount Olympus*, because the court would have gathered here while the great chamber was prepared for dinner, or waited to enter the next room, the presence chamber. In the presence chamber, now called the Music Room, William would have sat in a chair of state holding court and receiving petitions. The ceiling by Laguerre reflects this exactly by showing Apollo, the sun god, being petitioned by his son Phaeton. Ovid tells the story as taking place in the Palace of Helios when Phaeton asks his father to grant a wish. Unfortunately the young demi-god asks for the use of the sun chariot that travels across the heavens from sunrise to sunset. The request is unwillingly granted, with the inevitable result – an accident; Phaeton, unable to control the horses, goes too near to the sun and in falling seems likely to set everything on fire. On the coving Jupiter is shown stopping the disaster with a well-placed thunderbolt. The moral is plainly one of not asking for too much.

From the presence chamber we pass into a bed chamber, and again the ceiling subject is appropriate, for it shows the *Triumph of Diana* with Diana as goddess of the moon, a favourite subject for bed chambers. Diana as night is being chased away by dawn in the person of Aurora. We have now reached the penultimate room of the range of apartment chambers; only the most favoured would be allowed into the bed chamber, and the whole system was designed to act, as at Hampton Court and Windsor, as a filter to keep the unworthy away from the superior being at the top of the pyramid.

The final room in the Chatsworth sequence of state apartments is the closet; originally this had japanned-lacquer Coromandel panels – another compliment to William; he had installed similar panels at Windsor and they were much in fashion due to exotic imports by the Dutch East India Company. The panels, too valuable to scrap when removed in 1702, are thought to have been remade into the coffer and cabinets now in the withdrawing room. The closet would have been used as a very private office by William, and the ceiling subject, by Laguerre, is of Mercury, messenger of the gods, being sent off with the apple of the tree of knowledge by Juno, Venus and Minerva. The presence of Minerva, goddess of wisdom, is yet another compliment to William.

The total cost of rebuilding Chatsworth was £40,000; what part of that sum was applied to the creation of the state apartments is not known, but as an investment to lure William to Chatsworth it was totally wasted, for no sovereign came until Queen Victoria arrived with Prince Albert in 1843, and they did not use the state apartments. The only reigning monarchs to use the apartments were Edward VII and Queen Alexandria in 1906 and George V and Queen Mary in 1933. However, on both occasions the state bed, in which George II died – he died at court but the 5th Duke was Lord Chamberlain and his perquisite was the royal death-bed – may have been moved out of the bed chamber as it is hardly likely that either king would have snuggled down in it with his queen! Another bed chamber may have been provided for both queens and possibly an alternative bed for the kings.

When going through these high baroque apartments of state it must never be imagined that the families themselves ever inhabited them; impressive though they are, they must be the most uncomfortable accommodation ever devised. Families lived in far more comfortable quarters, often called the 'rustics' in the eighteenth century – an obscure reference to the fact that they were in the basement, which, on the exterior, was distinguished by rusticated stonework (large plain masonry with deeply grooved joints giving a strong texture to the surface). At Blenheim, the family lived in smaller rooms in a compact layout in the west wing; at Chatsworth they lived on the first floor beneath the state apartments, and in both houses the families occupy the same quarters today. Other families used the attics, a word which does not have the same connotation today that it did in the eighteenth century. Families lived on the attic floor – the upper floor – and servants were accommodated in the garrets in dormitories. At Nostell Priory, Yorkshire, in the 1750s, the family had their rooms on the attic floor. Lady Shelburne at the same date was delighted with her attic accommodation at Fonthill Splendens, Wiltshire (demolished 1790). In 1728 the attics at Houghton in Norfolk had 'twelve good handsome bed chambers, four of which are pretty large' and all were fourteen feet high. At Houghton, however, the family lived in a self-contained range in the south front; at Holkham, also in Norfolk, the Coke family was housed comfortably in a pavilion that would be perfectly adequate as a country house on its own; likewise the Curzons at Kedleston, Derbyshire, in the 1780s, used the state dining room and drawing room in the main block during the day and retired to their pavilion at night.

As a reaction from heavy painting, ceilings were more usually whitewashed from the 1740s when fashion had tired of Kent's 'grotesques' or deeply coffered ceilings with a central painting. Robert Adam, returning from three years in Italy in 1757, brought a radical change. His lightly moulded plaster ceilings, using swags of stylized foliage, plaques and inset roundels with mythological landscapes by Angelica Kauffman, Antonio Zucchi, Cipriani and Francesco Zuccarelli, were taken up with enthusiasm. In 1758 Nathaniel Curzon, seeing Adam's proposals for Kedleston, already half-built by Paine and Brettingham, confessed himself 'knocked all of a heap' and couldn't wait for Adam to begin. Unfortunately many of Adam's ceilings have been redecorated in the wrong colours and this gives us an incorrect view of his interiors. The 1930s saw Syrie Maugham, the fashionable decorator of the moment, recommending completely white interiors, and under this impetus Adam's ceiling were often toned down. Many of Adam's watercolour sketches for ceilings have survived and the National Trust and the National Trust for Scotland, where funds permit, have restored Adam's ceilings to their original colours. The only hint Adam has left us of his theories is from his *Works in Architecture*: 'light tints of pink and green, so as to take off the glare of white, so common on some ceilings, till of late', created 'a harmony between ceiling and side walls with their hangings, pictures and other decorations'. It is precious little to go on! At the beginning of his career Adam used soft colours; later he introduced colours such as clear blue, pink and 'pea-green'. When a ceiling has been restored to the original colours the result can be startling, as at Osterley Park, for example.

French influence again brought change; by the end of the eighteenth century the simplicity of white and gold replaced Adam's colours. French influence also moved the bed chamber to the first floor; at Erddig, Denbighshire, lost on the Welsh borders, the state bed was moved upstairs in the 1770s, and Attingham Park in Shropshire, built for the 1st Lord Berwick in the 1780s, had its bedrooms on the first floor. The ground floor of Attingham was given over to three huge rooms for entertainment, separating two wings containing private suites, one for Lord Berwick and the other for his wife; this was a very French plan. The nineteenth century, as we have seen, re-created every past style and even Adam came into his own again in the early 1900s. A major influence on the nineteenth-century interior was the introduction of gas lighting, which also gave off heat and smoke, effects that remained until the introduction of the incandescent mantle in 1887. Consequently rooms were made high to take away the fumes, a height which gave rooms uncomfortable proportions.

Finally, it must be borne in mind when historic interiors strike us as overdone that we are not seeing them in the way intended. Rooms of parade were designed to be crowded with courtiers in ornate costume; the interiors, designed to compete with bright clothes, are now faded, their gold leaf tarnished; and they would have looked very different by candlelight. Dining rooms, used only in daylight, were invariably white, and even today some of these are not fitted with electricity, as at Claydon.

It requires less of an effort to realize that with servants to do everything, time could hang very heavy in the vast rooms of country houses. How to occupy the time was often a problem, particularly when we remember that every occupation was self-generated, unlike today when we can at any time summon music and films from radio, television and tapes. Contemporary diaries, specially those of women, are filled with entries of minor activities to fill the yawning gap between waking and sleeping. Lady Margaret Hoby, who lived at Hackness in Northumberland and kept a diary from 1599 to 1605, spent a great part of her day simply praying. It had become compulsive. Her entry for 12 November 1599, not a Sunday, is typical: 'After private prayer I went about the house till some strangers came, whom I accompanied till dinner time: then I prayed: after, I was busy all the day till almost supper time, and then I examined myself and prayed: then I went to supper, after I wrought [with her needle] then I prayed, and so went to bed.'[2]

Margaret Hoby was running a household and therefore did have some-thing with which to occupy herself, but daughters in general did not. Nearly three hundred years later the unmarried daughter of a family living at Thrumpton Hall, Nottinghamshire, kept a similar diary. She certainly resorted to a good deal of praying but she was not compulsive in the matter. Her domestic tedium was enlivened by taking soup to bedridden cottagers and reading to them. For women in every century until the twentieth, the days could be unbelievably long.

Men, on the other hand, had the business of an estate and local politics to keep them occupied; most were Justices, others served in the Army for a spell, and therefore the question of how to fill the day was not often a problem. As we shall see in the next chapter, when it came to acquiring and displaying the contents of a house, it was the men who set the pace.

It is little wonder that some enterprising women kicked over the traces of convention and took themselves off. One such was Lady Mary Wortley Montagu, born 1689, daughter of the 1st Duke of Kingston. She married

Edward Montagu who was for a time Ambassador to Constantinople, where she learnt Turkish and responded to the life and customs of the East, even going so far as to wear Turkish trousers. Later, back in London, she left her husband for no better reason than a severe infatuation with an Italian. The rest of her life was passed, first in France then in Italy, with a succession of paramours and in writing with considerable wit and verve. This behaviour in a man would have been unremarkable and it is a tribute to her personality that she, notwithstanding many raised eyebrows, largely got away with it. Best known for her interest in inoculation for smallpox, she died of cancer in London in 1762.

Lady Hester Stanhope, born 1776, eldest daughter of the 3rd Lord Stanhope, was a similar rebel but also an embarrassment to the British Government. In 1806 she left England for ever with a friend, Miss Williams; by 1814 they had arrived on Mount Lebanon where they lived and dressed as Arabs in the Arab community. Hester Stanhope built her own village and surrounded herself with a trusted retinue and half-tamed animals; she also made something of a name for herself among the desert people as a prophetess. She died in 1839 after shutting herself up in her own fortress in a self-imposed siege. Her body was found by the local British Consul; she had been deserted by her servants who had decamped from their eccentric mistress with all her possessions.

For women like Lady Mary Wortley Montagu, intelligent, interesting and interested, and Lady Hester Stanhope, an independent and forceful personality, the lifestyle of the upper classes could be appallingly dull. The wonder is that more did not take off as they did.

Yet even in Lady Margaret Hoby's time, life in some few remote country houses was not dull. When Bess of Hardwick was living at Hardwick Hall in the early 1600s, although she by then was in her seventies, it was not by any means a dull household. Many of her staff could play instruments and frequently did. As a rich woman she rewarded those who pleased her and consequently travelling players often visited Hardwick; the Queen's players, in September 1600, may have performed Shakespeare in the High Great Chamber. Lord Ogle's players made two visits in 1594 and 1595, the Earl of Huntingdon's in 1599, the Earl of Pembroke's in 1600, as well as singers, trumpeters and other entertainers. When all these distractions lacked, they could fall back on card games such as Faro, standing (not sitting) at the high card table still in the state withdrawing room, or any of the games shown inlaid on the famous Eglantine Table in the High Great Chamber – draughts, backgammon and an angled board game whose rules have long since been forgotten.

Needlework was very much a pastime for women in the sixteenth and seventeenth centuries. However, it must not be thought that Bess of Hardwick, Countess of Shrewsbury, worked any of the large table carpets and cushion covers displayed at Hardwick Hall. She would have worked on a piece small enough to be held in her hand. In fact the only piece of needlework one can be sure she worked is a centre panel in the hangings at Oxburgh Hall,

Norfolk. The designs were taken from woodcuts; many of the flower designs at Hardwick come from a herbal published by Mattioli in 1568 and 1572 and are worked with an amazing 400 stitches to the inch. Other flower designs, called 'slips', are taken from gardening woodcuts; the oblique cut at the stalk was for grafting. The design would have been drawn out on fine canvas by, in Bess of Hardwick's case, a male embroiderer and she would have worked the small flowers, leaving her ladies-in-waiting to fill in the backgrounds.

In addition to the considerable display of needlework at Hardwick Hall and the hangings at Oxburgh there is an interesting collection of sixteenth- and seventeenth-century needlework at Parham, Sussex; a seventeenth-century screen at Wallington Hall, Northumberland; and large collections at the Victoria and Albert Museum, London; the Burrell Collection, Glasgow; and the Royal Scottish Museum, Edinburgh.

Indispensable in any Elizabethan great house was the gallery – only later called a long gallery. By 1600 the gallery had become an important recreation space; no house of any size could omit the feature. The long narrow rooms were used for games, as a view-point from which to admire the decorative parterres of the gardens, for proposals of marriage – a gallery with embrasures made an ideal place for such intimacies – and for exercise in wet or cold weather. Usually they were furnished with little else but portraits of the family, portrait sets of kings and queens and a few hard chairs. Galleries were deliberately placed away from the main living spaces, with little furniture, not comfortable enough to tempt anyone to pass a cosy hour or two there; private discussion, therefore, could be carried out in galleries with little fear of interruption. Arabella Stuart and her cousin Mary Talbot were pacing up and down the gallery at Hardwick Hall in the winter of 1603 when they remembered that the rush matting was newly laid and not to be spoilt; they consequently went into the High Great Chamber to continue their discussion, where presumably the matting was older.

At Knole, Kent, is a remarkable surviving piece of gallery equipment: the Knole Dumb-Bell. It was probably installed over the Leicester Gallery in c.1603 by the Earl of Dorset. The machine consisted of a spindle with counterbalances mounted on a frame – something like a windlass. A rope ran round the spindle and went down into the gallery through a hole in the ceiling. It was a form of exercise machine; by pulling on the rope an impetus was generated causing the rope to go up and down, against which the person in the gallery pulled. There must have been more of these ingenious machines but the example at Knole is the only survivor. Joseph Addison in 1711 tells us: 'I exercise myself an Hour every morning upon a Dumb Bell, that is placed in the corner of my room, and pleases me the more because it does everything I require of it in the most profound silence. My landlady and her daughters . . . never come near me when I am ringing.' In their time galleries were an invaluable recreational space. Later, when their purpose had passed, some were converted into libraries: that at Syon in Middlesex was converted by Adam in the 1760s; Blickling, Norfolk, in 1800; Chatsworth in 1815, and Lanhydrock, Cornwall, in the later nineteenth century.

Libraries, surprisingly, were latecomers in country houses. Only two Elizabethans, Lord Lumley and Lord Burghley, had collections totalling over a thousand books which could really be called libraries, and these would not have been displayed on bookshelves as we might expect, but stacked in cupboards with titles written on the fore-edge, as the early seventeenth-century books at Charlecote Park, Warwickshire, still show. It was only when the number of books became an embarrassment that serious thought was given to their storage. Sir Thomas Bodley introduced double tiers of shelves reached by ladders in Duke Humphrey's Library, Oxford, in 1610.

After the mid-seventeenth century, when the gentry began to be interested in learning, the number of books in country houses increased. Even so, open-fronted bookshelves were unusual in private houses until the mid-eighteenth century. In the tiny library at Ham House, Surrey, made by the Lauderdales in 1675, the shelves are open, while at Chicheley Hall in Buckinghamshire the equally small library in the attic, made fifty years later, gives the appearance of being a panelled room until the panels are opened to reveal bookshelves. There is a similar secret library at Blithfield Hall, Staffordshire. An early recognizable library is at Holkam; designed by William Kent in the 1740s, it is 54 feet long, attached to Thomas Coke's own private apartments and not part of the state rooms. Even by that date a gentleman's library was not used to impress visitors with the owner's culture but kept for his own use. Later libraries were incorporated into the public rooms and became male domains. They could also become centres of learning. In the 1770s Humphry Repton, the landscape gardener, used the library of his neighbour William Windham at Felbrigg Hall in Norfolk. At Stourhead, the library, built in 1792, had by the 1820s become a focus for the study of local history. Colt Hoare, the owner of Stourhead, wrote his two-volume history of Wiltshire in this room; meetings of local gentry who were fascinated by history, including the Bishop of Bath and Wells, were convened here. John Skinner, the vicar of nearby Camerton in Somerset, a curious unhinged cleric, counted Colt Hoare almost his only friend and his greatest delight was to stay at Stourhead to use the library. Skinner recognized the library as a bright beacon of culture in a countryside otherwise occupied by the dull and ignorant. In Skinner's mind the uncultured were not worth knowing; he did not hunt and therefore that aspect of local society was of no interest to him.[3]

Lawn tennis, a sport in which women could and did take part, was a comparative latecomer in 1874. It sprang from the long established Royal Tennis, a game for which there is still an indoor court at Hampton Court Palace, with another still in use at Holyrood Palace; it was played as early as 1539 at Falkland Palace.

Until outlawed by Act of Parliament in 1849, cock-fighting was yet another essentially male sport. Popular by reason of the heavy bets wagered, the sport flourished in the eighteenth century. Once it was outlawed the cock-pits built for the game were used for other activities, demolished, or even disguised as something else so that an occasional illegal game could be played. At West Wycombe Park, Buckinghamshire, there is a so-called cock-pit above an archway built in 1767 leading into the stables. However, the rakish reputation of the builder, Sir Francis Dashwood, founder of the Hell-Fire Club, seems to have been exaggerated and the stories of goings-on at West Wycombe may have lent a never intended purpose to this building.

These amusements were all outdoor activities. When it came to indoor occupations men again tended to dominate. Billiards was played in country houses from the sixteenth century (the earliest mention of a table is at Howard House, London, in the inventory of the Duke of Norfolk, 1588; the earliest known rules were printed in 1650). The table was traditionally set up in the hall and all could happily join in, as at Ham House in 1679, but Celia Fiennes noticed one in the gallery at Euston Hall when travelling in Suffolk in 1697. The oldest table surviving in any house is at Boughton, Northamptonshire. Supported on twelve, spiralled, 'barley sugar' legs, it was in the house before 1690. The Victorians, with their passion for classification, stopped the haphazard placing of billiard tables; large country houses were usually equipped with a billiard room and smoking room annexed to it. Billiards therefore became essentially a male pastime. The reception rooms of Victorian houses were, perhaps unconsciously, sexually segregated; the withdrawing room was feminine, while the library, billiard room and smoking room became male domains, with the dining room and conservatory as neutral territories.

At least three historic houses still have shovel-boards for playing shove-ha'penny. At Littlecote, Berkshire, the great hall contains a vast table dating from *c.* 1600, converted to shovel-board by the mid-seventeenth century. Too big to move, the table has remained in the room in which it was built, serving as a table to eat off and play on. Stanway House, Gloucestershire, has one in the great hall, where it was made in about 1720. At Boughton House, there is a shovel-board in the Audit Room, which was made in 1702 for the sum of £3.17s.4d. These tables are found in rooms then used by servants and the game was a servant recreation.

In entertaining, which required the hostess's total involvement, women came into their own. Dances and balls were something that both sexes could enjoy. In the early 1700s dinner would be served to guests at around 11 am in the saloon, then once the tables were cleared out of the way, dancing would begin. In unaltered houses from the previous century, which were without the convenience of a saloon, dances and balls would be held in the great hall on special occasions: at Christmas, weddings, births and comings of age. Hogarth has brilliantly caught the atmosphere in the *Wedding Dance* of 1745, now in the South London Art Gallery. Here the celebrations, suitably held at full moon to light the way home, have carried on far into the night. The dance is probably held in the assembly rooms of a country town; the guests are a mixed lot of country gentlemen, some wearing the new, short bag wigs, others more conservatively holding on to old-fashioned, full-bottomed periwigs. What is clearly apparent is that all present are immensely enjoying themselves. The painting is filled with vivid movement and is one of the earliest domestic interiors to catch unposed enjoyment. The eighteenth century, once baroque formality ended, became more relaxed and assemblies turned into balls; in county towns, assembly room balls would be staged regularly. County families opened their houses to a wide circle of acquaintances by holding balls and, when they rebuilt or enlarged their homes, ballrooms that only came to life on a few occasions were added. A small string orchestra would provide the music, supper would be served and the local rustics, attracted by the unaccustomed light from the big house and the sound of music, would peer through the windows with amazement and, if taking themselves to the service entrance, might be rewarded with the leftovers from supper.

Music played its part in the medieval dinner; the screen passage made a very good base for a gallery in which minstrels played. In addition, when each course was carried out through the screen it could be announced by a ringing fanfare from trumpeters in the gallery. The masques acted in great chambers in the second half of the sixteenth century required music and ended with dancing. Music rooms were an eighteenth-century feature. Although not used exclusively for music, the walls might be decorated with musical instruments. At Kedleston, Derbyshire, there is an Adam music room with an organ of which the case was designed by Adam. At Killerton House, Devonshire, is a music room with a chamber organ of *c.* 1807, and at Traquair House, Borders, there is a very fine harpsichord, dated 1651, with original decoration. Fenton House, London, has an important collection of musical instruments, the earliest being a five-sided Italian spinet of 1540.

By the mid-nineteenth century, the railways had made the 'weekend' possible, although it was never called a weekend, being referred to as Saturday to Monday. Guests could arrive from as far away as 150 miles for a ball on a Saturday evening. Deene Park in Northamptonshire had a nineteenth-century ballroom tacked on to the end of the house; the room has now been demolished. An early ballroom is that at Hopetoun House, Lothian, created by William Adam in the 1720s. More usually the balls would be held in the saloon, as at Saltram in Devon, or in the galleries, as at Hagley, West Midlands, and Harewood, Yorkshire. The best balls, however, were those held during the Season in London, where every large town house had a room big enough for balls and rooms for supper. Guests at London balls would be the whole of London society, including those whom the host wished to cultivate politically. They would arrive in town carriages with servants, who were left to wait in the servants' hall until called. Guests at country balls were always from local society, and again people who might be politically useful. In the 1780s at Hatfield, balls for four hundred guests were given regularly, with weekly balls during the Christmas season. Staying overnight was unusual except for close friends and relatives. Again it was the railway that altered the pattern; with travel so much easier, guests arriving from a distance of 200 miles obviously had to stay the night and would arrive with their own ladies' maid and valet, who would sleep in rooms conveniently near to their masters and mistresses.

Amateur theatricals were another activity in which both sexes could take part. Jane Austen in *Mansfield Park*, written in 1811, shows how the Bertram family set about amusing themselves with forbidden private theatricals as soon as their father Sir Thomas Bertram had unexpectedly been called away on business. However, amateur theatricals go back much further than Jane Austen's time and sprang from the masques of the late sixteenth century. The earliest to be illustrated is that played at the marriage of Sir Henry Unton and painted after his death in 1596. It is probably taking place in the great chamber, with gentlemen members of the household, friends and family performing; a six-piece orchestra is sawing away and the masquers are dressed as black and white cherubs and exotically attired women with red faces. Exactly what is going on is as unclear to Lady Unton as it is to us because one tiny cherub is handing her a note of explanation. The masque usually ended with the players and the audience joining in general dancing. The court masques of the early seventeenth century, devised for Queen Anne by Ben Jonson and Inigo Jones, became our public theatre but the dance remained a private function. Hogarth obliges us by painting not only a public production of Gay's *Beggar's Opera* in 1729 but also an amateur production in 1732 of *The Indian Emperor* by Dryden. This was a dramatized version of the conquest of Mexico, lavishly produced in the London house of John Conduit, wealthy master of the Royal Mint, and played by his children and those of his friends. The audience includes the younger children of George II, one of whom has become bored and is causing a lively diversion in the front row. This type of extravagant family production was the exception, and most people were content with more makeshift scenery and costume.

Amateur theatricals held their appeal into the present century. The 6th Duke of Devonshire built a theatre at Chatsworth in 1833, the only survivor amongst others, since demolished, at Blenheim, Wynnstay in Denbighshire and Wargrave in Berkshire. The 5th Marquis of Anglesey has the distinction of having been the only peer to bankrupt himself by lavish expenditure on amateur theatricals, fancy-dress and jewellery. The three extravagances came together in his love of extraordinary dress and personal adornment. He built a theatre in the chapel of his house, Plas Newyd, in Anglesey, and financed his own company of players with whom he performed, unfailingly dancing the butterfly dance whatever the production. Bankrupt to the tune of £250,000 in 1904, he died in Monte Carlo the following year, aged only thirty.

Fanny Burney's diary gives an early mention of 'Fancy Dress' in 1770, although earlier the practice of going to a party in disguise was imported by the Grand Tourist from the Venetian carnivals. Charades came in by the mid-eighteenth century and even if the game was frowned upon by Sir Thomas Bertram in *Mansfield Park*, the real life, minor gentry family of Sperling, at Dynes Hall, Essex, had no inhibitions about playing them, as Diana Sperling's water colour, dated 1818, shows. However, not all households offered such lively entertainment. Charles Greville, the diarist and politician, stayed at Belvoir Castle in Leicestershire for the Duke of Rutland's birthday party in

January 1838. The Duke kept a very ducal state during the four months of the year he lived in the castle:

> In the morning we are roused by the strains of martial music, and the band marches round the terrace, awakening or quickening the guests with lively airs. All the men hunt or shoot. At dinner there is a different display of plate every day and in the evening some play at whist or amuse themselves as they please, and some walk about the staircases and corridors to hear the band, which plays the whole evening in the hall. On the Duke's birthday there was a great feast in the Castle; 200 people dined in the servants' hall alone, without counting the other tables. We were about forty at dinner.[4]

What Greville omitted to tell us was that the band announced dinner by playing 'The Roast Beef of Old England'. For those who hunted or shot, these events were occasions to be remembered but for those who didn't the tedium was excessive. Disraeli and his wife Mary Anne stayed at Belvoir ten years later. Disraeli neither shot nor hunted and the joys of slaughtering five hundred birds in one day were lost on him. Mary Anne later told a friend, 'Whenever we go to a country house, the same thing happens: Disraeli is not only bored, and has constant ennui, but he takes on eating as a resource: he eats at breakfast, luncheon and dinner: the result is, by the end of the third day he becomes dreadfully bilious; and we have to come away.'[5]

The Disraelis were not alone with their problem; in 1854 a guest at Middleton, Oxfordshire, built in 1830 by Lord Jersey at a cost of £200,000, complained that the household was devoted to 'whist, billiards, racing and betting'.

By the second half of the nineteenth century the railways brought sophisticated London folk to the country for a visit from Saturday to Monday. They had not travelled a long distance to be bored for three days; games became very popular, with charades and whist firm favourites. The Hon. Mrs John Mildmay White, daughter of the 1st Lord Mildmay, recalled busy evenings at her father's house, Flete, Devon, after the First World War: 'After dinner we nearly always played games of some sort, but we were not one of the really intellectual households like Taplow Court, where you had terrifying games. We played Clumps and Coon Can and guessing games, and things like bezique and piquet and rummy, with bridge for those who liked it.' Viscountess Hambledon remembered some of the same games at Greenlands, near Henley, in the 1930s: 'After dinner we played charades and paper games, and perhaps somebody might sing at the piano . . . With youngish people, one had these round games – Clumps and things. Older generations had more sedate games, and bridge.'[6] Chips Channon recorded the Prince of Wales's enthusiasm for one of the most ridiculous of pastimes: the players sat in a circle round an empty bottle and in turn placed a match stick on the open top. The loser was the one who upset the perilous edifice. As a pastime, the bottle game was probably as tedious as Lady Hoby's praying.

Between the wars, Lord Berners at Faringdon, Oxfordshire, was well known for his eccentricities which must have enlivened visits: getting his guests to wear grotesque masks when being driven in the car, having his white horse to tea in the drawing room and installing a piano in the back of his Rolls-Royce. Nancy Mitford in *The Pursuit of Love* modelled the character of Lord Merlin, whose whippets wore diamond necklaces, on Lord Berners.

For the Edwardian hostess, to know who was having a discreet affair and which affairs were over was essential; lovers liked to have adjacent rooms. Some spirited guests would enjoy swapping around the cards with the occupants' name on the bedroom doors, with the inevitable result that blunders were made by the blissfully ignorant lovers.

If, for the majority, entertainment was a problem, there were a lucky few with the means to indulge in a passion for collecting fine art – for them no day was long enough. The evidence of their passion is obvious in many houses today, as we shall see.

CHAPTER 6

The Collectors

In 1805, the 2nd Lord Berwick added a picture gallery to his Palladian house, Attingham in Shropshire. A picture gallery at the time was a rarity and indicative of a serious approach to art. It was also very expensive for Berwick, and the total cost of construction and decoration was over £13,000. In addition the glass roof leaked! Joseph Nash, his architect, used cast-iron ribs to support the glazed roof, another novelty, and water poured in and damaged the new scagliola columns. The walls were covered with fabric in Chinese vermilion, the capitals of the columns were gilded and the floor surrounding the carpet was inlaid; the white marble chimneypieces were in the Egyptian style, which had been stimulated by archaeological interest following Napoleon's invasion of Egypt in 1798. Lord Berwick's picture gallery was built to the latest fashion; the pictures it contained were the result of his Grand Tour and likewise represented the most up-to-date taste. Unfortunately the greater part had to be sold in 1827 as a result of Lord Berwick's bankruptcy, though the 3rd Lord Berwick bought back some of his brother's pictures.

On the walls of the gallery are twenty-three Italian paintings by minor artists from the sixteenth and seventeenth centuries; there are also six copies of major old masters. The unanswered question is whether the 2nd Lord Berwick knew they were copies when he bought them in Italy, or was he taken in by wily dealers? It is unlikely that he cared either way; at that time a good copy was regarded as highly as an original.

Lord Berwick was able to indulge in a new gallery due to his increased income from agricultural rents. If Britain had not enjoyed an agricultural revolution in the eighteenth century, giving landowners increased wealth, museums and art galleries in Britain would be poorer places. Many of the wealthy went on the Grand Tour and returned loaded with antique statuary, old masters, contemporary views of the places they had visited by Bellotto, Canaletto, Guardi, Piranesi, and more often with a quantity of useless junk eventually consigned to the attics, where some of it remains to this day. In the Cabinet Room at Lamport Hall, Northamptonshire, are several good Italian paintings bought in Rome by Sir Thomas Isham (d. 1681), and at least one which he must have regretted buying.

The thirty years of peace enjoyed by Europe from 1763 until Napoleon's invasion of Italy in 1793 marked the peak of the popularity of the Grand Tour. It was immediately followed, from 1795 to 1870, by the greatest period for the accumulation of paintings in Britain. The heyday of collecting was from 1770 to 1830; the decline of European aristocratic families and Napoleon's rampages throughout Europe released huge quantities of art treasures at the precise moment when British wealth, generated from improved agriculture, allowed the rich to snap up bargains. In 1835 Britain had the greatest number of outstanding pictures, antiquities and *objets d'art* of any European country except Italy. Since the early part of this century this national treasure has been steadily and wantonly dissipated through taxation.

However, collectors and collecting began long before the age of the Grand Tour; Henry of Blois, brother of King Stephen, displayed classical antiquities in the Bishop's Palace, Winchester, in the twelfth century. This was unusual for the period; the usual collections, up to the early seventeenth century, were family portraits – the dynastic idea again. By the late sixteenth century the approach to pictures had gradually changed from that of dynastic glorification to an appreciation of art.

Goethe (1749-1832) saw that a collection added prestige to a connoisseur and said of art collections: 'They outweigh any splendour which the richest man can gain for himself,' a point already made by the Medicis in the fifteenth century. Thomas Howard, 2nd Earl of Arundel (1585-1646), was the first Englishman to build a great collection. It is one of the regrets of history that this lover of art lost everything in the Civil War. The famous collection of Leonardo drawings now at Windsor was Arundel's, and although he had a deep affection for Italy he bought northern paintings and confessed to a 'foolish curiosity' for the works of Holbein. The main collection was destroyed and lost and all that is left of his collections are some fragments of Roman and Greek statuary in the Ashmolean Museum, Oxford; some in the British Museum; remnants until recently at Fawley Court, Henley-on-Thames; and oddments of drawings, paintings and cameos that are scattered throughout European museums and private collections.

Arundel was not just a collector for collecting's sake; he lived with and deeply appreciated art objects. He was ruthless in his acquisitions: in 1618 the Countess of Bedford reacted angrily to 'a tricke my Lo. of Arundel putt upon me yesterday to the cusning [cheating] me of some pictures he promised me'. Horace Walpole later called him 'the father of vertu in England'.

As an intimate friend of Prince Henry, Arundel undoubtedly helped the young man begin what would have been another great collection, had not the Prince died in 1612 aged only eighteen. His collection passed to his brother Charles who built up one of the greatest collections of paintings ever to be seen in England. Charles I's biggest coup was to acquire the Gonzaga collection under the nose of Philip IV of Spain at the enormous cost of £80,000. He not only bought paintings but commissioned works from

Rubens and Van Dyck. This collection too was broken up and dispersed in the Civil War. The Duke of Buckingham, seven years younger than Arundel, built up a spectacular collection of paintings at York House, London, in a very short time. Balthasar Gerbier, his art adviser, told Buckingham in 1625: 'out of all the amateurs, and Princes and Kings, there is not one who has collected in forty years as many pictures as your Excellency has collected in five.'

These three extraordinary collectors were not the first to have their agents scouring Europe, listening for rumours of sales so as to get in first and buy bargains. Sir Francis Walsingham, Queen Elizabeth's chief of the secret service, kept a man in Paris to buy and to spy, but he was only interested in paintings and could not really be classed a collector of virtu. Walsingham's contemporaries, Robert Dudley, 1st Earl of Leicester, and Archbishop Parker, both had galleries hung with portraits and therefore could not be classed as true collectors either.

The Civil War, as well as dispersing three great collections, also prevented the founding of any new collections until the eighteenth century. The wealthy of both sides suffered severe losses and from 1660 they were more concerned to re-establish themselves, with little inclination or money to spend on art; it has been called 'a century of darkness'. On the continent of Europe there was no such hindrance; Philip IV of Spain was able to acquire some of the Gonzaga collection when Charles I's pictures were sold after his execution in 1649. Others too took advantage of the chance to buy first-rate paintings; Louis XIV of France, inspired by the collection of Archduke Leopold Wilhelm in Brussels, built up a splendid gallery of paintings which in turn was dispersed in the French Revolution of 1789-97. Cardinal Mazarin, a private collector, was still on the lookout for items from Charles I's collection as late as 1653 when he wrote to his London agent telling him that 'there are still some unsold paintings in the King's palaces.'

Notwithstanding the Civil War, one collection did survive. Wilton House, Wiltshire, boasts one of the oldest collections in England, begun by the 3rd Earl of Pembroke (1580-1630) who, like the Earl of Arundel, married one of the daughters of the 7th Earl of Shrewsbury. A disastrous fire at Wilton in 1647, besides consuming a large part of the building, destroyed early family portraits. However, the greater part of the collection was in London at Durham House and included Italian old masters as well as the huge painting by Van Dyck of the 4th Earl and his family, installed by 1654 in the Double Cube room at Wilton. In addition there were other family portraits by Van Dyck. The Civil War inevitably reduced the Pembroke fortunes; the rebuilding of Wilton after the fire made further inroads and in the 1650s the 4th Earl was forced to sell many of the pictures acquired by his father. These included Titians, a Bassano, a Giorgione and a Correggio. The family portraits by Van Dyck and Lely were retained, but of the Italian pictures possibly only one is still in the collection today: *Christ Washing the Disciples' Feet* by Tintoretto. A sad note at the end of a short list of paintings at Wilton, dated 1652-3, states, 'others most or all to be sold and divers already sold'. The Wilton collection received unexpected additions in the last year of the 5th

Earl's life when he entertained Cosimo III, Grand Duke of Tuscany, at Wilton in 1669; the grateful guest made a parting gift of eight Italian old masters, five of which are still in the collection. They include *The Virgin and Child, St John and Two Angels* by Andrea Del Sarto, which can be seen on the west wall of the Corner Room. One other painting of this generous gift, attributed to Correggio, was sold at Christie's in 1951 for £273.

The Wilton collection was added to on a large scale for fifty years by the 8th Earl of Pembroke, who succeeded his brother in 1683. The 8th Earl bought not only paintings, including the well known Wilton Diptych, but, in the true spirit of a collector of virtu, he also acquired antique sculpture, coins, medals and a large library. The 8th Earl was responsible for the greater part of the Wilton collection of today; at the sale of Cardinal Mazarin's collection he bought a large quantity of marbles and busts, whereas his distant relation Arundel had lost his paintings to Mazarin eighty years before. The Wilton Diptych was sold to the National Gallery for £90,000 in 1929.

Little is known about how or where the Wilton paintings were hung, except for those in the Double Cube room which are still in the position in which they were placed in the 1650s. This gives a unique example of picture-hanging in a room of state of *c.* 1650, in which the paintings become part of the decoration; the procession of family portraits is interrupted by portraits of Charles I and his queen, Henrietta Maria, with their children, in the prime position over the fireplace. However, the baroque fashion for picture-hanging in smaller rooms was markedly different; the paintings would have been hung in rectangular, set patterns with the higher frames canted forward and with little regard paid to the subject of the pictures in the arrangement. The chains or cords might be covered with ribbons and bows.

The taste for Italian paintings, so obvious in the Wilton collection, was maintained until the end of the seventeenth century, with Dutch paintings becoming fashionable from the 1740s. English painters throughout the eighteenth century were rightly valued for their skill at portraiture. The 'conversation piece', by such painters as Arthur Devis and Zoffany, became popular from the first quarter of the eighteenth century on the grounds that several members of one family could be portrayed at a far lower cost than having them painted separately. There are examples by Devis at Upton House, Warwickshire, and by Zoffany in the Tate Gallery. Family portraits had always been popular and because they were accumulated through generations in a haphazard fashion and friends gave each other portraits, they can hardly be called collections. The head of a family would have himself painted in Garter Robes to commemorate his becoming a member of the order, and a rise in the peerage would stimulate another portrait. But on the market portraits fetched little money until this century.

Advice on where to hang paintings was given in 1624 by Sir Henry Wotton: 'Lastly that they bee as properly bestowed for their quality as fitly for their grace: that is, cheerful Paintings in Feesting and Banqueting Rooms: Graver Stories in Galleries: Landscaips and Boscage, and such wilder works, in open Terraces or in Summer Houses.' Fifty years later a handbook gave a different view of suitable subjects for different rooms: the hall was reserved for shepherds, peasants, milk-maids and flocks of sheep, the staircase was to have architectural scenes, either new or ruined. In the great chamber the recommendation was for landscapes (unusual for the time), hunting, fishing, fowling, histories and antiquities. The withdrawing room, being a less public place, was to have portraits of 'Persons of Honour' and intimate friends and acquaintances. In the 'banqueting rooms' the suggestion was for 'merry paintings of Bacchus, Centours, satyrs, syrens and the like', with a warning to avoid obscene pictures. The bed chamber was reserved for portraits of 'wives and children'.[1] The writer made no recommendations as to which artists were desirable; at the time attribution of unsigned work was merely hopeful – art history was unknown.

Until photography made reproductions of paintings available to everyone there was no means of comparing pictures except on auction room walls. Engravings were available which went some way towards establishing the background history of fine art and painting, but there were, understandably, large areas of ignorance. Consequently many collectors were perfectly happy to have copies hanging on their walls. Moreover the subject was more important than the execution; pictures were bought in the eighteenth century for the ideas they expressed and were meant to be 'read'.

A glance at any sale catalogue of paintings even as late as the nineteenth century will reveal that pictures were given optimistic attributions to make a better sale; Titians, Correggios, Rubenses and Rembrandts turn up in amazing quantities. Inventories are just as misleading in their attributions simply because scholarship was lacking. However, there were some knowledgeable collectors who went to great lengths to gain their knowledge, as was the case of the 2nd Duke of Devonshire.

One of the wealthiest families which suffered least in the Civil War was that of the Earls of Devonshire (the Dukedom was conferred in 1694); at Chatsworth they were one of the earliest to build up a collection. Even so they did not begin until the time of the 2nd Duke, who inherited in 1707 and died in 1729; his collection remained intact until very recent years. The 2nd Duke's interests were chiefly in drawings and coins; not the sort of objects for impressive display. The greater part of the Duke's collection was kept in his cabinet at Devonshire House in London and shown only to those specially interested. Exactly what the 2nd Duke contributed is difficult to assess simply because the accounts of the majority of his purchases do not exist. However, he was in close touch with the most distinguished connoisseur of drawings in France, a wealthy banker, Pierre Crozat, who was happy to give the Duke the benefit of his advice. Crozat was not so happy when the Duke pulled off the purchase of the Flinck collection of drawings in Rotterdam, a collection that Crozat particularly coveted, most of which is still in the Devonshire collection. Nicholas Flinck's father had been a pupil of Rembrandt. In 1722 Crozat arranged for the Duke the purchase, at a cost of £1,800, of Domenichino's *Expulsion from the Garden of Eden*, a painting still at Chatsworth. Another of the Duke's contacts was the Venetian collector, Antonio Zanetti the elder; he and Crozat met when Zanetti travelled to Paris with the painter Rosalba Carriera and stayed with Crozat in 1720. There was obviously an international exchange of views, one collector assisting another, and good-humoured envy if a spectacular coup were pulled off. One of the Duke's principal agents was Hugh Howard (1675-1737) who, although a gentleman, was forced to earn his living as a painter. Howard studied under Carlo Maratta in Italy from 1697 and later was instrumental in obtaining for the Duke two Van Dyck sketchbooks; one, acquired for the nation in lieu of death duties in 1957, is now in the British Museum and the other, which some doubt is by Van Dyck, is still at Chatsworth. Howard's acquisitions for the Duke may have included three paintings by Carlo Maratta. There are six by this painter at Chatsworth and a seventh was sold in 1976.

The four paintings by Maratta not acquired by the 2nd Duke belong to the second stage of the Chatsworth collection. In 1748, Lord Hartington, the heir to the 3rd Duke of Devonshire, married the only child and heiress of the 3rd Earl of Burlington, on whose death, in 1753, the Burlington wealth and his very large art collection, including the four Marattas, went to the 4th Duke.

While the Devonshire collection is the greatest and least altered of the early collections, that of Lord Methuen at Corsham Court, Wiltshire, is particularly noteworthy, not only because the collection of pictures formed during the first half of the eighteenth century by Sir Paul Methuen is intact, but because the rooms, furniture, and hanging pattern basically remain as they were in the 1770s. Sir Paul's collection is typical of the taste of the period: Italian old masters of the sixteenth and seventeenth centuries and Flemish paintings which became popular around the mid-eighteenth century. The collection received some very valuable additions in the mid-nineteenth century from the Rev. John Sandford, whose only daughter married the 2nd Lord Methuen. Sandford had the good fortune to be living in Florence when so much fine art was thrown on the market after the Napoleonic Wars. He not only bought Italian masters cheaply, but Italian primitives before they became popular. However, the basis of the collection was made by Sir Paul, who died aged 85 in 1757. He served as Ambassador to Portugal and to Spain and consequently was able to profit from being in Europe, the market place for paintings.

Undoubtedly the pride of Corsham is the picture gallery, designed by Capability Brown in the 1760s. The proportions of this treble cube room were planned around the pictures destined to hang there; the sizes and frames are carefully matched in balanced patterns, hanging on a background of rich crimson damask – from the late eighteenth century, red was recommended as a background, particularly for Italian paintings. The care with which the complete design was put together can be appreciated when it is seen that the double nail pattern on the seats of the chairs matches the double line of brass pins holding the edge of the damask wall covering. The carefully thought-out groups of pictures incorporate pier glasses, tables and seat furniture. It is noteworthy that the key painting above an overmantel is a studio replica of Rubens's *A Wolf and Fox Hunt*, framed to match the pier glasses – the original belonged to Lord Ashburton and is now in the Metropolitan Museum of Art, New York. Again, the effect was more important than the attribution.

The Corsham collection is exceptional, owing to the expertise of its founder. Other collectors of the eighteenth century were content with benefiting from the Grand Tour alone and the range of their collections is consequently narrower. The Cabinet at Felbrigg in Norfolk, designed by James Paine in 1751 for William Windham to show views of the Roman Campagna by Busiri which he commissioned on his Grand Tour, is typical of this taste. Unable to afford the expensive works brought back from Italy by his neighbour, Thomas Coke of Holkham, he was content with a great deal less. Nevertheless, he took enormous care over the arranging of his tiny collection and his pictures still hang in exactly the positions and patterns he planned over two hundred years ago.

Although paintings are easily displayed in rooms used for everyday living, this was not the case with marble busts and vases which are overpowering *en masse*, and should be seen from all angles. The 3rd Earl of Burlington was the first to address this problem when he built his villa at Chiswick in 1724 to include a sculpture gallery for statues and busts collected on the Grand Tour. Of course Burlington was referring back to Arundel's gallery, reserved for the display of antique statues. Other galleries quickly followed: Holkham, Norfolk, in 1734; Petworth, Sussex, in the 1780s; Woburn, Bedfordshire, 1754; Newby, Yorkshire, 1768; and Chatsworth, 1825. It was about the mid-eighteenth century that the plaster fig leaf appeared; naked statues in the garden were one thing, but with women taking an interest in antique art and with the figures in the house, modesty was important. A variation on the design of a gallery for displaying classical marbles was the circular gallery, taken directly from the Tribuna of the Uffizi in Florence; for example, the rotunda at Newby, 1768; the Pantheons in the garden at Stourhead, Wiltshire, 1758; and at Ince Blundell, Lancashire, in 1802. The Tribuna in fact was so popular that Queen Caroline sent Zoffany to paint it in the 1770s. The picture summed up the way in which all Grand Tourists liked to think of themselves: as connoisseurs and collectors of classical antiquities. Dr Johnson, who never made the Grand Tour, said in 1776, 'A man who has not been to Italy is always conscious of an inferiority.' To build a sculpture gallery, to show Canalettos or other Italian views, clearly demonstrated a superior intellect and taste.

The true collector, however, was not concerned with displays of superiority, he was only concerned to get the best and enjoy it. Typical of the type was the 3rd Marquis of Hertford, who took advantage of the flooded European art market of the early 1800s. From this beginning his son, the 4th Marquis, built up the largest and finest collection of the century, now known as the Wallace Collection, in London.

The 4th Marquis of Hertford (1800-70), who never married, lived a life of scandalous eccentricity in Paris for the greater part of his existence. He was only following the example set by his notorious father, the 3rd Marquis. The 4th Marquis began buying paintings in the 1840s and continued almost until the day of his death during the siege of Paris. During those thirty years he bought widely: porcelain, furniture, bronzes, marbles and tapestries, but mainly French paintings of the seventeenth and eighteenth centuries. By the time he died the collection was enormous – far too big to live with – and the greater part was stored in Paris and London. Hertford had the flair to recognize quality when he saw it; he began buying French eighteenth-century furniture twenty years before it became popular, and also bought paintings by living French artists. He maintained a mistress, Madame Oger, but never lived with her. She was half-French, half-English, and he had eloped with her to London in 1834 and gone through a marriage which she believed to be legal – the officiating 'clergyman' was Hertford's valet. Madame Oger forgave Hertford everything, even his many liaisons, and remained faithful to the end; she bore him a daughter.

Earlier, Hertford had seduced Agnes Jackson, the daughter of Sir Thomas Wallace, a woman ten years older than he, and temporarily separated from her husband. In 1818 Richard Jackson was born, the illegitimate son of Agnes and Hertford. Although Hertford never publicly acknowledged the relationship, the child was brought up by Hertford's mother. Jackson later changed his name to Wallace and eventually became Hertford's secretary. On his death in 1870 the 4th Marquis left his collection and the greater part of his fortune to Richard Wallace. Wallace, like his father, had kept a mistress for many years, Amelie Castlenau, and also like his father did not live with his mistress. On Hertford's death they married and moved to London. Wallace continued expanding the original collection formed by his father, buying heavily but only for some three years. He generously permitted his collection to be exhibited by the Victoria and Albert Museum and in return was made a baronet. Sir Richard Wallace died in 1890, leaving everything, apart from small bequests, to his widow. The future of the collection was of considerable concern to Lady Wallace and on her death in 1899 it was left to the nation. The gift posed many problems, not least where to put it. A committee was formed and Hertford House in Manchester Square was acquired from the trustees of the estate; the collection remains there to this day.

This was an extraordinary gesture on Lady Wallace's part; she never learned to speak English, was never happy in England, and the greater part of the collection was French. The gift, however, represented only half of the collection; the remainder was in Paris and Lady Wallace specified items on only two floors of Hertford House for inclusion.

The most bizarre part of the story now begins. The Wallaces' only and illegitimate son, who had no interest whatsoever in the collection, died in Paris before his father, leaving four illegitimate children. Thus Sir Richard Wallace had no recognizable heir. He employed as his personal assistant, rather oddly, an unintelligent man, John Murray Scott, who had no interest in fine art. On Lady Wallace's death the remainder of her estate, worth over a million pounds, went to Murray Scott. Two years later Murray Scott met the wife of the 3rd Lord Sackville, mother of Vita Sackville-West, who unscrupulously collected millionaires. Murray Scott stood no chance; by the time he died in 1912 he had been persuaded to leave his millions to Lady Sackville. The second half of the collection was sold and dispersed throughout Europe and the United States – the sales were only interrupted by the First World War. Some of this inheritance was put to good use in the repair and restoration of Knole House, Kent, which in turn came to the nation in 1962. When the money came to Vita, on the death of her mother in 1920, she was able to buy Sissinghurst Castle, also in Kent, and that too came to the nation in the same year as Knole. In ways that could never have been foreseen, the vast wealth of the 4th Earl of Hertford was given to the nation in three different forms within a hundred years of his death. Although the Wallace Collection in Manchester Square represents only half the original, it is nevertheless the biggest and finest collection of French decorative arts in the world.

A collection that might possibly have come second to Wallace's was that built up by the eccentric Bishop of Derry and the Earl of Bristol, nicknamed the Earl-Bishop, who died at Albano in Italy in 1803. Unfortunately practically all his collection was taken by Napoleon's armies when they invaded Italy in 1798. Ickworth in Suffolk, the house he built to contain his collection, but never saw, was left to heirs to complete and remains as his memorial.

The Earl-Bishop began his plans for Ickworth in 1794 when he was following a peripatetic existence in Italy. The house consists of a giant central rotunda, which he planned to live in, connected by curving corridors to two large flanking pavilions in which his collection was to be housed. He wanted his pictures to show 'an historical progress of the art of Painting both in Germany and Italy . . . to be divided into its characteristic schools – Venice, Bologna, Florence, etc.' Had the Earl-Bishop been able to achieve his object, he would have produced, for the time, a uniquely sensible way of exhibiting paintings.

With Napoleon's armies invading Italy, it was hardly the moment for an Englishman to continue journeying. In fact the Earl-Bishop saw no reason for his interests to be interrupted for anyone. His erratic peregrinations were due in part to buying for the collection and in part attempting to regain captured treasures that he had stored in Rome and Leghorn. Ignoring the fact that the French were watching his movements closely he happily spied on their army, openly sending reports to Sir William Hamilton, an old school-friend and British Minister to the court at Naples. The Earl-Bishop was astonished and affronted when he was arrested and imprisoned in Milan for nine months. Many who knew him felt that it was no more than he deserved. He was still trying to regain his possessions in 1803 on a journey from Albano to Rome when he was struck down with an old complaint he called 'flying gout in the stomach'. Taken from his carriage into a peasant's cottage, he was shortly afterwards removed when the Catholic peasants discovered that their sick visitor was a heretic bishop. The Earl-Bishop died that same day in an outhouse. Thereafter his troubles were not over because superstitious sailors refused to sail with a corpse and, before his executors were able to ship his body home to be buried at Ickworth, his coffin had to be crated up and labelled as antique statuary.

Some of the collection was rescued, possibly that stored in Rome, but how much is represented at Ickworth today, is impossible to say. The Earl-Bishop mentioned among his purchases 'large Mosaick pavements, sumptuous chimneypieces for my new house, and pictures, statues, busts, and marbles without end, first-rate Titians and Raphaels, dear Guidos and three old Carraccis.' Like the Rev. John Sandford, he bought Italian primitives before they were valued. He also bought urns, Etruscan vases and antique fragments; most, if not all, were lost. It is just possible that some of the chimneypieces and sculpture at Ickworth formed part of the Earl-Bishop's treasures. Even so, something of his personality can be appreciated; the main rooms are all thirty feet high because he believed that he was unable to breathe properly in lower rooms, and that the atmosphere was tainted by the disagreeable odour of bodies unless there was sufficient height to take away the noxious gases!

Another collection that vanished and about which very little is known was created by Gregory Gregory in the first half of the nineteenth century. Gregory, over a space of twenty years, built Harlaxton Manor, Lincolnshire, to contain his collection. Although the collection is gone the house remains. Even though Gregory had no title, nor any expectation of one, Harlaxton is ducal in concept, so confounding the principle of dynastic achievement, for Gregory was unmarried and the estate was entailed on a disliked cousin. The building represents a statement of how Gregory saw himself and his collection. But although the collection went to distant relatives, the Welbys of Denton, the next village to Harlaxton, the house today contains many fittings and fixtures bought by Gregory before it was built: French panelling from Parisian town houses demolished after the Revolution, expanded to fit the higher rooms at Harlaxton; Italian marble grave furniture turned into overmantels, with mirrors in place of an inscription. Floors are paved with eighteenth-century Italian tiles, two door frames are crowned with busts representing four of the seven deadly sins, another has a carved royal coat of arms from the late seventeenth century, worthy of Grinling Gibbons, another overdoor has two carved wood figures of Hercules and Samson. The Gregory collection, inherited by the Welbys, was so vast that they demolished their house and built a larger one to contain it. Even so they were unable to accommodate the complete collection and had to get an Act of Parliament to break the entail before they could sell some two hundred items they had no room for.

Another aspect of collecting which gave heirs some embarrassment was the early nineteenth-century fashion for mounting animals and birds in glass cases. No nineteenth-century country house was complete without cumbersome glass cases filled with staring creatures of the taxidermist's art. Many collections have been thrown away, but Calke Abbey, Derbyshire, contains a remarkably large collection which, before the National Trust took over the property, was scattered throughout many rooms. The fashion was due to two things: the Victorian interest in science and improvements in taxidermy. The problem had always been to preserve skins; this was not difficult when applying methods used in preserving food – alum, saltpetre and sodium chloride, or simply tanning. The drawback was that the skins were very liable to become infested with insects which destroyed the specimen. Arsenic provided the answer in the early nineteenth century; not only were the skins preserved but the poison prevented any infestations. When mounted, the specimens were even coated and the feathers, in the case of birds, dusted with arsenic. The process solved the problem of preservation but proved fatal to the taxidermist! It is due to arsenic that so many nineteenth-century stuffed creatures have survived.

The reasons why collectors strive to build up collections are varied. Arundel was a collector who wanted and could afford the best. Hertford was in the same category; neither were particularly troubled about showing their treasures. The 2nd Duke of Devonshire delighted in showing his treasures to knowledgeable friends. Wallace had something of a conscience over what he had inherited and was pleased to have parts of his amazing collection exhibited to an admiring public. These were all very rich men for whom collecting provided excitement and an occupation. The exception was the restless Earl-Bishop who loved the items in his collection. He intended to exhibit everything at Ickworth in a unique and orderly way, but the viewers would have been those who had the pleasant habit of dropping in on country houses and, by dint of tipping the housekeeper, being shown round. In 1785, the Hon. John Byng, with a friend, was very put out at being denied access to Wroxton, 'when unluckily for us Ld G[uildford] was just arrived from London, and denied us admittance. Very rude this, and unlike an old courtly lord! Let him either forbid his place entirely; open it allways; or else fix days of admission: but for shame, don't refuse travellers, who may have come 20 miles out of their way for a sight of the place . . . '[2] Many houses did have regular opening times – the visiting habit has been with us for a long time. Many collectors of paintings and fine art preferred to keep their collections in their London houses; the Spencers' collection, for example, was always at Spencer House, St James's Place, until the building was let to commercial enterprise.

Another collector who never saw the finished result was William John Banks, who created an astonishing Italian palace in the Dorset countryside. Banks vandalized Kingston Lacy, which was built in the 1660s and was a remarkable building in its own right. We must forgive Banks the outrage because he succeeded in his ambition – the exterior of the house evokes a Roman palazzo and the interior transports one immediately to Italy. Starting with a good inherited collection of Italian and northern European paintings, Banks went on to buy Titians, Velasquezes, Murillos, an astonishing and unfinished *Judgement of Solomon* by Sebastiano del Piombo, and many other treasures. Banks himself had to leave England after a scandal with a guardsman; he never saw Kingston Lacy completed nor his collection in place. Curiously, taste in collecting changed little over the centuries; paintings that

Arundel was collecting in the early seventeenth century would happily have been bought by Methuen at Corsham. But Arundel's collection of Roman sculpture would not have appealed to Methuen, because he had no way to display it. The demand was for Italian old masters in big frames, with taste turning to smaller Dutch paintings in the 1740s. The Grand Tour provided the chance for many to buy views of places they had visited. By the early 1800s French paintings thrown on the market by the Revolution were in high demand. Italian primitives, such as those at Corsham bought by Sandford in the 1830s, became fashionable. The nineteenth century saw industrial fortunes made by those who had no understanding of art, but some who did have left us with canvasses which are only now fully back in fashion. Lord Armstrong's paintings at Cragside, sold in 1910, consisted of works by Turner, Constable and the Pre-Raphaelites. Now replaced by pictures from the De Morgan Foundation, giving a similar impression, they would have been less highly regarded fifty years ago, but today show Armstrong to have been a perceptive collector of contemporary art.

The collecting of porcelain is a taste that developed fully in the second half of the nineteenth century. Today we see dinner services of Oriental china with the family coat of arms, set out in special displays. Such sets were specially made and could take two years to deliver. Such pieces are seen in many historic houses, including Kedleston, Derbyshire, and Belton House, Lincolnshire. At Glemham Hall, Suffolk, there is a good collection of Oriental ceramics, including *famille verte*, *famille rose* and Imari porcelain, as well as English Chelsea, Davenport, Derby and Worcester. Althorp, Northamptonshire, has a China Corridor for the display of Earl Spencer's collection. Dyrham Park, Gloucestershire, has a collection of Delftware which, apart from the tulip vases given by William III, was inexpensive and consequently little considered. Newburgh Priory, Yorkshire, has good examples of English New Hall, Derby and Worcester. The House of the Binns, Lothian, displays a large collection of Dutch, Chinese and English Delft on the walls. Waddesdon Manor, Buckinghamshire, has what is possibly the most priceless collection of porcelain anywhere in Britain, including Sèvres in the tented Blue Sèvres Room, Meissen figures by Kändler, Chinese and Japanese wares.

A collection is a very personal thing, but we have seen how easily collections are broken up and items pass to other ardent lovers of art. A recent example is that of the Rothschilds at Mentmore, sold against a background of criticism in 1977. This collection, made in two generations, was of course unique to the contemporary taste of the Mentmore Rothschilds, but at the same time the Rothschilds at Waddesdon were acquiring something better, although similar, and this collection has survived. An accumulation of art built up over two generations is a history not only of a family's taste but also of the taste of the nation; it is a statement that can never be repeated. Once dispersed, part of our history is gone beyond recall and we are the poorer for it. It is also true that paintings, marbles and fine furniture were objects made to be lived with; a desk designed by William Kent for domestic surroundings in Chatsworth loses a great deal when displayed alone under the bright lights of a museum gallery. Museums exhibiting priceless items certainly make them available to a wide public but they are far easier to understand in the surroundings for which they were designed.

It is time for us to leave the extravagant life of the very rich and spend some time with the army of servants below stairs who made it all possible.

CHAPTER 7

Below Stairs

A t Erddig, Clwyd, the servants' hall remains much as it was in 1939. A large, scrubbed, plain pine table runs down the centre of the small-ish, low room in the basement. On each side of the table are benches and at the head is a simple chair with splatted back; there would also have been another chair placed at the opposite end. Some ten oil portraits of past servants in a 'primitive' style – the earliest is of a negro coachboy, *c.* 1730 – line the walls and three star-shaped displays of swords decorate the ceiling. The swords are those of the Denbighshire Militia, raised in the early nineteenth century by the Yorke family. Fire axes hang over the cast-iron range and on the table are two leather blackjacks, or jugs, used when the staff's free quota of beer was handed out by the butler. The room was lit by oil lamps – electricity was never installed by the Yorkes. Outside in the passage is a long line of bells – the bell-board – one for nearly every room in the house and each marked with the room to which it is connected; an experienced maid would recognize the tone of each bell. Further down the passage, near the still room, are the nursery bells, marked Night, Day and Middle Nurseries, and beneath are eight lines in excruciating, but typical, Yorke family rhyme:

> *May Heaven protect our home from flame.*
> *Or hurt or harm of various name!*
> *And may no evil luck betide*
> *To any who therein abide.*
> *As also who their homes have found*
> *Of any acre of it's ground.*
> *Or who from homes beyond it's gate*
> *Bestow their toil on this estate.*

Erddig was not a particularly grand house and consequently the servants' hall never contained a huge number of servants; in 1852, in a photograph of the staff hanging in the passage outside the hall, there were fifteen servants, not including the gardeners, five men, under a head gardener, and four boys.

By 1919 the indoor staff numbered seventeen; yet the earliest records show that in the 1720s the staff numbered twenty-five to thirty.

At twelve o'clock every day the staff met in the servants' hall for dinner. The housekeeper, always given the courtesy title of 'Mrs', sat at one end of the table and the butler took the chair at the other. Down one side sat the maids and on the other, facing them, sat the men. In fact, meals were the few times when the two sexes were allowed to meet – the carefully organized routine was designed to keep them apart. After the main course had been eaten the housekeeper and the butler left the hall, taking their dessert to be eaten in the housekeeper's room.

Etiquette among the servants, as late as 1939, was more strict than that above stairs, even more so in very grand houses. At Blenheim at that date the visiting valets and ladies' maids in the servants' hall were all called after their masters and mistresses: Mr Devonshire, Mrs Bath. The valet of the eldest son of the house always sat on the housekeeper's right, taking precedence over the valet of even the most distinguished guest. However, it was more relaxed at Erddig.

In the 1920s at Erddig there were five maids under the housekeeper, Mrs Brown, and they slept in the attics – their bedrooms have been restored. The under housemaid cleaned the rooms and made the beds of the other maids; the head parlourmaid and housemaid had a room each and the under parlourmaid and under housemaid shared a room. Mrs Brown had her own room in the basement. During summer the day began when the under housemaid made tea in the attic pantry at 6 am and brought a cup to the other girls. In other households the summer day began an hour earlier. At 6.30 all reported to the servants' hall to collect the mail to be given to the family and each guest with morning tea in their bedrooms. Before breakfast at 8 o'clock the reception rooms on the first floor had to be cleaned, the shutters opened, the floors polished, grates cleared out and fires laid; in 1904, 108 tons of coal were burnt in the house alone. Additionally as many as forty oil lamps had to be collected up, refilled with oil and the wicks trimmed. The butler and footman were meanwhile setting up the breakfast in the dining room. At 9 am the housekeeper and butler joined the staff in the servants' hall and all processed to the family chapel for morning prayers. Breakfast was then served to the family and guests, and the housemaids finished cleaning the main rooms. After morning tea at 11 o'clock the maids cleaned the bedrooms, and after dinner changed into their black and white afternoon dresses and spent the afternoon in the attic workroom making their own dresses and mending the household linen until tea was served in the drawing room at 4 o'clock. The main rooms were prepared after tea, fires lighted when needed and oil lamps put out. Then it was the turn of the bedrooms, when the beds were turned down and clothes tidied away. Evening dinner was served to the family at 8 o'clock; the staff had their supper at 9 and went to bed at 10 or 11 o'clock.

Erddig was a comparatively relaxed household; the staff were well looked after, a pension fund was founded, the hours were not long and the staff could have three late nights out each week. In stricter households the day would begin for all at 6 am in winter and 5 am in summer and not end for the staff until the last guest or member of the family went to bed; often a nineteen hour day. The Erddig servants were, however, underpaid; the Yorkes felt it was a privilege to work for them. In 1903 the butler was paid £55 a year, no more than an under butler would have been paid elsewhere, when he could have got £75 to £100. The housekeeper was paid the same wage; junior maids were paid £8 and £15 when a maid-of-all-work would be paid £18 in other households. In that remote part of the country there was not much in the way of alternative employment.

In other parts of Britain, where alternative employment was available, girls reluctantly went into domestic service and their occupation was looked down upon by their friends working regular hours in manufacturing. The concept of service being a demeaning occupation was a notion introduced in the nineteenth century when alternative jobs with more freedom were available. The long hours at the beck and call of others, the lack of free time and a restricted or non-existent social life, in contrast with a regular sixty-hour week and complete social freedom, gave domestic service the aspect of slavery. This was not always the case. In the sixteenth century serving in a great household was a sought-after privilege; something of the rank, the power and the authority of a great family rubbed off on those who served them and, as they went about the countryside on the family's business, doors opened and favours were granted that were unattainable to anyone beyond the influence of the family's authority. The family livery afforded a certain protection and it was worn with pride and confidence – a total contrast to the situation four hundred years later.

The reason for this influence went back to the medieval barons who maintained private armies for the protection of themselves and their households; their power was maintained by real force. By the sixteenth century the powerful maintained their authority by more subtle means: a landowner was a magistrate almost by right, and magistrates were appointed by the Lord Lieutenant of the County, who would be one of the largest landowners; these positions gave enormous scope for manipulation. The office of Sheriff of the county was another powerful position. A web of 'interest' built up through friendships, the doing of favours for neighbours, even of finding jobs for supporters. Until the reform bills of 1831 and 1867, when the power of the landlords was broken – by pressure from the rising middle classes – Parliament maintained the authority of the landed gentry. In the eighteenth century eighty per cent of the House of Commons and virtually the entire House of Lords were landowners. The landowner was to be respected, or offended at one's peril.

Any servant of a sixteenth-century household was therefore part of a carefully constructed enterprise. The greater the enterprise, the greater the number of servants – and power could be calculated by the number of servants. The larger the staff, the larger the hall required to accommodate it and consequently the larger the house. Yet the servant hierarchy of the sixteenth century was totally different from what we might imagine and within it there were circles of interest built up and maintained by officers of the household. The officers of the household were gentlemen by class, often sons of neighbouring landowners, with servants to look after them. These men occupied the prime positions of power within the hierarchy; the names of their positions might sound strange to our ears today, but the whole fabric was based on custom at court. The chaplain of the household would be a gentleman, often bearing an honorary title of 'Sir'; the steward would also be a gentleman and would be responsible for running the household. The gentleman usher was responsible for maintaining the state apartments and receiving visitors; in a large household this duty would be supported by a gentleman-groom-of-the-chamber and a gentleman usher of the hall. The gentleman-of-the-horse supervised the stables, the auditor and the secretary were two more gentlemanly positions.[1] None of these gentleman servants did any manual work – no gentleman did; they delegated this to the yeoman servants. They were heads of department and they appointed beneath them whomever they wished and so made a sphere of 'interest' for themselves. The relationship with the family of both gentleman and yeoman servants was that of an identity of interest: to be part of the family group was a privilege based on trust and security; to fail in that trust brought instant dismissal.

To distinguish one household servant from that of another household and to differentiate the gentleman from the yeoman, the former usually had a livery cloak with the family's coat of arms on it and the latter a coat to match the cloak. In the following century – the century of civil war – servants wore their own clothes below stairs, except footmen and the staff who would be seen by visitors. Footmen, once they became part of the smart carriage equipage in the eighteenth century, were supplied with full livery. It was also the footmen who received visitors at the front door and who passed around wine at dinner and cordials in the saloon. So that no guest should suffer the embarrassment of mistaking a footman for a guest, it became the practice that footmen's livery was deliberately designed in a past fashion; powdered hair and short wigs continued even into the present century. When women, becoming parlour maids, took over some of the footmen's duties in the nineteenth century, they too were put into a uniform unlike anything a guest might wear.

When Bess of Hardwick died at Hardwick Hall in 1608 her steward, Timothy Pusey, had bought himself a nearby estate, no doubt helped by Bess. He retired a wealthy man in his early thirties to become head of a county family and obviously a strong supporter of Bess's dynasty. Lord Burghley, Bess's contemporary, employed twenty gentleman servants of independent means with incomes of £1,000 a year and many of his lower servants owned land to the value of £1,000 to £20,000. Clearly none of these had any financial need to work for Burghley. By being part of the powerful Burghley's staff they were in a political centre where, for the able opportunist, a fortune might be gained. At the height of his power Burghley's household numbered a round hundred.

In principle the number of servants varied according to the rank of the head of the family, but in practice it was wealth and power that dictated the size of the staff needed to run the enterprise. In 1605 it was recommended that an earl should have 85 servants, yet in 1613 the Earl of Dorset at Knole, Kent, felt the necessity to have 104. In the late sixteenth century the 2nd Lord Burghley, a mere baron, maintained 100; the 1st Lord Petre, also a baron, had 63 in 1594, while Lord Paget, at Beaudesert Hall, Staffordshire, in 1575, made do with a more modest 45. The 2nd Earl of Derby had 240 servants. The discrepancies here arose because Derby was an old man who had not adapted to changing circumstances and Burghley was a courtier who might have to entertain the court, whereas Paget was a Catholic out of the mainstream of court life. Petre, who supported the Established Church, although the family are now Catholics, had the right size of household for his rank.

The greater part of these households consisted of men, the exception being laundry-maids and ladies-in-waiting; the latter were paid companions for a nobleman's wife. Some members of the household staff seem to have been old servants kept on the payroll because they had nowhere else to live; Mother Henley at Beaudesert in *c*.1600 was paid £1.2*s*.8*d*. annually for undisclosed duties. At Knole in the 1620s there were two 'blackamoors', Grace Robinson in the laundry and John Morockoe in the kitchen, who were probably unpaid slaves. Also in the kitchen at Knole were the oddly named Diggory Dyer and Marfidy Snipt.

Wages were paid quarterly or half-yearly; a steward at Bess of Hardwick's Chatsworth in 1593 was paid £20 annually and five gentleman servants got £5 each, except one, a nephew of Bess, who had an extra £1.12*s*.4*d*. The yeoman servants averaged £2.15*s*.4*d*. Additionally they received a yearly livery of a cloak for the gentlemen and a coat for the yeomen. A total of 40 on the staff – well below the average for a countess – cost £280 annually. This compares with Lord Paget's staff of 45 at Beaudesert, where the wage bill totalled only £107, who were thus paid less than half the Chatsworth rate, and Lord Petre's at Thorndon Hall, Essex, where 59 servants cost £148 annually. The marked difference in costs was because Bess was paying well for first-class men – for example her constant lawsuits made her need to have a lawyer on hand, and it is likely that her steward was trained in law.

Contrast these figures with the annual earnings for a building labourer in 1600 of £6.10*s*. and the skilled mason's wage of £13, both having food provided. It is easy to see why employment in a household was preferable; the work was not hard, the hours no longer, the food and conditions far better, there was scope for advancement and the job was secure.

A gentleman servant was not expected to do a great deal for his wages. He was there to provide the pageantry and background for family life. The yeomen-of-the-chamber set up the tables in the great chamber for dinner, the yeomen-of-the-ewery the cups, the yeomen-of-the-pantry the wine and bread and the yeomen-of-the-buttery the beer. The yeoman carver carved, the yeoman server served, the yeoman waiters cleared away the dishes. It was all done with great panache and flourish but it was far from being arduous work.

At Knole in 1613 the ladies-in-waiting and the gentleman servants ate with the family in the parlour. After this, two clerks of the kitchen presided over a table in the hall at which sat the principle yeoman servants, two cooks and two gardeners, while at another long table, overseen by seven gentleman servants who had been involved in serving the meals in the parlour, sat footmen, grooms, an armourer, a scrivener, a falconer, a bird catcher and the lesser servants. In addition there was the laundry maids' table in the hall, and the kitchen staff ate in the kitchen when all the others had eaten.[2]

It is very difficult to describe the daily life of Elizabethan servants in a great house; there survives but one memoir, and for the rest one must rely on 'Household orders' which only tell a fragment of the story. In 1572, Sir Francis Willoughby at Wollaton Hall, Nottinghamshire, had forty-seven gentleman and yeoman servants. At the head was a gentleman steward paid £6.10s per year and his income would have been considerably augmented by the custom of 'gifts'. At the bottom of the hierarchy was the kitchen boy at 13s per year. The only women were three of Lady Willoughby's waiting women and a laundress, with three under her. The usher of the hall, at £2 a year, was to keep the place clean and, with his groom, to see that 'no dogges come there'. Additionally, 'all disorders in the hall are by the usher to be reformed', and 'no stranger be suffered to pass without offering him a drink and that no rascall or unseemly person be suffered to tarry there'. John Penne was the botelier at £2 a year; he was in charge of the beer and his office was to be open only between 8 and 9 am, 11 am to 2 pm and from 5 to 9 pm, the meal times. He was to allow no servant to remain 'tippling' and he was to wash his plate and cups twice a day. He also provided cards and dice 'whereof he is to have the profit'. Unusually he, with his under-butler, were to clean the great chamber, generally the responsibility of an usher-of-the-chamber, make the fires and provide lights there, also supplying table linen for the family's dining.[3] The work was obviously not arduous, except for the job of clerk of the kitchen, another gentleman, who was responsible for buying all the food, running the kitchen, accounting to the steward for the silver, and seeing that all were fed. The number of servants was an indication of how Willoughby saw himself; in 1634 the 2nd Duke of Buckingham ordered that servants should be about him so that there would 'not be any wanting, and my service thereby [not] disappointed to my dishonour'. In the cause of ostentation the great houses were overmanned and a contemporary writer, William Harrison, referring to 'great swarms of idle serving men',[4] was probably not far off the mark.

When the day was done only the steward and the receiver, or accountant, retired to their own rooms to sleep. The gentleman servants would have beds, but slept two to a bed and only gentlemen together. The remainder slept where they could, on trucklebeds in passages or bedded down on the rushes in front of the fire in the great hall.

A hundred years later the scene had changed unrecognizably. The great hall was no longer used and servants ate in the servants' hall below stairs and slept in garret dormitories. The gentleman servant barely existed; only the gentle-man-of-the-horse and gentleman usher survived in grand households. They had not been swept away by the Civil War, but had found better things to do; commerce was expanding, the law, government service and the armed forces all offered better opportunities. In the vacuum caused by the gentlemen's departure the yeoman servants moved up the rungs and the gap between the served and the serving grew. Wages increased and half the indoor staff would by then have been women, who were cheaper. A new position of power was created: that of housekeeper. The women in the household staff were under her control and all victualling, except the wines and beer, was her responsi-bility; she had taken over part of the job formerly held by the clerk of the kitchen and some of the steward's responsibility.

Staffs were smaller in 1700 and considerably reduced by the end of the century. At Petworth, Sussex, the 6th Duke of Somerset employed a hundred servants in 1690, reduced to fifty in the early years of the new century; the 4th Duke of Bedford's London home was staffed by forty in 1753 and about the same number in 1771. With forty servants – about half the number needed in the sixteenth century – a peer of the realm could rub along quite comfortably. In fact he had to make do with fewer, because by 1700 wages were double what they were in 1600 and they had more than doubled again by 1800. The position of butler became all-powerful and was maintained until the very end. Although the number of unseen servants declined the number of footmen increased.

Originally a footman ran behind the coach, but by the 1700s he had come into the house and worked under the butler, waited at table now that the yeoman waiters had gone, and escorted his master and mistress when they went out – the more footmen kept, the more splendid the impression given. While the noble families were managing with fewer servants, the expanding mercantile classes were creating more and more domestic jobs.

The cost of maintaining a large household was high; in 1774 Clive of India, the 1st Lord Clive, paid out £700 at Powis Castle, Clwyd, for a staff of thirty-three that included sixteen women and permanent staff in his London home. A year earlier at Audley End, Essex, the future 1st Lord Braybrooke paid £510 for a staff of thirty including twelve women and the permanent staff at his London home. The differing cost again is accounted for by the fact that Clive was paying his upper servants more than Braybrooke – at one time he had eight footmen at his Berkeley Square house. It also happened that Braybrooke increased the wages of his upper servants; his annual wage bill had risen by £137 over five years and his staff by only four, but he managed with less display and only two footmen.

A man typical of his time was John Macdonald (1741-96), a very exper-ienced eighteenth-century footman – he performed all the duties of a nine-teenth-century gentleman's gentleman – who, curiously enough, also intro-duced the umbrella to Britain. During his career Macdonald worked for an earl, the son of a peer and a baronet, but more often was happy to be employed by lawyers, merchants and a historian. In the sixteenth century

Macdonald would have worked his way up to be a yeoman servant in a noble household; in the eighteenth century he was content to work for the professional middle classes. He was independent enough to give notice if his master failed to please, and the middle classes, anxious to employ so good a man, were more than happy to offer him a comfortable place. His ambition was to save enough money to retire – servants could earn quite a lot in tips. Retire he did, but not in the way he had foreseen, for he married the daughter of a Spanish hotel keeper in Toledo.[5]

In other ways Macdonald was ideally suited to his employment, for his father was a tenant farmer in Scotland, who lost all during the 1745 rebellion. Farmers' children took over the old domestic places of the sons of the landed gentry in the eighteenth century. Country-born servants were considered best – the city-bred had picked up bad habits, and married servants living in were very rare; when dormitories were the rule, accommodation was a problem. Macdonald, country-bred, was ideal from both points of view and he only married when he left service.

By Macdonald's time the quality of service began to give cause for complaint, and it was then that the middle classes generated a minor campaign for improvement. Defoe, the son of a London butcher, published a pamphlet in 1725 calling on Parliament to give magistrates the power to discipline servants: 'if Servants misbehave they ought to be . . . punished.' His mind was still on the subject in 1727 when he published *Everybody's Business*, and, in 1728, *Augusta Triumphans*; both books proposed better rules for servants' contracts. Swift, son of a Dublin lawyer, published a satire, *Directions to Servants*, in 1745; with tongue in cheek he suggested that the cook stir soot into the soup when it chanced to fall there, to give an authentic French taste, that the footman should warm the plates by putting them under his armpit, and to use them instead of a handkerchief when he sneezed or coughed, that the housemaid should empty chamberpots out of the windows instead of taking them down the back stairs. In 1759 another satirist, James Townley, a schoolmaster, wrote *High Life Below Stairs*. These publications were calculated to improve servants and they were read by the middle classes who faced the 'servant problem'. Fortunately for the landowner his rents increased dramatically in the eighteenth century and helped cover the cost of rising wages. This increase, however, was to come to an end in the following century.

With the end of the Napoleonic wars in 1815, the rich could afford to employ rather more staff, due to lower wages, although this was only a temporary lull. The 1st Earl of Verulam increased his staff at Gorhambury, Hertfordshire, from twenty to forty by 1820, only to drop back to thirty-five by 1830.[6] After the 2nd Earl inherited in 1845 – the repeal of the Corn Laws in that year caused many to lose nerve – there was another retrenchment to a mere twenty staff. For a wealthy man and an earl this was too low and by the 1850s he was cutting a rather more prosperous figure with thirty-seven staff. The Earl of Darlington at Raby Castle, County Durham, followed a similar policy. At the beginning of the century his wage bill was around £2,500; in

1825 it had increased to £3,000, but by 1845 it was reduced to £2,000.[7] Wealthy families such as the Grosvenors and the Percys made no economies and maintained large households. This was an Indian summer; there were only a few decades left of the grand life for many of this exclusive sector of society.

Wages generally moved steadily up, apart from the 1820s; at Milton, Cambridgeshire, a butler with Earl Fitzwilliam in 1800 was paid £50 a year; this was reduced to £43. 15s in 1822, while at Gorhambury, Hertfordshire, the 2nd Earl of Verulam paid £63 a year to his butler in 1847, £84 in 1864 and £90 in 1868. The Duke of Manchester at Kimbolton Castle, Cambridgeshire, was having to pay £84 for a butler in 1881. A nobleman's butler would command about twice the salary that he would in a gentleman's household. A house-maid paid £12 in the 1830s would expect to be paid £16 in the 1880s; it made little difference what household she was in.

One thing that did not change, however, were the rules below stairs. In a few servants' halls the faded boards still display the rules which, surprisingly, varied very little from house to house. There is one in the servants' hall at Chirk Castle, Denbighshire, another in the service passages in the basement at Holkham Hall, Norfolk, another is fixed to the kitchen wall at Cotehele House, Cornwall. At Wasing Place in Berkshire, burnt to the ground in the Second World War, the rules on a board from *c.*1750 were typical:

RULES and ORDERS
to be observed by the Servants of this
House and other people who may
occasionally happen to be there
First: That the hall shall be cleaned every
day by one of the Servants who shall take
his turn weekley and observe that a Fire be
made in due time, the Cloth laid, and after
Meals to put every thing in it's proper place
Secondly: That any Servant who shall
have the Management of the Hall agreeably
to the aforesaid Article shall at the Expiration
of the Week deliver to his Successor all things
belonging to it clean and in good Order
Thirdly: That if any one shall take any
thing belonging to the Hall out; or
displaces anything, cuts more bread than
is necessary, makes unnecessary Waste,
wipe their Knives and Forks on the
Table Cloth or Hand Towell, say any thing
indecent at Meal Times, give Lie to any
one, shall forfeit the Sum of Two Pence or receive
Six Strokes of the Boot on their Breech
Fourthly: That if any one shall leave dirty

Boots or Shoes or make any Dirt whatever
without immediately cleaning it, or shall be
guilty of any indecency whatever shall be
subject to the Fine or Punishment mentioned
in the foregoing article.
Fifthly: That if any one be heard to swear he
shall forfeit for every Oath the sum of one Penny
Sixthly: That if anyone shall by Accident
or otherwise break any utensil it shall
be left to the Decision of our Mistress
Whose Decision shall be final.[8]

It was more usual to include an order against gambling, and the two pence
fines at Wasing are twice as high as elsewhere – in the case of a housemaid on
low wages, very high indeed, and she might well have preferred to take the
boot. In some households this was not restricted to six strokes but a
'Punishment of a severe Booting'. The brushing of clothes in the servants'
hall was another prohibited occupation; the dust would get into the food and
many households had brushing rooms for cleaning outdoor clothes after
hunting or riding. In the nineteenth century the fines, along with the cost of
living, had more than doubled and the option of a 'booting' was rare. At
Llanbedr Hall, Ruthin, in Wales, the first order in hall was 'No Welch to be
Spoken'.[9]

William Gladstone, the nineteenth-century Prime Minister, also lived in
Wales, at Hawarden, and he seemingly had no objection to Welsh being
spoken or, more likely, his servants were mainly recruited in London. He,
like many others, moved his household easily to London from his country
estate, leaving behind a housekeeper and a few housemaids on board wages,
all other servants going with the family.[10]

In 1828 Petworth was run with typical Regency ease by ninety-seven
servants. Thomas Creevey stayed there and noted that the servants were
'very numerous, tho' most of them very advanced in years and tottered, and
comical in their looks'. One of the family explained that at Petworth there
were more servants 'of both sexes, and in all departments, than in any house
in England, that they were all very good in their way, but they could not
stand being put out of it, and were never interfered with, that they were all
bred upon the spot and all related to each other.'

The eccentricity of the Petworth household amused Creevey because even
though the house had guests staying the family and servants were all in bed by
10.30 pm. Creevey tried to get a glass of wine before retiring but the butler
had gone to bed and he had to do without. The lapse was more than made up
for the following day when he was offered anything for breakfast in any room
at any time between 9 am and noon.

Eleven years later Creevey stayed at Holkham where he was given a room
on the ground floor 'with a door at hand to go out of the house if I like, and
another equally near for nameless purposes. A maid lights my fire at seven

punctually, and my water is in my room at eight.' In fact the maid would have already been up since six in winter and an hour earlier in summer; parlour maids would have sprinkled the reception room carpets with wet sand before sweeping them, dusting, cleaning and laying fires.[11]

Upper servants, the housekeeper, cook, butler and lady's maid, got up an hour or so after the junior staff. Both housekeeper and cook in many houses were called with tea. The kitchen maids and the housemaids had the hard time; carrying coal for the many fires – when one grate used three to four tons in a year this represented enormous physical labour for young girls. Polishing floors with beeswax on hands and knees may have given a mirror-like finish and pleasant smell to rooms, but it also gave servants 'housemaid's knee'. They carried water for the many baths, then took it away again, before they collapsed into bed after the family had gone to theirs.

There was certainly companionship among the staff; meal times in the servants' hall, when the housekeeper and butler had left to take their dessert in the housekeeper's room, were often an occasion for fun. Servants' halls at Raby Castle, County Durham, and Erddig, Clwyd, have been restored to something like their nineteenth-century state, and at Waddesdon, Buckinghamshire, and Kedleston, Derbyshire, the servants' halls are converted to restaurants – a use not very different from the original! At Longleat, as in most grand houses, there was an annual servants' ball at Christmas in the nineteenth century; the Marquis of Bath led the dancing with the housekeeper, and the steward with the Marchioness. At Belvoir Castle, Leicestershire, in January 1838 on the Duke of Rutland's birthday, Charles Greville reported in his diary: 'We all went into the servants' hall, where one hundred and forty-five retainers had just done dinner and were drinking the Duke's health, singing and speechyfying . . . '[12]

The Victorian household was carefully organized so that the female servants, in the course of their daily duties, should not meet any of the male servants. In the morning, while the butler and footmen were setting up breakfast, the housemaids were calling guests and lighting bedroom fires. When breakfast was being served, the housemaids were making beds and cleaning the bedrooms, and so the routine was organized through the day. The only time the male and female servants officially met was at meals, although at least one butler recalled that the system was easily short-circuited.

A carefully organized routine for the staff requires a careful floor plan, and an examination of purpose-built nineteenth-century staff quarters should clearly show the thought behind the positioning of the service rooms and passages. The kitchens should be a long way from the dining room yet near the servants' hall. The route for food from the kitchens to the dining room should have at least one bend to prevent smells percolating into the main part of the house. At Stoke Rochford, Lincolnshire, there was a short underground railway carrying a hot cupboard from the kitchen to a lift in the servery; there are others at Petworth, Sussex, and Belton House, Lincolnshire, and beneath Welbeck Abbey is a complicated warren. The butler's pantry, something like the bridge of a ship, should be convenient for the dining room for serving meals, and for the front door so that he could see visitors arriving and send a footman to receive them. It would also have a silver vault attached, with the butler's or footman's bedroom nearby, to guard the vault. Routes to the family rooms should have alternatives so that guests were not disturbed – servants were not to be seen. Polesdon Lacey in Surrey, where Mrs Ronnie Greville entertained Edward VII, had no fewer than three service routes in the main house, with very wide passages. This was an ideal that few could attain, but such a plan avoided the embarrassment of butlers, going one way with loaded trays, colliding with housemaids going in the opposite direction with ash cans full of hot cinders. The housekeeper's room should be near the butler's pantry so that her adjoining linen room was convenient for the butler and footmen – this was seldom achieved. The servants' bedrooms should be as far away from the family and guest rooms as possible so that privacy was maintained. The arrangement of the male and female servants' sleeping accommodation gave great trouble because they had to be kept apart at all cost; J. C. Loudon's *Encyclopaedia of Cottage, Farm and Villa Architecture*, first published in 1833, took a Regency attitude to this problem by recommending that 'the menservant's bedrooms should, if possible, be apart from those of the females'. Later opinion hardened and usually the maids slept in the attics and the footmen in the basements or near the butler's pantry. At Welbeck Abbey the late Winifred, Duchess of Portland, deliberately christened the maids' dormitory 'The Virgins' Wing', and the housekeeper saw that this reputation was maintained. To be discovered in any sort of compromise with the opposite sex usually invited instant dismissal for both servants, although in practice it was usually the more easily replaced servants who left in disgrace. Barbara Charlton, in *Recollections of a Northumbrian Lady, 1815-1866*, faced just this problem: 'The butler Hinckley began his games and both the [childrens'] nurses had fallen madly in love with him . . . the conduct of [nurse] Josephine and the infamous Hinckley had been scandalous.' As Hinckley was almost irreplaceable, it was Josephine who was sacked. There was a grain of truth in the old saying about sex being too good for the lower orders! In practice it was accommodation that was the problem, with maids sharing rooms and dormitories and the male servants similarly accommodated, there simply was no room for married servants.

The chink in the armour of the Victorian household organization was in the old, historically independent laundry; the laundry maids had to go outside to hang up washing in fine weather – they were the only females whose business took them outside – and here the male outdoor staff could trap them. They frequently did, and the parish registers near country houses show many baptisms to illegitimate babies of laundry maids.

The outdoor staff were as crucial to the smooth running of any establishment as those indoors; Hatfield in the 1880s numbered over a hundred outdoor staff. Apart from the stable personnel of a boy and six men to look after nine riding horses and eleven carriage horses, with nearly twenty vehicles to clean and maintain, there were a gas maker, a smith, a building department with a wide range of skills, nine parkmen, seventeen woodmen, nine keepers and twenty-two male gardeners, with two women and nine boys for the gardens around the house and the kitchen gardens. To accommodate all these essential trades there were two harness rooms, a surgery for sick horses, a slaughterhouse, a dairy, a saw mill, a nail room and a brewery with twenty-one 36 gallon casks and a huge vat holding 144 gallons of beer.

The complications of nineteenth-century planning often caused the service wing to be larger than the main house. The vast Victorian country house has been likened to a dinosaur stranded in the English countryside. It is a very good comparison; only a hundred years ago they were going full blast and it looked as though they would continue to do so. Now they seem as archaic and as dead as the dodo. The bells on the bell board, once ringing so insistently, are tarnished and hang askew; the maids' bedrooms (two to a room) cause us to wonder how anyone could have been asked to use such places or to work in such conditions as existed in the damp, cold passages below stairs.

However, not all service wings were depressing; at Clouds, Wiltshire, in 1879, the architect Philip Webb provided his client, the Hon. Percy Wyndham, with light and airy rooms for servants. After a serious fire, when the servants' wing was untouched, the Wyndhams were grateful for the luxury of moving into the wing. 'It is a good thing our architect was a Socialist, because we find ourselves just as comfortable in the servants' quarters as we were in our own,' was Mrs Wyndham's comment. This comfortable wing has since been demolished but the main house remains.

Servants' conditions improved remarkably between the wars; the improvement had begun in the 1920s. Detmar Blow, another Socialist architect who had no objection to making money out of his patron, the capitalist Duke of Westminster, began building his own house, Hilles, Gloucestershire, in 1914. There were no servants' rooms as such and the family and staff ate together; this was so embarrassing to all that he abandoned the experiment. Blow was an idealist who continually bruised himself on the hard facts of life. Americans buying country houses in Britain saw little reason why servants should not have pretty bedrooms with washbasins and central heating. Mrs Ronald Tree, a Virginian, modernizing Ditchley Park, Oxfordshire, in the 1930s, provided the servants' rooms with fitted carpets and antique furniture. In consequence the Duke of Buccleuch told her that she had cost his generation a great deal of money.

It was all a stop-gap; by the time peace came in 1945 no one could afford to pay the wages for staffing large houses, even if the staff could have been found. Yet these houses had been built to be run by large staffs and the design was uncompromising in that respect. The investment in the land was the first priority, and redundant buildings came very much in second place. In many cases, the damp, chilly service wings, often badly built and with no pleasing outlook, proved themselves unamenable to all remedies and were demolished. Many servants' quarters, like the servants before them, have vanished, taking their ghosts with them.

CHAPTER 8

Transport

Hovingham Hall, Yorkshire, is a unique house; it was dedicated to the horse! Built in the 1750s by Sir Thomas Worsley, the entrance is by way of a tunnel-vaulted archway which the visitor can well imagine is high enough to ride through on horseback. The archway leads directly into the Riding School and not to the house. From the Riding School the visitor enters the stables, consisting of three rooms as palatial as any house interior and which once had as a centrepiece a marble sculpture of *Sampson and the Philistines*. Finally one is allowed to mount the stairs into the domestic rooms of Hovingham. Unusually, there is a first-floor ballroom, placed there because of the importance of the horses on the ground floor, and uniquely there is a bay window looking down into the Riding School. Although Worsley worshipped his horses, his peculiar design of house gave a problem to his heirs, who may not have been so enthusiastic, because in high summer the smell from the well stocked stables below unmistakably percolated to the best rooms above.

As Sir Thomas Worsley knew, the importance of the horse was overwhelming – until this century. We can judge this by the care and cost devoted to building stables; for many owners of historic houses the comfort of the horses almost took precedence over the comfort of the family. Certainly in many cases the horses were better housed than were the servants. Before the steam railways of the 1840s no one could move far on land without a horse. If we look carefully at almost any old building we can find iron rings and hooks to which horses tied, although at grand establishments there would be a groom to take the horse.

Up to the mid-seventeenth century the horse was little considered, hard ridden, over-worked and ill housed. Rising costs brought a more considerate approach to transport livestock. This attitude is reflected in the better quality of stabling; at Peover Hall, Cheshire, the stables, built in 1654, have decorated plaster ceilings and loose boxes with finely carved ornamentation. Sir Francis Delaval, builder of the now ruined Seaton Delaval, Northumberland, finished his stables in 1768 – they are palatial. So splendid indeed that Sir Francis held a banquet in them to celebrate their completion.

Another eccentric was the 5th Duke of Portland. Although he already possessed two riding schools, one designed in the early seventeenth century at his home at Welbeck Abbey in Nottinghamshire and another built after the Civil War at Bolsover Castle only eight miles away, for the 5th Duke these were not enough. At Welbeck in 1860 he began building another riding school on a massive scale, 52 feet high, 385 long and 122 feet wide, second only in size to that in Moscow. Its arched glass roof, supported on cast-iron columns, gives the impression of being a hothouse more than anything else. The Tan Gallop nearby was 422 yards in length. The 5th Duke's new hunting stables built at the same time cover an acre in area. Yet the man never hunted nor was he particularly interested in horses. He went on to construct a vast range of underground rooms and kitchens for entertainments he never gave. Why he did all this remains a mystery, for Welbeck was large enough for anyone and the Duke was rabidly antisocial.

In towns, even in London until 1720, the countryside was near enough for horses to be grazed outside the walls and a coach housed in a shed. The first mews was built when the Grosvenor family laid out Grosvenor Square in the 1720s. In this development the square was surrounded by four unbroken terraces of adjoining houses with gardens behind. At the bottom of the gardens were the stables and coach houses, served by access roads called mews. Where the US Embassy now stands were nine houses and to the rear of these was Blackmans Mews. This was convenient for the rich inhabitants of these properties because the horses and their smells were well out of the way, while the stable staff and coachmen were accommodated over the stables. Moreover the household rubbish, ordure and horse-dung was inoffensively taken away through the mews.

With the appreciation of the value of horseflesh came the desire to have horse portraits. John Wootton (1682-1764) established his reputation by painting racehorses at Newmarket, where sporting painting originated. Many of his paintings of unbelievably huge horses are too big to hang anywhere but in the halls of country houses. Althorpe, Northamptonshire; Badminton, Gloucestershire; and Longleat in Wiltshire all have fine sets of Wootton's paintings in their halls. A man before his time in his appreciation of horses was the 1st Duke of Newcastle who had his horses painted in 1625, and their portraits, bigger even than Wootton's, hang framed in the underground picture gallery at Welbeck Abbey. After Wootton came Stubbs (1724-1806); Ben Marshall (1767-1835); John Ferneley (1782-1860); and finally the coach painter who found more profit in painting Derby winners, John Herring (1795-1865). All painted their patrons' horses in a more manageable size and many are found hanging on dining-room walls. By Wootton's time the horse was recognized as an expensive investment; the best fetched very high prices and great trouble was taken to import Arabian stock to improve the breed, changing the shape of the horse. When the horse was bred only for work, for pulling coaches and for carrying knights in heavy armour, the deep-chested breed was favoured. The Arab, a lighter horse noted for endurance, intelligence and courage, was known, but until racing became a court pastime at Newmarket in 1640, the need for a lighter horse was not evident. Once Arab blood was introduced, the horse became more like the riding horses of today; in particular the Arab made an ideal cavalry horse. With the development of better turnpike roads, and consequently lighter carriages, greater attention was paid to breeding harness horses, and from the foundation stock of Scandinavian horses came the lighter and faster Norfolk Trotter, Cleveland Bay and Yorkshire coach horse.

In a society that depended on the financial return from agriculture, it is understandable that the practice of selective breeding from the best stock should have been used for improving horses. With this obsession for creating horses perfect for their purpose went a love of racing. Fortunes were lost and some made out of this passion. The 1st Lord Grosvenor, of whom his lawyer remarked in 1779, 'I know no nobleman's Affairs so reduced, nor anyone who has so small an income from so large a One,' was in a serious financial position due to his love of racing. Out of a gross income of £20,000 he had outgoings such as allowances to his mother and a younger brother, provision for an estranged wife and the payment of interest on debts of £151,000, which left him a net income of practically nothing. This did not stop him maintaining a Newmarket establishment costing some £7,000 a year. This sort of extravagance could only end in one way and by 1792 his financial position was perilous. He was saved by enormously increased rents from his London properties.[1] At the turn of the nineteenth century the 4th Earl Fitzwilliam at Wentworth Woodhouse, Yorkshire, was spending between £1,500 and £3,000 a year on his racing stables and about the same on his riding horses,[2] but his income was double that of Lord Grosvenor and he could afford the expenditure. In the case of Lord Grosvenor his racing winnings and losses just about cancelled each other out, while Lord Fitzwilliam could afford to lose.

Hunting too was always expensive. King Cnut recognized the right of any man to hunt on his own ground. William the Conqueror saw it differently: 'He loved the tall deer as if he were their father,' says the Anglo-Saxon Chronicler, and he introduced forest laws forbidding hunting even if one owned the land. The penalty for killing hart or hind was loss of sight. Even in the time of William IV it was illegal for any man to trap, shoot or sell game unless he had a property qualification of at least £100 a year. Landlords, therefore, had things very much their own way for a thousand years and they took advantage of the fact. From the beginning, hunting and shooting with bows was very much the same pastime. The hunters did not gallop for miles after animals but the prey was driven into traps for the sportsmen to kill off unsportingly. The lack of wild prey for hunting – the last wild boar was killed in 1683 – sent the huntsmen after the fox in the eighteenth century; by then shooting was a separate activity. The first man to breed hounds specially for hunting was Lord Arundel between 1690 and 1700. Arundel's hounds would not have hunted foxes exclusively, but by 1782 his pack had descended to Hugo Meynell who was dedicated to foxhunting. The first pack of pure foxhounds was hunted by Thomas Boothby of Tooley Park, Leicestershire. When he died in 1752 he had ridden to hounds for fifty-five years.

The very rich spent huge sums on foxhunting; the 4th Duke of Portland at Welbeck Abbey was pouring out £2,000 annually by 1800. What is now the Goodwood Golf Club House began as kennels, erected at a cost of £6,000 by the 3rd Duke of Richmond in 1787. The Duke of Beaufort kept more than a hundred horses for hunting at Badminton in Gloucestershire just before the First World War – but Badminton was the centre of foxhunting. Every groom had two horses and the Duke kept a full-time smith. Sandbeck Park in Yorkshire, built in the 1760s, gives the impression of having been built for hunting parties – a hunting lodge – and the now empty and forlorn stables are almost as large as the house. By the nineteenth century foxhunting had become a highly organized sport which took over the lives of many rich men. So much so that, by the mid-nineteenth century, the case for hunting keeping down the vermin fox was inverted to the fox being preserved for hunting, and other means of destroying foxes were severely discouraged. An agent of the Duke of Cumberland wrote in 1858: 'There has been foul play with foxes . . . a tenant of yours has made it his business to destroy foxes.' Until the First World War hunting was chiefly a male occupation, although women often hunted. Lizzie Greystock in Trollope's *Eustace Diamonds* tried a day out with Lord Eglinton's hounds and was not impressed: 'If this is hunting,' commented Lizzie, 'I really don't think so much about it.' The first female Master of Foxhounds was Lady Leighton who took over from her husband, Sir Baldwin Leighton of Loton Park, Shrewsbury, when he sailed off to the Boer War.

The late Duke of Beaufort, reminiscing about earlier days at Badminton, recalled:

> Hunting was always the main thing at Badminton. We started in the middle of August and went right through the first of May, six days a week in those days. We would get off very early in the morning – breakfast at six o'clock, because one was out on a horse by half-past six.'
>
> When I was a boy, there were one hundred horses here (my father died in 1924 and we moved straight into the big house); then there were about fifty. Every groom had to do two or three horses, but there was a head groom over them, and two or three rather senior ones who were second horsemen. We had our own blacksmith, who had a full-time job looking after the horses. The hunt had a huntsman and two whippers-in. At the end of the season we used to have a party for everyone connected with the stables.
>
> I bought my own horses. I used to get practically all of them from a well-known horse-dealer: two men, the Drage brothers, who lived in the Pytchley country. Odd ones I bought from local farmers.[3]

For centuries travel was uncomfortable, slow and expensive; travellers put up with conditions we should find intolerable. Riding accidents were frequent, causing broken bones or at least a shake-up which, in the case of the elderly, often led to pneumonia. The Marquis of Tavistock, heir to the 4th Duke of Bedford, was thrown when his horse stumbled in Houghton Park, Bedfordshire, in 1776; he was a young man of twenty-five and only two years married. He fractured his skull and was dead within two weeks. His broken-hearted young wife died a year later. A runaway horse pulling a carriage almost inevitably caused injury to the passengers and carriage accidents were frequent; the Countess of Lathom was killed in a carriage accident near her home, Lathom House, Lancashire, in 1897. When Edward Gibbon, the historian, crossed Europe by coach in 1793, taking three weeks to cover 650 miles, he noted that in the fourth century Caesarius took only six days to cover an identical distance from Antioch to Constantinople by chariot; there had been no improvement in fifteen hundred years! Until the eighteenth century most people chose to travel on horseback rather than in a wheeled vehicle. Women, however, felt obliged to travel in some sort of conveyance. In 1601 Parliament, in a fit of puritanism, passed a bill designed to prevent the effeminate habit of men riding in coaches; it was repealed in 1625. The first coach in England was made for the 3rd Earl of Rutland in 1555; the 16th Earl of Arundel imported a coach from Germany in the year he died, 1580. But these were primitive, unsprung carts and on unmaintained roads, pock-marked with craters and with gradients too steep for horses, they were kept mainly for town work. It is understandable that sixteenth-century women preferred to travel in a horse litter when living in the countryside and to use a coach in towns. But improvements were coming.

Samuel Pepys in 1665 noted with wonder, 'After dinner comes Colonel Blunt in his new chariot made with springs, and he hath rode, he says, now this journey, many miles in it with one horse, and outdrives any coach, and outgoes any horse, and so easy, he says.' Pepys clearly disbelieved his friend. 'So for curiosity, I went in it to try it, and up the [Shooters] hill to the [Black]heath, and over the cart rutts and found it pretty well, but not so easy as he pretends.'[4] That was in 1665 and Colonel Blunt's chariot, since its body was made of wickerwork, was probably a light open carriage, and Pepys was referring to the latest steel C-shaped springs from which the body of the chariot would have been suspended. Previously the body of a carriage was suspended on leather straps that did little to absorb the heavy jolting caused by very bad road surfaces. The steel springs were much lighter than the earlier suspension, which accounts for the high speeds claimed by Colonel Blunt. When Pepys's report is looked at closely one can see that the two friends were discussing the new vehicle and comparing the speeds and ease of driving as new car owners would today.

Pepys did not, however, have to put up with vehicle taxation which was introduced in 1747 and which, by the 1850s, had risen to £2.2s for a four-wheeled vehicle; if the conveyance had less than four wheels and was under 4 cwt the tax was 15s. Any two-wheeled vehicle costing less than £12 was taxed at a few shillings – provided that it had painted on it the words 'tax cart'. These rates continued unchanged into the Second World War. There was also an armorial tax of £2.2s for those who had their arms painted on their carriages; that sum covered all the vehicles in a household. The vehicle tax became the motor vehicle tax which has risen with increasing ferocity, but the armorial tax was only dropped between the wars, when the ownership of motor cars became so common that in general the practice of showing arms on vehicles was discontinued.

It is ironic that, just as they were to be dismissed by the motor car, improvements to and more types of carriages were developed. What Colonel Blunt called a chariot in 1665 was not the same vehicle that Gladstone would have called by that name. Both would have been four-wheeled, but Blunt drove his own chariot and Gladstone would have been driven by a coachman on a box and would have been under cover in a two-seater body. The original brougham, invented by Lord Brougham in 1838, was another version of the chariot; the Hansom cab was introduced in 1834, the wagonette in the 1840s, the brake in the 1860s, the spider phaeton in the 1880s and the governess cart around 1900. These apart, the nineteenth century produced a multitude of carriages with exotic names: the crane-necked phaeton, the Dennett gig, the Stanhope gig, the tilbury, the sulky, the high-cocking cart, and many other variations on the basic two-wheeled and four-wheeled vehicle. The biggest step forward in travelling comfort was the invention of the leaf-spring in 1804 which enabled light, fast vehicles to be designed with bodies that could never have been carried on the old C-spring suspension. This invention was mainly responsible for the many new models of vehicle produced in the nineteenth century.

The carriages we see in transport museums and in the stableyards of historic houses are no more than a chance selection of mainly nineteenth-century vehicles. At Erddig in Denbighshire, for example, the survivors comprise a governess cart and a gig (open, two-wheeled vehicles used for local journeys) and two late nineteenth-century phaetons, which are four-wheeled, light, open vehicles. There is not one closed vehicle the family could have employed for winter journeys. The well-used carriages would have worn out and been scrapped, and what are preserved are the little-used and often peculiar variations ordered by wealthy owners to meet their particular requirements. A stage coach, for example, would not have been kept by a private owner, yet some are displayed in the coach houses of what were private homes. At Raby Castle, County Durham, there is a more balanced selection of vehicles: two travelling chariots from the late eighteenth century, an early nineteenth-century state coach that would have been kept in London, a governess cart, a light, caned whiskey which, drawn by a pony, 'whisked' over the park at high speed, a station cart and an estate wagon. At Charlecote, Warwickshire, is a travelling coach of some magnificence, upholstered inside with the Lucy family's colours of claret and scarlet. In this coach the family crossed the Mont Cenis pass in 1841 and one of their children died of the cold when they were held up by snow drifts. There are also at Charlecote a barouche, to carry six persons; a victoria, a lighter vehicle which superseded the barouche; and a brougham of the late nineteenth century with a very primitive hand-brake.

A wealthy, nineteenth-century titled owner, with a house in London and a place in the country, would almost certainly have possessed a state coach, seating four, for formal city occasions, or he might have compromised and had a dress chariot, seating two, a brougham for visiting and going out in, with a clarence, seating four, for travelling. All these were closed, practical, four-wheeled vehicles; for summer he might have had a very stylish open, two-wheeled, two-seater curricle with a small boy, dressed as a footman and called a 'tiger', perched on a precarious seat behind. The tiger's job was to ring door bells, present cards and leave or collect parcels for his master and mistress. Another smart two-wheeler for town use was the open cabriolet. On the other hand such a fashionable man would have a wide choice of other open, four-wheel carriages and might have settled for any of them; a barouche, a phaeton or, a great favourite, the open landau. The choice of vehicle was entirely a matter of taste and fashion. For country use there were small dogcarts, originally for carrying shooting dogs, but used generally as a light two-seater – there is a smart one at Lanhydrock, Cornwall. After 1900 there was the useful governess cart, or the ubiquitous gig from which all two-wheel vehicles seem to have developed. For shooting parties a body-brake, a two-horse char-a-banc, or a wagonette was available. There would have been a closed carriage for taking family and guests to parties and balls; this vehicle could easily have been the town clarence that brought them all from London. This selection would have answered all the travelling needs of the wealthy family unless, like the Rothschilds at Tring in Buckinghamshire, it was felt necessary to cut a dash with a zebra cart drawn by three zebras and a leading pony!

Fire engines by Merryweather are often seen in the coach houses of historic houses. A serious fire at Hatfield House in 1835, when the myopic Marchioness of Salisbury apparently held her newspaper too near a candle to read the small print and set fire to herself and a complete wing of the house, alerted other owners to the danger of fire, and from then Merryweather pumps and fire engines were to be found in most country house stableyards. Quite how much use these primitive engines were in the case of a serious blaze is doubtful; that at Lanhydrock must have been ineffectual c.1880 when the house was nearly burnt down completely. Other houses with fire engines are Polesdon Lacey, Surrey; Tatton Park, Cheshire; Raby Castle, County Durham; and Compton House, Dorset.

The cost of carriages varied enormously and, like that of motor cars, was whatever an owner felt prepared to pay. In 1597 the 5th Earl of Rutland paid £40 to his coachmaker for a basic coach;[5] then it had to be fitted out, but the cost for that is not given. In 1623 the 8th Earl ordered a new state coach at a cost of £50; the provision of harness, upholstery, very expensive fringeing, hammer-cloths for the coachman's seat and gilding, was an extra £123.[6] King's College, Cambridge, paid out £43 in 1634 for the Provost's new coach. Twenty-four years later Pepys paid £53 for a coach; and in 1777 £88 was paid for a coach and accessories. These three vehicles were not for state occasions; they were everyday town and travelling coaches and, since they were not for the nobility, expensive fittings could be left off. In 1682 the 5th Earl of Bedford ordered a chariot; this was a light, closed, four-wheeled two-seater. It cost him £53 for the coachmaker; £24 went on velvet for the interior, £14 to the fringemaker for vehicle and horse-cloths, £10 for glass. After all this the carriage still had to be painted and japanned for a charge of £25. When all was settled this nobleman's little runabout vehicle had cost almost £130 – a cautious estimate of present-day equivalent value would be £13,000. Eleven years later another chariot cost the earl, by then a duke, a more modest total of £56.[7] In 1802 the upper-class Wynne family living in Buckinghamshire paid £160 for a completed but unspecified type of carriage and £80 for a two-wheeled gig. The painting of carriages contributed to the high cost, something like eighteen to twenty coats of paint and varnish being applied for a first-class job, with a drying time for each coat adding up to a month to completion. The resulting high gloss was felt to be well worth the expense.

A coach in the seventeenth century would require four horses to pull it; as the horses worked in pairs, coach horses were usually sold in pairs. In 1654 the 8th Earl of Rutland paid £62 for a pair at Northampton fair and £24 for a single coach horse.[8] His ancestor, the 2nd Earl, in 1537 paid £2.13s.4d for a gelding intended for riding. Another riding horse, obviously rare, was given to the King of Denmark in 1605; it cost £60.[9] An enormously expensive import from France, a Barbary, cost £140 in 1609, and the additional charges for getting it back from Marseilles were felt to be well worth his while by Viscount Cranborne. But that may have been for racing;[10] the 7th Earl of Rutland paid the same sum for a racehorse in 1618.[11]

These, of course, were special prices for special horses; a better idea of cost can be gained from the inventory taken in 1709 after the death of Queen Anne's husband, Prince George. His breeding mares were an average of £25 each, his four stallions averaged £53 apiece, the hunters £33 each and his coach horses £20. The state coach was £150, which is about in line with other costs already quoted.[12] By 1911 a broken-in carriage horse which was six years old would have cost around £50.

In fine weather and in summer, travelling in a coach could be moderately comfortable although the undamped springing threw passengers about on rough roads, giving rise to nausea similar to sea-sickness; dust blown up from the dirt roads could be suffocating. In winter, coach travel must have been abysmal, with leaking roofs and unglazed windows letting in both rain and draughts unless wooden shutters were fitted, in which case the journey was completed in darkness. Against piercing cold, passengers could resort to muff-warmers – little heaters held in the hands – and foot-warmers like large metal hot water bottles (there is one in the back hall at Lanhydrock) and piles of fur rugs. Straw on the floor gave a closed carriage a particular smell; Vita Sackville-West recalled that her father's coach-of-all-work at Knole in Kent, used to collect visitors from the railway station, smelled of musty hay. A journey of any length in winter required endurance from the passengers, not to mention the coachman on his box outside. With the coming of the railways in the 1840s, new and undreamed of standards of comfort were available for the long distance traveller and journeying became a less hazardous, more relaxed undertaking.

The railways killed off the stage coach routes and did away with the need for any family to have a travelling coach, except for those who lived in Scotland. The town carriage could be loaded on to a flat truck at sixpence a mile and, with its passengers sitting inside an extra twopence a mile, be delivered to any station, at a time, in the 1840s, when the first-class fare was threepence a mile. The Countess of Zetland suffered a terrifying experience travelling in this way from Darlington to London. Red-hot ashes showering down on her open carriage set it on fire; her maid panicked and fell off the train but the Countess, made of sterner stuff, stayed on board as the flames, fanned by the speed of the train, all but consumed her carriage before she was rescued at Rugby. Probably the last person to use this uncomfortable service was Mrs Caroline Prodgers in the 1890s, who, regarding trains as 'a vulgar method of locomotion', resolutely travelled in her open barouche on a truck hitched to the back of the train, to arrive red-faced and smut-stained at her destination. This procedure soon gave way to a preference for more comfortable travelling in first-class carriages built, of course, like a horse-drawn vehicle. Family saloons, introduced in the late 1860s, were the most civilized way of travelling ever devised. These had a large open compartment with seats round the sides and some fixed armchairs; the servants travelled in the back second-class section with, between the two sections, a water closet, a luxury denied to other travellers. For a fair-sized family and household the cost was no more than travelling in ordinary carriages.

Railways brought a social and economic revolution to Britain. From the first there were landowners of the old diehard brigade who saw no good in the improved transport and others who backed the innovation to the full. The Duke of Wellington, whom one would expect to have been against the railways, was a supporter and used to travel regularly between Walmer Castle in Kent and London in his own railway carriage, built in 1838. The railway company, the old South Eastern & Chatham, as a compliment adopted brown, the colour of the Wellington livery, for its carriages. The old Duke did, however, have reservations about rail travel; he felt that it was all right for some but pointed out that in his opinion, 'it would encourage the lower classes to move about'. At Rugby, the famous Dr Arnold took an opposite and more far-seeing attitude: 'I rejoice to see it [the railway that ran past his school] and think that feudality is gone for ever. It is a blessing to think that any one evil is really extinct.'

Arnold was right, but for the wrong reason; the railways brought great prosperity to those in manufacturing and fortunes outside the aristocracy were frequently made, so bringing new families into society. Perhaps the old order suspected this, which would account for their resistance. Scotland was the exception; transport was a problem and Scottish landowners, such as the Dukes of Buccleuch, assisted and invested in the railways in order to open up the highlands. The main resistance was confined to England, with battles between landowners' servants and surveyors setting a route for a proposed rail track. The Duke of Grafton energetically opposed the laying of the London to Birmingham line out of Northampton in 1831 – he was a Master of Foxhounds and was convinced that trains would destroy his sport. Some landowners proved resolutely obstinate when it came to selling their land to the railways at any price; a proposed new seaside resort between Mundesley and Overstrand in Norfolk had to be abandoned in 1898 because the principal landowner refused to sell. The nearby Earl of Leicester at Holkham took an opposite view and in 1854 enthusiastically invested £10,000 to bring a line to his remote part of Norfolk.

The compensation for disruption and the price paid for land could be enormous; Lord Petre at Ingatestone Hall was paid £120,000 (with which he bought a new estate) and his neighbour received £35,000; this was for a mere six miles of narrow track. Other co-operative landowners made arrangements for trains to stop at halts for them when required; the Marquess of Ailesbury had his own private station at Great Bedwyn and the Great Western Railway stopped there whenever he wished to travel from his home at Tottenham Park, Wiltshire. Great Malvern station came to be built in 1860 because of the claustrophobia of Lady Mary Foley, who should have caught her trains at Stoke Edith, but tunnels, of which there are two, terrified her. The new station got round this difficulty and Lady Foley commuted ten miles in her carriage. Some had special facilities at stations; at Melton Constable a private waiting room for the local nobleman was so badly placed that it blocked the provision of a relief line for many years. As was the case in so much of the industrial revolution, fortunes were made out of the railways, but few great houses were created from railway money.

Thomas Brassey was the most successful of those associated with the railways. He was an organizing genius and assembled armies of navvies to dig cuttings and tunnels all over the world. In 1867 he built Normanhurst in Sussex, which, despite its fireproof construction, was burnt down and had to be demolished. It was not Thomas Brassey but his descendants who made their mark architecturally and socially; his son, in 1870, bought and restored Heythrop Hall, a burnt-out shell in Oxfordshire, while his grandson bought Apethorpe Manor in Northamptonshire; he married into the family of the Duke of Richmond and Gordon and became a peer in 1938. George Glyn, who became Lord Wolverton in 1869 and was a banker and director of what became William and Glyn's bank, made a fortune out of financing railways, and the railway town of Wolverton was called after him. His son built a vast gloomy house in Dorset at Iwerne Minster in 1878; it is now a school. Thomas Hudson, who was the most involved of all in railways and who was not thought to be honest, made a huge fortune but lost everything before he could build a house. Canford Manor, Dorset, was remodelled in 1848–52 for Sir John Guest, a Welsh ironmaster who made his fortune manufacturing rails for railways. Somerleyton Hall in Suffolk, a house of little architectural merit, except that it had what was once the biggest winter garden in Britain, was built in the 1840s for Sir Morton Peto whose fortune was made out of building railways all over the world. Peto over-reached himself and crashed in 1866; Somerleyton was sold in 1865 to the Crossleys who had made their money in Yorkshire out of carpets. Textile money was more stable than railway money; the Crossleys are still at Somerleyton. Historically, the railways had a very short run of prominence; just as they were approaching their peak at the end of the nineteenth century, the motor car was invented and developed in Germany.

From the beginning the motor car was looked on as a carriage without horses. Logically the engine was put where the horse would have been: in front. The driver was perched high up where the coachman would have been, the bodywork was made by coachmakers and so looked like a coach – although no motor car has ever been so elegant as an open four-wheeled carriage – and the old leaf-spring was used for suspension. Moreover, because most coach drivers were right-handed, and therefore sat on the right-hand side, traffic drove on the left so that the coachman could see the road ahead and the steering wheel of a motor car was consequently on the right. On the Continent, where coaches were driven on better roads by a postilion riding on the left hand of a pair of horses and controlling the unsaddled horse with his right-hand whip, traffic drove on the right to give the postilion a clear view. Inevitably, across the Channel the steering wheel was on the left.

In the early days any journey by car was more fraught with mischance than a journey by horse-drawn vehicles. Punctures were frequent and with no spare tyre – because carriages never carried spares – journeys were of unpredictable duration. Due to the archaic laws of Britain, by which, from 1878 until the act was rescinded in 1896, the 'man with a red flag' was required to precede any self-propelled vehicle travelling at no more than 4 mph, the motor car stood no chance of being developed in Britain. Some of the wealthy wouldn't have anything to do with them; the Harpur-Crewe family at Calke Abbey in Derbyshire banned all motor cars from their park until the 1920s. Others took to the novelty with enthusiasm, like the Duchess of Sutherland who regularly drove an unwieldy Mercedes in London, with her chauffeur sitting in the back seat in case of breakdowns and to swing the heavy starting handle. The 20th Earl of Shrewsbury, whose family name was Chetwynd-Talbot, founded the Clement-Talbot motor company in 1903, which later became the British Talbot Car Company. The Earl was an early victim of speed-traps when the limit was 20 mph (imposed in 1903); in 1908 the *Daily Telegraph* reported: 'at Dumbarton the Earl of Shrewsbury was convicted of excessive driving near Garlockhead, and was fined 3 guineas. The Earl covered a measured half-mile in 58 seconds, giving a speed of 31 m.p.h.' Once the petrol engine's reliability and economy over the horse had been demonstrated, the coach houses became motor houses, the coachman became the chauffeur and the shady horse dealer became the dishonest car dealer.

In Britain development of the motor car moved more slowly than in the United States, France and Germany. Consequently it was only the rich who could afford motoring in the early days. They demanded more efficiency than they would have expected in a horse-drawn vehicle: windscreen wipers, a spare wheel, a horn, more efficient acetylene headlamps, safer brakes (coaches never had them until the late nineteenth century), speedometers and rear view mirrors. Self-starters only became general in the 1930s and heating in cars only in the 1960s. The majority of the early cars were sporty, open tourers, with canvas hoods and side screens which, in winter, let in piercing jets of freezing wind at any speed; motoring in this type of car was regarded as an interesting fair-weather hobby by many. Undoubtedly Edward VII, who acted as a magnet to the racy set and who was an early motorist, helped to make motoring acceptable in Britain. After that it was only a question of time before the motor car would outnumber horse-drawn traffic on the roads of Britain, but the Second World War intervened and at Cowley William Morris, 1st Lord Nuffield, had to wait until after the peace of 1918 to market his little, and immediately popular, two-seater. At Erddig the first car, a second-hand 1907 Rover, was bought in the 1920s and it was in service until 1924. The vehicle is still there in the coach house along with two Austins which succeeded the Rover and which were made in 1924 and 1927. While not as conservative as the Harpur-Crewes at Calke Abbey, the Yorkes at Erddig certainly did not rush into motoring and like many continued to drive around in the governess cart or the gig even when there was a perfectly serviceable Austin in the motor house.

As late as 1919, George Bernard Shaw summed it all up: 'Go anywhere in England where there are natural, wholesome, contented and really nice English people; and what do you always find? That the stables are the real centre of the household.'

CHAPTER 9

The Setting

On 18 March 1765, Lord Bruce, later the 1st Earl of Ailesbury, received a letter from Tottenham Park, Wiltshire, written by his agent who was reporting progress on the new landscaping of the park being undertaken by Capability Brown:

Mr Brown came here on Sunday to dinner. In the afternoon he took a view of the gardens in a storm of snow. Early this morning, which proved tolerably favourable, he allowed lining out and finally settled the serpentine walk all round the garden, marked such trees as were proposed to be taken away and gave general directions to Winckles [Lord Bruce's house steward] upon everything that occurr'd. He thinks it best to keep [the] Howse [open] a fortnight or three weeks longer to get the levelling Business forward. In general he approves of what has been done except the taking away [of] a few large trees in one or two places. If the high bank and trees had been taken down, great would have been the fall indeed, Brown would have excommunicated us all . . . '[1]

Autocratic Brown certainly was, but he had made his reputation by providing exactly what his clients wanted. Lord Bruce was having his old-fashioned parterre gardens swept away, the grass was brought up to the house and the whole was surrounded by a distant belt of trees with eye-catching clumps of trees creating a multitude of views to be appreciated from the serpentine walk. The whole provided complete isolation from the outside world and was thought of as an Elysium, a place of happiness and a retreat from the cares of the world.

The epitome of a Brown landscape is that at Blenheim, Oxfordshire. When the Palace was completed in the 1720s after designs by Vanbrugh it was surrounded by formal gardens and the intended approach was by a straight avenue leading over a massive bridge crossing the river Glyme and arriving in front of the main door. Today the visitor arrives from the village of Woodstock by another more spectacular route devised by Brown in 1763.

Entering by the Woodstock gate one skirts a lake made by damming the Glyme to raise the water level and the Grand Bridge, now serving no purpose, is seen in silhouette against a background of trees. The Palace, instead of bearing down on the visitor, is enticingly glimpsed through clumps of trees, until turning to the right one arrives before the stable court. The whole approach subtly leads up to the climax of the Palace itself, rather than prefacing it with Vanbrugh's formidable and military avenue, and it is typical of Brown.

We have become so used to the imprint on landscaping made by Brown, his successor Humphry Repton and their imitators that we tend to take them as 'natural'; Brown, Repton and their clients would have been flattered. Yet the greater part of the British landscape is man-made and very far from natural; hedges and trees grow where they have been planted, almost every mound, ridge and hollow is evidence of someone's labour. There is a sense of order in disorderliness. Long before the building is seen we become aware of the setting of a large country house. This imprint is the result of eighteenth-century landscaping and planting; the trees, lakes and hills seem to be placed where all are seen to the best advantage.

The history of garden design is a story of rebellion; Brown was reacting against the baroque garden, which in turn replaced the Jacobean garden that had evolved from the Tudor garden. Unlike buildings, which are comparatively permanent structures, gardens, once abandoned, soon revert to the wilderness. Nothing of the early gardens is left, and we have to recreate them from illustrations and descriptions.

The story of the English garden is naturally bound up with the Englishman's reaction to nature. At first nature was feared and left to itself, then attempts were made to force it into unnatural shapes and geometric patterns; these reached an apogee at Versailles, which was copied all over Europe. Finally, under Brown, gardeners, full of self-confidence, recruited nature on their own terms, allowing it to develop its own way under their control. Unfortunately they destroyed what had been before and we are both the poorer and richer for their efforts. In fact old gardens were common even in Jane Austen's day, until obliterated by Repton and his imitators.

The Romans were the first to garden in Britain, and medieval monks were the second gardeners, planting herbs to make healing potions and flowers for devotional purposes. The *Glastonbury Leechdom*, an early medical herbal written *c.*960, gives a prescription: 'Against Lice: pound in ale oak rind and a little wormwood, give to the lousy one to drink.' Eglantine, the wild rose, although only mentioned twice in the Bible, was, if red, symbolic of martyrdom, if white of purity, while the lily was the flower of the Virgin; the flowers would have been carried in church processions as well as used for decoration. The medieval castle had no room within its walls for gardening and so gardens were cultivated beyond the moat. Here were grown the same healing herbs, but also herbs to flavour food, lettuce for salads and aromatic plants to sweeten the air within the thick walls. The Tudor garden was very little different; it was recognized as a pleasurable place to be in and we get a glimpse of this through the doors of Whitehall Palace in the painting by an unknown artist, *The Family of Henry VIII*. There we can see straight paths edged with painted rails bordering rectangular beds and, because flowers only bloomed in spring, painted poles support heraldic animals carrying banners to supply colour. Nature is clearly something to be kept under strict control. In other Tudor gardens the colour lacking after the spring flowers faded was provided by filling the geometric beds with red brick dust, coal dust and coloured pebbles. The courtier who did not understand the meaning of flowers was no courtier; Shakespeare in *Hamlet* has Ophelia in her madness explain: 'There's rosemary, that's for remembrance; pray, love, remember: there is pansies, that's for thoughts.' Mazes provided an intellectual puzzle and the unnatural shapes of topiary caught the eye. The visitor was intended to be amused and amazed. In these strangely fortified gardens nature could only attack with weeds, and Tudor household accounts have many payments to 'the women for weeding'. The Tudor garden was above all a place for contemplation, for recreation and, in season, for courtly love. In Scotland, however, gardens did not develop until the eighteenth century; the quarrelling clans, the border wars, inhibited any such civilized elaboration. An exception to this was Edzell Castle, Tayside, which still has an early seventeenth-century walled garden.

The Spanish wars in the Netherlands brought refugees to England and army officers abroad saw what could be done in the way of alternative gardens. Travellers brought home exotic plants; waterworks, as seen in Italy and France, were constructed and the first herbals printed. Hatfield House in Hertfordshire, partly built with imported stone in 1607-12 for the 1st Lord Salisbury, had the latest of imported garden schemes: fountains whose waterworks were designed by a Frenchman, terraces, fishponds, statues, a great range of plants and even trained fruit trees. The Queen of France sent 500 fruit trees and the wife of the French minister sent 30,000 vines – Salisbury was influential as Lord Treasurer and Secretary of State. The whole was overseen by John Tradescant, Thomas Chaundler and Cecil's gardener, Mountain Jennings. It was all very impressive and although most of Hatfield's garden has since been altered, traces of the original are still there.

Haddon Hall in Derbyshire also shows traces of an early seventeenth-century garden. Italian renaissance gardens in hilly Tuscany were not flat areas and the Derbyshire landscape oddly lends itself to the 'Tuscan garden' tumbling down steep slopes. The terraces on the hillside at Haddon and the wide flight of steps leading down from what was once a bowling green to what once was, perhaps, a knot garden, are a distant echo of something seen in Italy.

Almost certainly at Haddon there would have been a knot garden – beds in geometric patterns enclosed by low clipped hedges. If so it was perfectly placed for it could be seen from above, which was necessary to appreciate the intricate patterns. Ideally a knot garden should have been looked down on from state apartments or long galleries, as at Hatfield or Montacute in Somerset. In the case of lower houses set on flat land, gardeners had no such advantage and they threw raised terraces around the gardens, like those at Lamport Hall in Northamptonshire and the raised double terrace at Northbourne Court, Kent, or more economically mounds like those both at Little Morton Hall and Dunham Massey, both in Cheshire. The effect of both mounds and surrounding terraces can be appreciated by the modern visitor to the reconstructed garden situated behind The Queen's House at Kew Gardens.

In Italian gardens the hot summer sun was shaded by leafy trees trained over pergolas; the renaissance garden in England had the same feature – again nature was being forced to assume unnatural forms. We can see one in the background of Isaac Oliver's exquisitely painted miniature of an unknown man reclining against a tree; a couple, perhaps lovers, wander out from the pergola into a knot garden. It is a place given over to pleasure.

In July 1634 the 1st Earl of Newcastle entertained Charles I, his queen and the entire court at Bolsover Castle, Derbyshire. The walled garden, overlooked by the tiny Gothic revival keep, was the theatre for a masque by Ben Jonson, *Love's Welcome to Bolsover*, the theme being that of mutual love. An ungainly statue of Venus stands over the 'Venus Fountain'; the king and queen strolled in this 'garden of love', for that was the meaning of this one surviving Carolean garden. One can imagine cavaliers and their ladies engaging in courtly dalliance in an eternal golden twilight.

Inevitably the fussy, busy form of garden gave way to something else, and again the inspiration came from abroad: from France and the gardens that Le Nôtre, under Louis XIV, was making on a giant scale at Versailles. Grand alleys taking the eye in a straight line through thick forests and ending in a temple, a monument, or an obelisk provided hunting country as well as a view to contemplate. Vistas with intersecting alleys, straight canals and square pools with elaborate fountains and basins were created on the same principles as before – the taming of nature – but on a grander scale. In place of hedges, tree-lined alleys; instead of ponds, stretches of water – nature was forced into straight lines. Tumbling water was compelled to flow into lead pipes to supply dolphins and tritons spouting into geometrical basins, before it came to rest in rectangular ponds. There are few of these formal gardens left; they needed numbers of foresters to keep them in shape and later generations never troubled to replant. Bramham Park in Yorkshire, however, maintains many miles of intersecting alleys, laid out around 1700; Ham House in Surrey, Erddig, Denbighshire, and Melbourne Hall, Derbyshire, have something of their original formal gardens from this period, still with a feeling of Versailles. Melbourne garden was designed deliberately 'to suit Versailles' by George London, who had visited France, and his partner Henry Wise, who was royal gardener to Queen Anne. Wrest Park, Bedfordshire, has a grand canal terminated by a domed pavilion made in 1709. Ledston and Ebberston, both in Yorkshire, have traces of formal gardens. As with the baroque style of architecture, the baroque garden was superseded in the early eighteenth century and a glance at Knyff's 1712 engraving of Chatsworth, laid out by London and Wise, quickly shows what has been lost.

Celia Fiennes, who rode 'through England on a Side Saddle in the time of William and Mary', visited Chatsworth in 1697 and was fascinated by the waterworks: 'by the Grove stands a fine Willow tree, the leaves barke and all looks very naturall, and all on a sudden by turning a sluice it raines from each leafe and from the branches like a shower, it being made of brass and pipes to each leafe, but in appearance is exactly like any Willow . . . '[2] A reproduction tree from 1829, repaired and vandalized in turn, still exists. The cascade she saw still tumbles down steps from a pavilion where the water pours from, and down, its dome; it can surprise us as it amazed Celia. All the tricks and wonders of Chatsworth had been born at Versailles on a far grander scale.

Of course it had to end. Maintaining the formal gardens was labour-intensive and consequently costly, and like the baroque style in architecture such gardens were associated with the Stuart monarchy tainted with Roman Catholicism. It may strike us as odd that the encouragement for change in gardens should have come from writers, but Joseph Addison visited Italy in 1701-3 and, on his return, derided the Italian gardens that inspired the French, from whom we borrowed. Addison recommended the natural Roman Campagna and, for those who could not make the visit, pictures by Albertini, Claude and Poussin, showing imaginary, classical landscapes set with ruins and temples and peopled with gods and goddesses, demonstrated what he was talking about. The 'Claude Glass' became an indispensable piece of equipment for any eighteenth-century tourist. Consisting of a slightly convex mirror about four inches square and lightly silvered, it gave a darkened and romanticized reflection of a landscape. Yet another writer, Alexander Pope, was one of the first to laugh at man's pretentious distortions of nature and in 1719 designed a more natural garden at his home in Twickenham. Charles Bridgeman, who died in 1738, worked for London and Wise and is credited with being the first to design the 'natural' garden. If Horace Walpole is to be believed, Bridgeman introduced the ha-ha to England from France to replace the 'unnaturalness' of walls. A ha-ha is a sunken wall having the double advantage that it does not interrupt the view and at the same time keeps animals out – the first English illustration of this feature is dated 1712. If more was known of Bridgeman he could, perhaps, be credited with much of the achievement that has been given to William Kent for developing the 'natural' garden. Nothing remains of a complete Bridgeman garden as his schemes were overlaid by his contemporary Kent and later gardeners; his work at Stowe, Rousham, Chiswick and Claremont is fragmentary.

It was William Kent who saw Pope's conception on a grander scale and in 1733 invested Stowe with glades and walks. A year later Sir Thomas Robinson wrote with enthusiasm to Lord Carlisle:

There is a new taste in gardening just arisen, which has been practised with great success at the Prince's garden in Town [Carlton House], that a general alteration of some of the most considerable gardens in the Kingdom is begun, after Mr Kent's notion of gardening, viz., to lay them out without either level or line . . . this method of gardening is the more agreeable, as when finished, it has the appearance of beautiful nature, and without being told, one would imagine art had no part in the finishing . . .]'[3]

Nature, instead of being clipped, trained and distorted, was about to be let free, within limits, and Kent's work was only the beginning. It would be unrealistic to expect any of Kent's gardens to have survived unaltered but at Rousham House, Oxfordshire, one of Kent's early gardens, his temples, groves and water-gods still survive surrounded by overgrown trees. This garden was designed around two walks, an inner and outer route. The inner walk is restored and provides a good example of the effect Kent intended to achieve as one walked along it, with surprise views of meadows, a corn mill, a ruin, and at one point a view of Rousham House which appears as a castle. At Stowe in Buckinghamshire, later 'improved' by Brown, Kent's pantheon, exedra and monuments line the banks of the small Serpentine River (in 1770 it was called the Styx). The garden at Claremont, Surrey, restored by the National Trust, shows successive layers of 'improvements' imposed by Bridgeman, Kent and Brown on a garden designed in the first place in 1715 by Vanbrugh. Kent's gardens were not an exercise in large-scale planting but like his furniture they were an architectural exercise. He was attempting to create landscape architecture that did not interfere with nature and in this he succeeded. Although to us it might seem bizarre that anyone should have attempted to re-create a classical landscape in Britain, the idea had been in circulation for a long time that England was the inheritor of the grandeur of ancient Rome.

One good example of a surviving 'natural' garden is Stourhead in Wiltshire, although the labour required to create it in 1740-60 indicates that it was in fact far from 'natural'; two streams were dammed, culverted and piped to form a lake, a grotto and a cascade. The result is a highly effective, contrived and intimate landscape offering a long walk round the banks of the lake with views of temples, a pantheon and bridges. It is all reminiscent of paintings by Claude and Poussin, which is the effect that the banker Henry Hoare, who made the garden, was trying to achieve – Hoare had a Poussin that still hangs in the picture gallery at Stourhead. Today, some of the original buildings have gone but the intended effect is immediately recognizable; the only intrusion is the unfortunate nineteenth-century planting of azaleas and rhododendrons giving a seasonal display of colour that Hoare never intended. The banks were originally planted with beech and larch and under-planted with cherry laurel. Stourhead garden was immediately popular with visitors, so much so that an inn was built to accommodate them. Kent's influence went far, but it was left to Lancelot Brown to carry his theme further.

Lancelot Brown, nicknamed Capability from his habit of saying that a landscape had 'capabilities' and no more, worked at Stowe and so was well acquainted with Kent. Like Kent, Brown could turn his hand to architecture, chiefly through his partnership with Henry Holland, a master builder from Fulham, whose son, also Henry, joined Brown in 1771 and married his daughter Bridget. Brown built Croome Court in Worcestershire, which was said to have cost the Earl of Coventry £40,000; he designed the picture gallery at Corsham Court, Wiltshire, the stables at Burghley, Northamptonshire, and remodelled Broadlands in Hampshire. In all he was involved in twenty-two major architectural operations, although the greatest part of his architectural experience was in constructing lodges, bridges, temples and other landscape buildings.

Kent had started something that was to become essentially British and the British landscape garden, after Brown and Repton, would be exported all over Europe: to Russia, France, Germany and, surprisingly, even to Italy, the home of earlier inspiration. Lancelot Brown left more of his personal imprint on the English landscape than any other man; he was responsible for just over two hundred landscape gardens, many of which still exist. The primary feature of their design consists of a thick cordon of trees around the estate to isolate the real world beyond from the ideal to be created within. The driveway was devised to take a circuitous route so that 'picturesque' views were glimpsed between the trees, the house might be sighted only to vanish; an extreme example of this is the park at Woburn, Bedfordshire (not by Brown), where the drive passes the front of the Abbey at a distance and then follows a route of over a mile before one arrives.

Brown cleared away the old gardens round the house and brought the park right up to the drawing-room windows. Trees were never planted on top of hills, but grace the rolling grassland in carefully placed clumps; water is glimpsed at a distance, and the overall impression is of a natural, peaceful Elysium. Yet the whole thing is most carefully contrived; Brown's plans show that he devised many viewpoints and the landscape was arranged to be seen from differing angles; not least of all is the surprise view under trees browsed to a level by cattle or deer. The light and shadow cast by the evening sun, the complex patterns of shade and light following fleeting clouds like brushwork on the canvas of the parkland and the changing colours of the seasons were all part of Brown's schemes. Neither Brown nor his patrons ever saw their landscapes as they planned them to be; in their lifetime the clumps had grown at most fifteen or twenty feet. Today we see them past their maturity but more easy to appreciate than they ever were in Brown's lifetime. However, we lose one effect by using the motor car; the eighteenth-century landscape was never planned to be viewed from any vehicle moving faster than a horse's pace.

If Kent had started the idea of the landscape garden, it was Brown who popularized it during the thirty years of his professional life. It was left to Horace Walpole to have the last word in 1785: 'Men tire of expence that is obvious to few spectators . . . The Doric Portico, the Palladian Bridge, the Gothic Ruin, the Chinese Pagoda, that surprise the stranger, soon lose their charms to their surfeited master. The lake that floats the valley is still more lifeless, and its lord seldom enjoys his expence but when he shows it to a visitor. But the ornament whose merit soonest fades, is the hermitage, or scene adapted to contemplation. It is almost comic to set aside a quarter of one's garden to be melancholy in. Prospect, animated prospect, is the theatre that will always be the most frequented.'

On his death in 1783, Brown, aged sixty-seven, had been in one way lucky; there had been no worthwhile competitors. Within four years Humphry Repton had stepped into Brown's shoes. Repton's career in landscape gardening began late, at thirty-six, when he deliberately set out to make himself Brown's successor. He died in 1818, aged sixty-six. In thirty years he created nearly two hundred landscapes, an output almost equal to Brown's.

Like Brown, Repton was concerned with architecture and, like Brown, he was untrained. He thought he had found the ideal solution when he formed a short-lived association with John Nash. In fact his architectural works are few: about fourteen commissions completed with the help of either John Nash or his own sons. Repton came within an ace of remodelling Brighton Pavilion in the Hindu style; it is perhaps as well that he missed the chance.

Although Repton's career paralleled Brown's and his early landscapes were similarly planned, he soon moved on and developed his own popular style. He reintroduced the terrace in front of the house and the flower bed. The greatest difference from his predecessor is that whereas Brown's landscapes lay around the house, with Repton the houses were part of the landscape.

Always conscious of the value of publicity and presentation, Repton is best remembered for his 'Red Books' produced for prospective patrons and showing, by means of folding flaps, the landscape before and after 'improvement', together with a reasoned explanation of the suggested changes – over seventy of these books survive today. Repton calculated that during his lifetime he had produced over a million and a half explanatory sketches and of those about 3,000 were in private hands. Since only seven per cent of these private owners engaged him to carry out his proposals a great many others must have followed his plans under their own supervision. In fact Repton recalled being shown landscapes and gardens claimed to have been made by him with which he had never been involved. In this respect the British landscape probably owes as much to Repton as to Brown.

Repton's landscapes and those of his imitators, like Brown's, are now past their prime but we can appreciate his skill in genuine examples of his work at Sheringham Hall, Norfolk; Attingham Park, Shropshire; Ashridge Park, Hertfordshire; Woburn, Bedfordshire, and Cobham Hall in Kent. He also has the distinction of being recommended in *Mansfield Park*, begun by Jane Austen in 1811. Mr Rushworth of Sotherton Court was dining at Mansfield Park and felt his own estate to be in need of improvement:

'I must try to do something with it, but I do not know what. I hope I shall have some good friend to help me.'

'Your best friend on such an occasion,' said Miss Bertram calmly, 'could be Mr Repton, I imagine.'

'That is what I was thinking of. As he has done so well by Smith, I think I had better have him at once. His terms are five guineas a day.'

Mr Rushworth did have Repton and the result amazed him: 'I never saw a place so altered in my life' – a comment made by many others of Repton's satisfied customers.

At almost the same time as Repton's death, W. A. Nesfield, an army officer retired on half-pay, started a notable career as a landscape gardener with no previous experience. Like Brown and Repton he allied himself with an architect, Sir Charles Barry. In that era of cheap labour and immensely wealthy clients they revived the historic parterres, the Jacobean garden and Italian Renaissance terraces which required numerous gardeners to maintain them. Trentham Gardens in Staffordshire is one example of their work, although the house, by Barry, was demolished in 1910; at Harewood, Yorkshire, in the 1840s, Barry, without Nesfield, undid Brown's work, surrounding the house with terraces and parterres. Of Nesfield's work without the assistance of Barry there are examples at Drayton, Northamptonshire, where he replaced what had been destroyed when the park had been landscaped; and Holkham in Norfolk where he created something that might have existed before it was destroyed by Brown. Broughton and Castle Howard, both in Yorkshire, are two other well-known Nesfield gardens. Nesfield specialized in the 'historical' formal garden which had a great vogue while the money lasted.

After Repton's death in 1818, his theories were developed by the great nineteenth-century gardener John Claudius Loudon, with results which we can still appreciate today; where Repton brought back the flower bed, Loudon went on to develop planting to an extent unimagined by his predecessor. With cheap labour readily available planting out was no problem, and beds on terraces before the house were not only planted out for the spring but, as soon as these flowers had finished blooming, they were replaced with later flowering varieties. Beds were sometimes cleared as many as three times in a season to provide a continuous display of colour. We can still see this effect in many municipal parks and busy traffic islands where the gardeners have progressed no further than the nineteenth century and are still planting out in labour-intensive, strict regimental rows, as recommended by Loudon, completing ignoring gardening schemes introdced by William Robinson and Gertrude Jekyll.

Loudon, in effect, evolved something similar to the busy baroque gardens of the early eighteenth century, and made villa gardens that were far from natural. With labour costs rising something had to change and in 1883 William Robinson published *The English Flower Garden*. Robinson abominated bedding-out and what he called 'pastry-work gardening'; he recommended the now familiar return to nature. Robinson was essentially a theorist; he was a writer of skill and imagination and although he made a garden at his home, Gravetye Manor in Sussex, he was not responsible for making gardens in the way that Repton or Loudon were. Robinson had a vision of the traditional cottage garden coloured with wild flowers and hollyhocks and, through his influential but uncommercial gardening publications and aided by an agricultural slump in the 1870s, when owners cut back on expensive labour, did away with the sweeping lawns and shapely beds. Robinson did not have it all his own way; Reginald Blomfield, a successful architect, published *The Formal Garden in England* in 1892 in which he tried to separate horticulture from garden design, claiming that design should be executed by an architect. This, of course, was nonsense but both Blomfield and Robinson had a point. There was room for both the formal and informal garden and much depended on where they were. The hilly stone country of the Cotswolds is more suited to the informal garden than, for example, flatter country. Moderation was unknown in either camp. When victory was won it was Robinson who gained the day. The victory, however, was not entirely due to Robinson; in 1875 he gained a valuable ally, Miss Gertrude Jekyll.

Gertrude Jekyll (1843-1932) realized what Robinson did not; that wild gardens need some discipline if they are not to revert to waste. A cottage garden is commendable so long as plants do not totally cover paths, wall-flowers take over every crack in a wall and moss smother a lawn. Further-more Jekyll's earlier career as a painter, which she had to give up owing to failing eyesight, taught her the use of colour which she carried into her gardening practice. Jekyll's influence was immense and is still with us today; Hestercombe in Somerset is a recently restored Jekyll garden in which she collaborated with her architect partner, Edwin Lutyens. Other gardens that carry her trademark, although they are not to her design, are at Hidcote Manor, Gloucestershire, made by Major Lawrence Johnston; Nymens in Sussex, by Lt-Col. J. R. Messel, and Sissinghurst, Kent, created by Vita Sackville-West and her husband, Harold Nicolson, from 1930 until her death in 1962.

Jekyll and her followers were somewhat different from earlier gardeners in that they used the colours of leaves and flowers in groupings. Of course they had a vast range of plants to use, a palette denied to earlier gardeners, but earlier gardeners were mainly architects as well and tended to create three-dimensional landscapes, although Brown and Repton both used trees in colour patterns. The former used cedars of Lebanon to give evergreen colour to his canvasses and Loudon, carried away by enthusiasm for exotic trees brought in by plant hunters, used American oaks, cork oaks, tulip trees and rhododendrons, not always with happy results. Although Loudon planted sequoias and redwoods he may not have been responsible for planting the monkey-puzzle (Chilean pine), introduced in the 1790s; it is difficult to think of another tree that looks more ridiculous in the British landscape. Sequoias and redwoods also look out of place unless they are planted in masses, and until the North American redwood forests have been experienced at first hand the majesty of this tree cannot be appreciated. Loudon was an architect as were Vanbrugh, Kent, Brown, Repton and Lutyens, and it is understandable that the landscapes and gardens they created should be scattered with garden buildings.

The earliest garden buildings are the Elizabethan banqueting houses, although the first reference is to a timber one at Kenilworth Castle in *c.*1414. We tend to think of them as garden houses, but their purpose was different from later garden houses. In them was served the final course of a dinner, the cordials and sweetmeats, and they are as likely to be found on the roof as in the garden, as at Hardwick, Derbyshire; Longleat, Wiltshire; and Wollaton in Nottinghamshire, or in the house itself as is the case at Hardwick. There are two of these structures in the garden at Montacute and three at Hardwick.

The orangeries of the second half of the seventeenth century were used not so much to produce oranges as to give winter protection to the tubs of orange trees put out in the gardens in summer – a fashion that came to us from Italy through France; at Versailles the Sun King had them in silver tubs. As early as 1561 Lord Burghley had a heated room which he called an orangery. What is claimed to be the first orangery, contrived in 1580 for Sir Frances Carew at Beddington near Croydon, does not sound like an orangery at all; in 1658 John Evelyn explained that in winter the trees 'were protected only by a tabernacle of boards and stoves.' Whatever the construction it must have been effective for the orange trees survived until the fierce winter of 1739-40 killed off the last of them. It is surprising that anything survived because the early orangeries had very little light. Evelyn realized this need when he suggested that 'light is half their nourishment'; nevertheless it was 1696 before an orangery with top lighting was built.

The earliest surviving orangery is Wren's 1704 building at Kensington Palace, and Chatsworth claims the earlist surviving greenhouse, built in 1697, but moved from its original position in the 1820s. A further development of orangeries and greenhouses was to attach them to the house for convenience, referring to them as winter gardens. Sezincote in Gloucestershire, where Repton advised on the layout of the grounds, has a sensuously curving orangery, dating from the early nineteenth century, which exactly demonstrates Repton's idea of connecting thee house to the garden. As soon as exotic and rare plants began to be available in the late seventeenth century, variations on the greenhouse proliferated; a camelia house at Wollaton in 1823 may be the first cast-iron and glass structure, or the claim may lie with the cast-iron palm house at Bicton, Devon, built around the same date. These were forerunners of Paxton's 'great stove' built at Chatsworth in 1836-40, which in turn was the forerunner of the Crystal Palace for the 1851 Great Exhibition.

Other less practical garden buildings are not difficult to find; typical of the taste of the time was the hermitage in Richmond Park, designed by Kent for Queen Caroline and later destroyed by Brown. A Hermit's House still exists at Badminton, another in a grotto at Chatsworth. Hermits were paid to inhabit the places to provide effects for visitors, but as they were often drunk the charm vanished. Grottoes, where water gods lurked and streams gushed – an idea imported from Tuscany – were another fancy; Stourhead, Wiltshire, possesses one, and a better grotto is at Wardour Castle in the same county; Hawkestone in Shropshire had no natural standing rocks and a grotto was tunnelled into the ground. The East inspired Sir William Chambers to build the Pagoda in Kew Gardens after he published *Designs of Chinese Buildings* in 1757. Yet another pagoda is at Alton Towers, Staffordshire, designed in the

1820s and once fitted with gas light, which had a 70-foot jet of water from the spire. A Dairy House is likely to have been no more functional than a shelter to sit in or play at milkmaids. Woburn Park, Bedfordshire, has a Chinese dairy and a small wooden pagoda; Sherborne Castle, Dorset, a gothick dairy; and Althorpe, Northamptonshire, has a splendid dairy of 1786 decorated with Wedgwood. Uppark, Sussex, has an elegant little dairy at the end of the west terrace. Most date from the 1780s when there was a desire for more informality and the idea that bucolic simplicity was a better way of life, an attitude initiated by J. J. Rousseau's 1754 *Discourse* praising the Natural Man.

Marie-Antoinette, to escape the monotony of court protocol, took the idea of returning to rural simplicity and innocence to the letter and built le Petit Hameau at Versailles in 1786, which included a dairy house.

One is left with a curious vision of fine ladies putting on their milk-maid outfits, wandering down to the Wedgwood, Chinese or Gothick Dairy, to spend a relaxing afternoon playing with the mysteries of making butter and cheese. A later dairy that was really used is a splendid 'ecclesiastical' dairy built at Manderston, Berwickshire as late as 1900.

When, unavoidably, a utilitarian building protruded into a view from the house it was often the custom to disguise it as something more attractive. Kent at Rousham faced the difficulty of a cowshed adjoining the new gardens and turned it into a castellated and turreted construction with a seat on the garden and a cowshed on the field side, which nicely solved the architectural problem but not the problem of the smells of high summer. The game larder of Farnborough Hall, Warwickshire, resembling an octagonal Roman temple and built in the 1730s, exactly complements three other small terrace buildings. Fort Putnam is a farm at Greystoke Castle, Cumbria, but it looks like neither a fort nor a farm and commemorates fierce rivalry between the 11th Duke of Norfolk, a Whig, who built it in *c.*1778, and his Tory neighbour the 1st Viscount Lowther, later 1st Earl of Lonsdale. The Duke, a supporter of the rebels in the American War of Independence, provocatively went on to build other fort-farms called after rebel victories, forts and leaders.

Bath houses, another feature of the landscape, were built following the fashion for cold plunges which became popular in the early eighteenth century; medical opinion followed the trend, and the recommended cold baths may have gone some way to cure the inevitable hangovers from too much port. The idea again came from Italy, but was adapted to the Anglo-Saxon view that the treatment was good for one rather than a luxury as in Italy; the Villa Garzoni in Tuscany has a bath house dating from the 1640s, built over a Roman bath, which must have been seen by many Grand Tourists. Again Rousham provides an early small British example from the 1730s, but Rufford Abbey, Nottinghamshire, has a Bath-cum-Garden-House of 1729. The majority of surviving baths date from the late eighteenth century; Wynnstay in Denbighshire has a bath house, *c.*1780, made like a classical temple; Corsham Court, Wiltshire, has a gothic bath house of the 1760s by Capability Brown. Cragside has a complete suite of bathing rooms built in 1870; from the Dressing Room one entered the Hot-air Bath, next a wash and a rinse in the Shower Bath before the cold Plunge Bath. At Wimpole in the 1790s Sir John Soane designed a Plunge Bath with a great segmental barrel-vault ceiling and a small warming room with a fire. In 1936, after a game of cricket between police teams, twenty-two policemen crammed into Soane's masterpiece.

An unplanned feature of the landscape are the monuments to favourite animals. Many graveyards for small animals can be found tucked away in some forgotten corner; Polesdon Lacey in Surrey has seventeen dog graves whose occupants shared their lives with Mrs Ronnie Greville; Dunham Massey, Cheshire, has a collection of dog graves going back to the eighteenth century. Woburn Abbey has a pretty classical temple to a pekinese, Che Foo, who died in 1916, while Newstead Abbey in Nottinghamshire has the biggest tomb of any for the poet Byron's dog, Boatswain, placed, as he thought wrongly, but with typical sacrilege, where the monk's high altar had been. William Kent with a similar sense of humour put a memorial to a dog on the back of the Temple of British Worthies at Stowe. At Rousham is a stone to Faustina Gwynne, a cow aged twenty-two that died in 1882. Shugborough Hall has a monument of the mid-eighteenth century to Lord Anson's cat; a racehorse has a monument at Longworth Hall, Herefordshire; and a pet pig called Cupid is commemorated by a thirty-foot obelisk, formerly at Mount Edgcumbe, now overlooking Plymouth.

However, nothing in the landscape can surpass the eccentricity of those buildings whose only purpose was to improve the view: the follies and eye-catchers. Kent, still at Rousham, closed a view with three arches on the skyline. George Durant, of Tong Castle, Shropshire, whose father made a large fortune in doubtful circumstances supplying the army in the West Indies, was a frustrated architect who built for himself a pyramid consisting of a henhouse on the ground floor and a dovecote in the upper five storeys. His main gate comprised ten-foot pyramids on top of ten-foot high gate piers, flanked by castellated walls, in which he had a pulpit from where he preached to passers-by. Durant's father was equally eccentric; he rebuilt Tong Castle himself in 1765 in a gothic style with castellated pediments and four domes; it was demolished in 1954. Tong, was and still is, a very small village but Durant managed to father some thirty illegitimate children with the wives of his tenants.

A mock castle ruin was a favourite eye-catcher, and the most celebrated provider of ruins was Sanderson Miller (1717-80). Wimpole, Cambridgeshire, has one built in 1772 and his ruined tower at Hagley, Worcestershire, built in 1747-8, had the full approval of Horace Walpole. Alfred's Hall in Cirencester Park, Gloucestershire, built 1721-32 by the 1st Lord Bathurst, is now sufficiently aged to be mistaken for a genuine medieval castle, but even in its early days an eminent historian was totally taken in by it.

Rock gardens are sometimes found in mouldering corners of historic house gardens. The fashion started in the late eighteenth century with the Romantic movement which was attracted to mountains and wild terrain, witnessed at first-hand in the Lakes by the Romantic poets. The first of such gardens was possibly introduced by William Beckford at Fonthill in Wiltshire, who made an alpine garden in a quarry in 1795; this has long since disappeared, along with Fonthill. In 1838 Lady Broughton of Hoole House, Cheshire, made a large model of the mountains surrounding the valley of Chamonix; it was a disaster – tree roots split the rocks and rain washed away the soil.

The popularity of alpine gardens was greatly helped by Robinson who published *Alpine Flowers for Gardens* in 1870. A later rock garden which still survives is that built by Sir Frank Crisp, using 7,000 tons of rock, at Friar Park, Henley, where the white-painted Matterhorn towers above alpine valleys but the herd of carved chamois, thankfully, is no more. Perhaps the most bizarre was the steep rock garden made at Lamport Hall, Northampton-shire, in 1847 by Sir Charles Isham. The rock garden is still there but not its surprising inhabitants; it was peopled by a tribe of gnomes from Nuremberg and Sir Charles must be held responsible for introducing this now popular foible. All but one gnome was removed by his daughter, it is claimed, to Longnor Hall in Shropshire and they have since vanished. The sole survivor now lives in a glass case in the hall at Lamport. Isham was not alone in his liking for German gnomes; two stone gnomes inhabit the recently restored conservatory at Harlaxton Manor in Lincolnshire.

Of far more practical use were the kitchen gardens, a subject of importance avoided by garden histories. We have seen how the Elizabethans grew their herbs, flowers, roots and vegetables all together. At the same time in France the vegetables had become established in their own *potager*; it was only a question of time before this became the custom in England – exactly when is difficult to pinpoint, but John Evelyn lived in France from 1643 to 1646 and made a final visit in 1649. In 1653 he was planting out gardens at his home, Sayes Court, Surrey – demolishd, alas, in 1925. In *Directions to the Gardiner at Says Court* he wrote, 'Notes for the Kitchin-Garden: Chervill is handsom and proper for the edging of Kitchin Garden beds.' Evelyn's garden was famous in his time and Charles II made a visit in 1662. It may be that we should credit Evelyn with the introduction of the kitchen garden to England. By the end of the eighteenth century the separate walled kitchen garden was well estab-lished. Many of Leonard Knyff's fascinating paintings of the late 1690s show walled kitchen gardens, notably Chatsworth, Derbyshire, and Hampton Court, London. The high walls sheltered the plants, kept out blown weed seeds, prevented animals breaking in and provided a warm wall for trained fruit trees. Cold frames brought on early plants, heated walls brought on fruit and the orderly kitchen garden became a place for family and guests to promenade. In Suffolk the crinkle-crankle wall evolved. Heveningham Hall has as good an example as any and it provided south-facing surfaces on a wall running north and south. Thomas Jefferson saw such walls in 1786 and, while ignoring British architecture, praised the gardens; he used serpentine walls when he came to build the University of Virginia at Charlottesville in 1817.

With the decline of the large household the purpose of the big kitchen gardens came to an end; there was no need for enormous quantities of fruit and vegetables to supply a house. None exist today with the massive production of a hundred years ago. The kitchen gardens at Erddig and at Montacute have been turned into visitors' car parks by the National Trust. At other houses the walled areas have been developed as garden centres, which at least continue the theme. Many more remain as overgrown wildernesses, with broken hot-houses and smashed cold frames littering the undergrowth, the vines and fruit trees rampant and neglected.

CHAPTER 10

Last Things

Any mention of priest-holes in a house usually brings a frisson of anticipation about the discovery of secret doors and traps in the floor. Alas, few of the so-called priest-holes are genuine. Real priest-holes were used as hiding places for Catholic priests when the practice of Roman Catholicism was forbidden from the reign of Elizabeth I until the relaxation of the penal laws in the late seventeenth century – a period of just over one hundred years. The spurious ones are often no more than voids left by builders in walls and beneath floors. Harvington Hall in Warwickshire has no less than seven genuine hiding places. The house was owned by the Catholic Pakington family and the ingenious hiding holes date from *c.*1630. The building is medieval, modernized in the 1570s and again *c.*1700; thereafter it was left alone, which is why so much has remained unchanged. Today the house would make an ideal setting for a spine-chilling gothic film.

The first secret room at Harvington is just inside the gateway and is entered from a trapdoor in a passsage above it. The space is a mere four and a half by two feet and must have been used only in the gravest emergency and for short periods. A seven-inch diameter hole with a slot was used to pass food to the hiding priest. A trapdoor near the altar in the chapel gives access to another hole possibly used for vestments when, as frequently happened, these had to be hurriedly stuffed out of sight. Another priest-hole is entered from a trap in the main staircase, and a final touch is a shaft inside the outer walls with a pulley for a rope to lower the priest to an emergency exit close to where a draw-bridge spanned the moat.

Another authentic priest-hole is in Carlton Towers, Yorkshire. Although the house gives the appearance of being high Victorian, due to rebuilding in the 1870s, an older building is hidden beneath the nineteenth-century walls. The Catholic Stapletons built a house there in 1615 and incorporated a hiding place entered through a trapdoor in a cupboard. When the house was altered in the 1840s by Thomas Stapleton, the 8th Lord Beaumont, and the Jacobean long gallery was converted into nurseries, the priest-hole was preserved, so providing the Stapleton children with one of the most romantic settings imaginable. Like many other houses there is a legend of a secret underground passage at Carlton Towers which is entirely imaginary. The story has come from the practice of having a 'safe passage', or quick route, above ground for a fleeing priest.

Both the Packingtons and the Stapletons were 'recusants', a term which came into being around 1570 to denote those Catholics who refused to attend the established Church and who, from the time of the penal laws imposed in 1581, risked a fine of £20 per month. In the aftermath of Henry VIII's break with Rome, church observance and beliefs remained basically Catholic until Edward VI's reign when, under Archbishop Cranmer and Bishop Ridley, a change was made; services were read in English and a Calvinist influence was established. The final break came in 1570 when Pope Pius V excommunicated Queen Elizabeth. This left a hard core of Catholic recusants who clung to the old faith. Many others, though outwardly conforming, privately kept their Catholic beliefs. Indeed, these beliefs remained widely prevalent. It was, for instance, still held that since no one led a completely good life and few led an entirely evil life, a period of torment in purgatory was the fate of the soul after death until grave sins had been atoned for, when the soul would be admitted to heaven purged of all wrong-doing. The time spent in purgatory could be reduced by the prayers of the living. Wealthy people would leave a stipend to a priest to say prayers for their souls and a common method was to pay for trentals – a set of thirty masses – to be said. Although trentals and similar observances for the souls of the dead were abolished by Henry VIII, the belief persisted and ways could be found round the edict; for instance, by founding almshouses for old people whose terms of acceptance included the promise to pray for the soul of the founder. The Puritan doctrines of the Commonwealth under Cromwell from 1653 effectively ended any lingering belief in purgatory and thereafter the funeral service became a ceremony only for the benefit of the living. The simplicity of Puritan church monuments gave way, at the Restoration in 1660, to a reaction of extravagance in huge and costly sculptural memorials which reached their peak of popularity in the early eighteenth century. The 1st Duke of Marlborough's tomb at Blenheim is a good example of this fashion.

On 24 May 1732, The Duke of Marlborough's widow, Sarah, wrote to Sir Phillip Yorke:

The Chappell is finish'd and more than half the Tomb there ready to set up all in marble Decorations of Figures, Trophies, Medals with their inscriptions and in short eveything that could do the Duke of Marlborough Honour and Justice. This is all upon the Wall of one side the Chappel. The rest of it is finish'd decently, substantially and very plain. And considering how many Wonderful Figures and Whirligigs I have seen Architects finish a Chappel withall, that are of no Manner of Use but to laugh at, I must confess I cannot help thinking that what I have designed for this Chappel may as reasonably be call'd finishing of it, as the Pews and Pulpit.

Marlborough had died in 1722 and Sarah paid £2,200 to Michael Rysbrack to make the tomb to a design by William Kent.[1]

The huge marble memorial still stands in the chapel where Sarah had it erected. It is a stodgy translation of Bernini's great Italian baroque monuments. The weight of a black marble sarcophagus crushes the last enemy, Envy, flanked by white marble figures of Fame with her trumpet and History with her quill. Above are larger than life size figures of the 1st Duke with his Duchess and two sons who died, one in infancy and the other of smallpox at the age of seventeen. To either side are two vertical panels of trophies of arms and instruments in white marble set on black and beneath the sarcophagus is a marble relief showing Marlborough accepting the surrender of Marshall Tallard at the battle of Blenheim.

The chapel has been altered twice since Sarah's day, once in 1850-70 and again *c.*1890 when the present pulpit, organ case, reredos and benches were inserted; therefore we cannot appreciate the complete design approved by the 1st Duchess. However, because the monument dominates the space we can forget the later alterations and concentrate on what it means.

To understand how our ancestors saw death, we have to adjust our twentieth-century sights. The words of the burial service, 'in the midst of life we are in death', do not have the same meaning today that they did. In 1640 life expectancy for the son of a peer was thirty-three years, although after this date the chances of survival began to improve. Infant mortality accounted for a large part of the figure; in 1640 34 per cent of children born to peers died before the age of fifteen. For the rest of the population the figures were worse; in London in 1764, for example, 49 per cent of all children were dead by the age of two and 60 per cent by the age of five. Death, therefore, was an everyday event and expected, unlike today when the majority complete their three score years and ten. It was impossible then to put death out of mind as is done today, and our ancestors viewed the celebration of death as something different from the modern funeral. Also we have to forget our modern outlook, by which we seek after happiness in life, and remember that this is a recent philosophy. Until comparatively recently it was enough in life to have been born, survived infections, married, lived a Christian life, and had sons before dying. If honour and glory had been won on the route, so much the better, and this could be shown on a handsome tomb designed and made before the subject died. In Marlborough's case Blenheim Palace itself is the real monument to him and the decoration on the exterior, carved by Grinling Gibbons, is martial in the extreme. Sarah could be more subtle when it came to her husband's monument. So subtle in fact that there is no mention of four daughters, through the eldest of whom the title descended – daughters were little thought of.

The monument to the 1st Duke of Marlborough is only part of the story of his death. When he died in 1722 there was an elaborate lying-in-state that marked the apogee of baroque funeral arrangements. No less than five rooms of the principal apartments were set aside for the lying-in-state – these are the rooms along the south front which the public see today. The great hall was hung with black 'from the Painting downwards to the floor . . . adorned with Escutcheons Crest and Badges of the Order of the Garter, furnished with black sconces and Wax candles'. The hall served as the ante-room for distinguished mourners. It was followed by a presence chamber with the inevitable black canopy and chair of state. The duke's body lay in the third room in a crimson coffin set on a state bed; covering the coffin was a black velvet pall and laid on the pall was a suit of gilt armour. The remaining two rooms were for the use of high-ranking mourners attending the funeral.

The pall covering the coffin comes from the Latin *pallium*, meaning a cloak, which it replaced and which originally may have been buried with the dead person. However, the pall eventually became the perquisite of the clergy and was used to make vestments. At funerals of the wealthy the family would present a number of palls to the church in which the ceremony took place. Eventually palls became heavily embroidered with heraldic devices, particularly those lent out by the London guilds for the funerals of their members. One from 1508 in crimson and gold still exists at the Saddlers' Guild.

In 1971, when the Octagon Room at Attingham Park in Shropshire was redecorated, traces of black paint were found on the skirting and pilasters, suggesting that the room had been used for the lying-in-state of the 1st Lord Berwick in 1789. The ground-floor plan of Attingham, dating from 1782, has Lord Berwick's suite of rooms in one wing and those of Lady Berwick in another balancing wing; the Octagon Room, with convenient accesss from outside and the last room in the suite, was Lord Berwick's study and would have been the logical room for a lying-in-state. The King's bed at Knole, Kent, was perhaps once painted in mourning black; at any rate, when the black was cleaned off, gilt and silver decoration was discovered underneath. The bed now shows its original splendid colours, but the feet have been left with the black intact.

When Sir Ralph Verney died at Claydon House, Buckinghamshire, in 1696, his son, Sir John, the 2nd Baronet, ordered that the hall should be hung with black baize, 'the entry from the Spicery door, and the best Court porch, likewise the Brick Parlour top to bottom', where a dozen chairs and three great tables were to be covered with black.

Sir Ralph was embalmed and his body lay in state before being put into the family vault in the church next to the house. Seven months after his father's death Sir John wrote from London: 'Pray let all the Black Bayes that's around the Hall, the Entry and the Summer Parlour be taken down, and off the Chaires, and Stooles, Tables and Stands (if you can measure it, do) and make it up in a bundle and sent it up to me by the Carrier . . . for the Escoshens About the Hall Lay 'em up until I come down, & then we'll distribute 'em among the Tenants. Doe not meddle with the Hatchment over the Doore in the best Court.'

Claydon was drastically altered in the last half of the eighteenth century and although the walls of a Jacobean house are concealed in the middle of the present building we cannot know where the room referred to lay. However, we can see Sir Ralph's monument in the church. He had this made at a cost of

£130 during his lifetime and 'before erecting the tomb on which he had lavished so much time and trouble, Sir Ralph seriously considered whether he should shift the Church in which he was to rest to a more convenient site . . . After three and a half years argument the tomb was finally erected in 1653 and dedicated before a notable gathering of Claydon friends.'[2]

To see a room in which an earlier lying-in-state took place we could stand in the unaltered High Great Chamber at Hardwick Hall, Derbyshire, where Bess of Hardwick, Dowager Countess of Shrewsbury, lay in state for three months after her death in February 1608. Enormous yardages of black cloth were needed to drape the Chamber, the Hall and stairs, and it was bought from as far away as Warwick. When she was buried at All Hallows, Derby, in May 1608, the procession was headed by a mourning-knight carrying a great banner painted with Bess's arms, followed by heralds and officials of the College of Heralds, then the coffin, covered by a black pall and carried by six gentlemen. Behind the coffin came her two household gentleman ushers, carrying their white rods of office, preceding the chief lady mourner, her daughter, Mary, Countess of Shrewsbury, supported by two hooded barons, and trailing behind, her servants, almswomen and hired mourning-women. At the conclusion of the funeral her household servants were dismissed and only a few were taken on by her heir, Lord Cavendish. The funeral was not, directed Bess, 'to be oversumptuous' nor to exceed a cost of £2,000. She may have had in mind the funeral for the Earl of Derby in 1572, at which the procession stretched for two miles and involved nearly one thousand mourners.

Bess's monument is still in All Hallows, now Derby Cathedral, and, like Sir Ralph's, it was made before her death. Designed by her architect Robert Smythson, who built Hardwick for her, it resembles nothing so much as one of the overmantels in her great house. Both Sir Ralph and Bess were well aware that their executors and heirs would not be inclined to spend money putting up anything so grand.

Extravagant monuments symbolizing power and wealth are just one aspect of the litter of artefacts the wealthy have left in our churches, and fashions for the dead followed each other like fashions for the living. There are four-teenth- and fifteenth-century brasses showing knights in full armour; palimp-sests, the term applied to re-used brasses, mostly of the sixteenth century; while shrouded figures and skeletons – reminders of mortality – appear from the mid-fifteenth to the end of the sixteenth century. Prior to 1500, effigies laid full length and in full armour on top of table tombs are shown in reverent attitude with hands in prayer, in the thirteenth century often with legs crossed; a kneeling prayer position became popular in the sixteenth century and by the seventeenth century the figures become far more relaxed. The effigies were painted to make startling lifelike figures, but before 1550 were unlikely to be actual portraits; the masons had a stock of figures ready carved. A knight would be buried in his vault with his crested helmet, sword, emblazoned shield, his coat of arms (literally a coat embroidered with arms) and sometimes gauntlets displayed above, high on the church wall; these were funeral 'props' and seldom genuine armour. We saw at Bess of Hard-wick's funeral that her painted arms were carried on a banner in the front of the procession; this was a hatchment. Women were forbidden the knight's right of arms and armour at their funerals. Hatchments, like that already mentioned at Claydon, were lozenge-shaped canvases framed in wood or sometimes entirely of wood, on which were painted the deceased's arms. They took the place of arms and armour from the early seventeenth until the mid-nineteenth century; a few were used as late as the 1920s. The custom was to hang one over the main entrance of the house for the period of mourning and another, carried at the funeral, was hung in the church, where many of them have remained. Others, presumably those placed over the front door, are displayed in houses; in the kitchens of Hardwick Hall is a hatchment with the arms of the 6th Duke of Devonshire, made for his funeral in 1858. Two other nineteenth-century hatchments hang in the restaurant – the old Audit Room – at Petworth, Surrey. Another hangs on the stairs at Milton Manor, Oxfordshire.

All the three funerals described here involved the College of Heralds which, until their power was broken in the early seventeenth century, had the monopoly of organizing funerals for a high fee. The ceremonial was built up from the heralds' experience over centuries and the particulars were committed to their library; manuscript tomes such as *Vincent's Precedents*, or the early sixteenth-century *The Manner of Ordering* [a funeral], now in the Bodleian Library, Oxford, provided detailed protocol to cover almost every event. They dealt with such technicalities as who the chief mourner at an earl's funeral might be, who should attend and in what order, what arms should be represented and where carried, along with other minutiae, which assured that equal ranks were buried with equal pomp and emphasized that nobility was based on the monarchy. From time to time there were disputes – as for example that of 1611, when James I, short of cash as usual, created the new rank of baronet and sold these titles at £1,095 apiece. This solved some of James's money problems but left the heralds with the puzzle of where the new rank fitted in. The question was finally settled by James, and the heralds proclaimed that a baronet had the right to 'two assistants of the bodie to support the Pall, a Principal mourner, and foure assistants to him at their funerals, being the meane betwixt a Baron and a Knight'. Where payment was involved the heralds could usually be counted on to find a solution. The customs and rules for public funerals for noblemen organized by the College of Heralds dates back to 1400 at least.

For the powerful in medieval times, there was always the danger of being murdered and it was the custom for the body of a peer to lie in state so that all could assure themselves that there had been no violence. Since some mourners would have taken a considerable time to arrive it was also the custom to embalm the body after removing the bowels and brain. A further reason for preserving the body was the time taken by the College of Heralds to organize the event. When Bess of Hardwick died, her funeral was controlled by the heralds and there was no avoiding the expenditure the heralds saw fit for her rank. The total cost of her funeral must have been about the figure of £2,000 specified in her will.

In the early seventeenth century the heralds' influence was undermined by a fashion for night burials, called 'private' funerals, which did not involve the heralds'. In 1616 Sir John Grimes was buried in London by the light of two hundred torches. Lady Haddington was buried by torchlight in 1618, and Lady Cave was given a night burial in 1623. In the case of the two women the heralds may have turned a blind eye because they were wives and of lower status, and Grimes, a Scottish courtier, was outside their influence. From the point of view of the organizers of the private funeral, there was the great advantage that the event could be run as they wished, they could invite whom they wanted, the ceremony could be held within a very few days of death, the sermon was dispensed with and there was none of the high expense or restraints which the intervention of the heralds involved. Once the way was shown the night-time 'private' funeral became normal among the aristocracy. The first royal night burial was that of Charles II in 1685 and it was observed by Evelyn on 14 February: 'The King was this night very obscurely buried . . . without any manner of pomp.' The funeral, without the body, followed on 14 March, again at night.[3]

Naturally the heralds fought back against the fashion that was taking away so much of their income and as early as 1618 they brought in retaliatory measures, including fixed fees such as £2 for a gentleman's burial, up to £45 for that of a duke, and the requirement that funerals should be registered at the College of Heralds. This had little effect on fashion; even the prohibition of night funerals by Charles I was ignored and by 1674 the heralds realized that they had lost this battle and would, if asked, officiate at night funerals. The Duchess of Newcastle was buried that year in Westminster Abbey with a torchlight procession in which the heralds were involved.

Once the heralds' hold on the burial of the aristocracy had been shaken, the way was open to a new profession, that of the undertaker. One of the earliest references to their employment at a funeral is in 1700 when the burial of Sir Samuel Grimston was undertaken by the 'Company of Upholsterers' in the Strand for £106. Since so many black hangings and so much funeral furniture was needed as well as mourning furniture, it was logical that upholsterers should offer the service. The funeral in 1723 of the illegitimate son of Charles II, the Duke of Richmond, in Westminster Abbey, was entirely organized by an undertaker, for the cost of £654. The first royal funeral involving an undertaker was that of Frederick, Prince of Wales, who died in 1751.

The undertaker-upholsterer probably came into his own soon after 1660, and it was a lucrative profession. In the case of a family in mourning for a year, the funeral furnishings would not only be rented but the mourning furniture put in the house for that period. Although the charge was high for the full service it saved a great deal of bother and there was no necessity to have one's furniture ruined by being painted in mourning black. Black was, and still is, associated with mourning; the custom came from France in the late fourteenth century. Crimson and purple were also to a lesser extent mourning colours.

Before the body could be buried it was embalmed, but the process was not particularly effective in preserving the corpse; it only served to prevent decay over the period of the lying-in-state. Furthermore there was reluctance by some to submit their own bodies to the embalmers' attentions. In 1572, Mary, Countess of Northumberland, directed in her will that her body was not to 'be opened after I am dead. I have not loved to be very bold afore women, much more would I be loath to come into the hands of any living man . . .'[4] However, the tradition of embalming a corpse continued until the nineteenth century, along with the macabre custom of the heart, bowels and brain being placed in an urn and carried on top of the coffin in the procession, or even buried separately. The embalmed body was then wrapped in 'cere cloth', a waxed linen sheet tied at the head and foot. In the thirteenth and fourteenth centuries the body was then dressed in rich and costly clothes in which it was buried. Occasionally a body resisted all efforts at embalming; the 1st Duke of Lennox who died in 1624 was one whose body had to be hurriedly buried. His funeral was later performed over an effigy.

There was a fear of being wrongly pronounced dead, and this discouraged embalming. John, Duke of Lancaster, in 1397 requested that he 'should not be buried for forty days, during which I charge my executors that there be no searing or embalming my corpse.'[5] This fear lingered until medical science became less a matter of chance and death could be established with certainty. Nevertheless, Lady Blanche Balfour, wife of Arthur Balfour, 1st Earl of Balfour, and sister of the 2nd Marquess of Salisbury, left clear instructions in 1872 for the disposal of her body after her death. 'I wish that my body should not be consigned to the coffin till unequivocal marks of corruption have shown themselves; I wish to have no leaden coffin or leaden wrappings about the body, and nothing more expensive than a plain oak coffin. I wish to have no stone on my grave.'

The problem of the lying-in-state for a long period of an unembalmed or badly embalmed body was solved by exhibiting a wooden effigy on top of the coffin; the corpse, wearing a simple chemise, would be wrapped in cere cloth or shroud, the whole covered by an outer wrapping of lead. An act of 1678, to encourage the wool industry, made woollen shrouds compulsory. Elizabeth I ordered that her body was to be neither embalmed nor disemboweled and, since she lay in state for a month, there was no question of her actual body being shown. Her wooden effigy, lying on top of her coffin, was displayed wearing a specially made crimson satin robe, lined with white fustian, with sabotans and a coif of cloth of gold. The custom of exhibiting royal funeral effigies had begun in 1327 with the burial of Edward II and it survived until 1688, when the politics of monarchy were changed by the arrival of William and Mary; although wax figures of sovereigns continued to be exhibited they played no part in the funeral. Like so much else, what was practised at court became the custom for the rest of England. The last time an effigy was used at a peer's funeral was at the burial of the Duke of Buckingham in 1735; his wax figure is still at Westminster Abbey.

High expenditure on funerals and monuments was only another expression of dynastic power and had nothing to do with piety. Furthermore, after the Reformation funeral ceremonies were performed for the benefit of the living. In Bess's case, as with all the aristocracy of her time, it was very reassuring for an heir to see his predecessor buried with high ceremony and his immediate family and household united in sorrow around him; the transition of power was thus assured without dissent. The emphasis was on continuity rather than loss. In her will of 1601 Bess said that her tomb was 'finished and wanteth nothing but setting up' because she knew very well that she would get nothing so grand if it were left to her miserly son William. As already noted, her tomb was set up in what is now Derby Cathedral, but her epitaph, which she could not prepare, was not composed until sixty-nine years later by her grandson, another William Cavendish, 1st Duke of Newcastle; it says a great deal about the Duke but the little about his grandmother is wrong; her age is exaggerated by three years. Her recumbent marble figure lies peacefully on her tomb wearing a countess's coronet and robes. Originally it would have been painted in lifelike colours; the gold leaf still shows, but her red hair, of which she was very proud and which was dyed when she was elderly, is now unfortunately painted black!

John Donne, Dean of St Paul's, had the gruesome notion of having himself drawn in his shroud while he was living. Isaac Walton in his *Life of John Donne* described the occasion: 'when nearing his end in 1631 [Donne] posed for his own monumental effigy . . . having put off his clothes, and his winding sheet put on him, and so tied with knots at his head and feet . . . as dead bodies are usually . . . shrouded and put into their coffin or grave . . . He thus stood . . . with so much of the sheet turned aside as might show his . . . death-like face.' On Donne's death that year, Nicholas Stone, a sculptor and architect, copied the drawing in stone, and Donne was buried in St Paul's. To this day the Dean's effigy in St Paul's is a startling sight as he balances upright on an urn, wrapped in his shroud. However, he did start a fashion for similar effigies in shrouds.

In the church of St Mary Magdalene at Croome d'Abitot, Worcestershire, there is a monument composed of a kneeling woman draped over the pedestal of an urn; it is to the 6th Earl of Coventry, who died in 1809. His epitaph points out charmingly that he deliberately employed the poor to create his landscape park, designed by Lancelot Brown, who was also responsible for Croome Court and the church in which the Earl lies. Both interiors were completed by Robert Adam. Brown himself died when he was working for Lord Coventry and a memorial near the lake he made at Croome commemorates him. In rebuilding the church Lord Coventry was, in the spirit of the time, attempting to store up treasure in heaven, for his epitaph also says: 'If you want a monument to his devotion to God, look around at this sacred abode, raised and embellished at the expense that befits the man himself.' When his wife, Maria, reputedly the most beautiful woman of her time, died aged twenty-seven, ten thousand flocked to see her coffin. Also in Croome church is a monument by Grinling Gibbons to the 4th Baron Coventry (d. 1687). Faith, with upraised arm, originally presented Lord Coventry with a 'starry crown'; in the rebuilding the crown vanished and his own coronet, which lay at his feet and was several sizes too small for him, was perched ridiculously on his head. The 6th Earl is not surrounded by all his ancestors; although most are there, the 1st Earl, who died in 1699, is absent. His widow went to considerable expense to have a monument made by William Stanton in London and had it transported to Croome church where, to her embarrassment, the 2nd Earl refused to let his father's monument be set up. The widow later remarried into the Savage family at Elmley Castle, only ten miles from Croome, and there the 1st Earl's monument, in black and white marble, was at last erected. Wearing a full-bottomed wig in the fashion of the time, he looks somewhat uncomfortable in a semi-reclining position, and surprised, moreover, to find himself surrounded by Savages, as if he had gate-crashed a party.

Other monuments with romantic backgrounds are not difficult to find. In the sumptuous Beauchamp Chapel of St Mary's, Warwick, is a sad memorial to the 'Noble Imp', the four-year-old son of Robert Dudley, 1st Earl of Leicester, who died in 1584. 'The Noble Imp' had been secretly promised in marriage to Arabella Stuart, then aged only eight. This was an ambitious plan whereby Leicester's power was to be allied to Bess of Hardwick's wealth and, since her grandchild Arabella had royal blood (her father, Charles Stuart, was descended from Henry VII's eldest sister Margaret), the children of such a union could have succeeded Elizabeth I. The premature death of the 'Imp' put paid to that scheme. Another romantic monument is in the chancel of St Mary's, Bottesford, Leicestershire, which is packed with tombs of astonishing magnificence and was used by the Dukes of Rutland as their private chapel; one, to the 6th Earl, has the well-known, and only, reference to witchcraft on a tomb. Three 'witches' were executed for the mysterious deaths of the 6th Earl's two sons in 1619. Two of the accused were sisters and, as servants, had been sacked by the Rutlands. Their mother was the leader of the 'coven' who, claimed neighbours, made a compact with Satan by means of gloves belonging to the two sons, a familiar in the form of a cat called Rutterkin, and holy water. The whole story is redolent with village hatreds and unpleasant vendettas against disagreeable neighbours.

Monuments of the Civil War period provide other romantic connections; in Buckinghamshire, standing next to Claydon House, the home of the Verneys, is Middle Claydon Church and in it is a monument to Sir Edmund Verney who died at the Civil War battle of Edgehill in 1642. Sir Edmund sided with the King without great enthusiasm; he had a conviction that he would not see the war out. He was standard bearer at the battle and foolishly advanced into the enemy's lines 'in order that the souldiers might be engaged to follow him'. Surrounded by Roundheads, he was offered the chance to surrender the standard in return for his life. He refused and the standard was captured, but not before he had killed sixteen Roundheads with his sword. Later that day the standard was recaptured with Sir Edmund's hand still gripping the shaft; his body was never found and his hand is all of Sir Edmund that is buried in the crypt. The ring given to him by the King, containing his miniature, was still on a finger of the hand and can be seen at Claydon.

Wealthy families sometimes provided themselves with side chapels in their own church with vaults beneath for burials and filled the chapel with their monuments. Examples of these are at Kedleston in Derbyshire; Chenies, Buckinghamshire; and the Bridgwater tombs at Little Gaddesden, Hertfordshire. Other historic houses have churches marooned in their parks because the village has either been moved or eradicated when the park was made. Examples include Dyrham Park, Gloucestershire; Lanhydrock, Cornwall; Staunton Harold, Leicestershire; and Chatsworth, Derbyshire. The really wealthy with a large household would invariably have a resident cleric. In this case they would have their own private chapel in the house, as at Audley End, Hertfordshire; Belvoir Castle, Leicestershire; Blenheim, Oxfordshire; and Alnwick, Northumberland. Almost all ducal households had their own private chapels.

It was only a short step from having a private chapel to building a private mausoleum in the park of a great house. Mausolea are named after the great tomb built in the fourth century BC at Halicarnassos by Queen Artemesia for her husband Mausolos, and they became fashionable in the eighteenth century when the Grand Tour brought the idea of Imperial Roman burial building to Britain. Undoubtedly one of the grandest, and possibly the first, is the great mausoleum in the park of Castle Howard. It was designed on a vast scale by Nicholas Hawksmoor in 1728-29 and built in 1731 for the 3rd Earl of Carlisle. A huge drum surrounded by tall columns and roofed with a shallow dome stands on a fortress-like crypt where the Carlisles are interred. The building dominates the landscape and Hawksmoor's intention was that no one should ever be allowed to forget that this is the ultimate resting place of the Earls of Carlisle. At Cobham Park, Kent, in 1784 James Wyatt designed a more modest building with a pyramidal roof for the Earls of Darnley. Although the mausoleum is sadly vandalized there are plans to convert it into a house for the living. Possibly the most elegant of all these buildings is the Pelham mausoleum in Brocklesby Park, Lincolnshire. Its bright, top-lit interior is filled, but not cluttered, with marble monuments to Pelhams from 1587 onwards and in the centre of the floor is an exquisite sculpture by Nollekens of Sophia Pelham, a young wife who died in 1787. A grand pyramid built in 1793 to designs by Joseph Bonomi at Blickling, Norfolk, commemorates the 2nd Earl of Buckinghamshire and his two countesses. The biggest memorial of any was built at Lancaster by Lord Ashton in 1906-9 in memory of his wife. It cost £87,000 and is capped with a similar dome to that of St Peter's, Rome. From the M6 motorway it looks like a misplaced town hall. The building has recently been restored at a cost of £600,000 and surrounded by a Victorian and Edwardian theme park.

Saint Augustine, who died in AD 430, made the point that funerals were for the living and not for the dead. Today when we enter the great houses of the past we should reflect that they too were designed for the living, who, were they to return, would be saddened to see them regarded as no more than monuments to a vanished way of life.

CHAPTER 11

An End and a Future

'Step back in Time' was an advertising slogan of English Heritage; it simply is not possible to do that and, even if it were, we should not at all like what we found. We all have romantic notions about the past, conditioned by our twentieth-century outlook; the state apartments we see in many houses are now filled with more people than ever used them in the past. In fact they would have spent most of the years unused, with furniture shrouded in dust sheets. Furniture is not now placed where it was historically used and some furniture, like the sofa table, was used differently anyway. The stables are empty and the servants' wing is desolate. No longer is it possible to know what it was like to run a household of servants and to ring for the fire to be made up rather than do it ourselves. There are countless other points of difference between us and the people of the past; it just is not possible to gain a complete picture of what life was like one hundred, two hundred or, even more difficult, three hundred years ago. Sometimes we can get a feeling for the past from objects we see in an historic house, or from reading contemporary letters, diaries and fiction, but glimpses are all we get.

Moreover, the way of life that went on in the historic house was always changing, as the philosophy behind the life was always changing. Yet from our point in time the lifestyle looks as if it had been unaltered for centuries. As long as land was a sound investment the great historic house was safe. Ownership was not restricted to the old landed families; wealthy society was fluid and penetrated by fortunes made first by the merchant and then by the entrepreneur in the industrial revolution of the late eighteenth century. In the same century the Hoare family at Stourhead and the Childs at Osterley showed how merchant-bankers could compete with established families. The Crossleys and the Brasseys, who made fortunes, one from carpets and the other from railway contracting, demonstrated the same lesson in the nineteenth century. The four families must have rung warning bells in the ears of many that the old ways were changing. To go further back, Thomas Hewitt left his Midland home for London where he made from cloth one of the biggest merchant fortunes of the sixteenth century. He became Lord Mayor of London and retired to Shireoaks in Nottinghamshire, near his birthplace, where he built a house that is now sadly mutilated, although recently rescued from becoming a ruin. The hall wing at Penshurst in Kent was built in the mid-fourteenth century out of new money made by Sir John de Poultney, a leading London merchant and financier. These too must have made many of the old guard regret the speed of change. These changes, although they may have appeared threatening at the time, were no more than changes in ownership. The way of life in the historic house proved remarkably resilient to change until the present century, when the whole system collapsed. A privileged way of life maintained for centuries was seemingly swept away in one lifetime.

There are many reasons for the collapse, ranging from the minor problem of servants – although if the economic return from running a large house could be justified, this problem would vanish – to taxation, politics and universal suffrage. So long as the wealthy could maintain their political power, shared between the Whigs and the Tories, through selective suffrage based on a wealth qualification, their position could be maintained. The first Reform Act of 1832 was seen by many as the death-knell of a way of life. They were right, but the Act only gave the vote to £10 householders and removed the scandal of rotten boroughs such as Dunwich, which for centuries had been beneath the North Sea, or Old Sarum, that was no more than a green mound, each of which returned a member of Parliament. Lord Verulam was so depressed by the whole thing that he was convinced that Reform would be the end of shooting.

Had Reform gone no further the old way of life would have been maintained, but the later Acts of 1867 and 1884 widened the voting qualifications and finally opened Parliament to a more democratic representation. With that, the power of the landowning politician was broken and the political purpose of the great house consequently declined; a politician could be a power in the land even if he was landless. He had no need of tenants' votes or of 'influence'; the political party took over the patronage and control of MPs. But politics was only a small part of the story; the main reason for the collapse of landed families was financial.

The financial return from land in the 1870s suffered a setback from which it only recovered in the Second World War. For the landlord whose wealth was traditionally in land the Great Depression of the late nineteenth century spelled disaster; from 1873 a series of wet summers ruined harvests, while cheap wheat from the USA, let in by the earlier repeal of the Corn Laws, undercut the price of what home produced grain there was. Tenants were unable to pay even the reduced rents that sympathetic landowners asked and before the end of the century many estates were bankrupt; some families were forced to sell up when the bottom fell out of the price of land – in 1878 15,000 acres of rich Lincolnshire land, which in the 1820s could have fetched £350,000, was valued at £16,541! The 7th Duke of Manchester at Kimbolton Castle, Cambridgeshire, was reduced to a staff of only nine in 1881, costing £360 a year. Other families just scraped through, but it was mainly those with commercial investments, who did not rely wholly on an agricultural income, who survived. Families not relying entirely on income from land could continue in the way to which they had become accustomed. The 3rd Earl Manvers, who had just spent nearly £250,000 on building Thoresby Hall, would have been badly hit had there not been a high income from Government stocks. In the 1880s he maintained a steward and thirty staff costing £1,000 a year, as he had in the past. The 15th Earl of Derby at the time of his death in 1893 employed 727 indoor and outdoor servants costing around £25,000 a year, but his case was exceptional; he managed to increase his agricultural income during the Great Depression. For those who survived there were more disasters to follow.

The effects of the Great Depression were still being felt when the broader based Parliament introduced Death Duty taxation in 1894. In fact the highest rate of eight per cent on very large estates worth a million pounds was not onerous and could be met out of income by insurance or avoided by giving the estate to the heir before the death of the owner. It was the incidence of the tax in the First World War that did the damage, when it might have to be paid several times in succession because of deaths of sons (in the next war death duty was not payable when the victim was killed in action). By 1919 the duty was forty per cent on an estate of £2 million. Moreover, the financial return from land was far below that from industrial investment. 'The old order is doomed,' wrote the Duke of Marlborough in 1919.

Notwithstanding the problems, some of the 'old order' survived up to the Second World War; E. F. Benson of the 'Lucia' novels pointed out that, 'Pockets of Edwardian manners survived long after that war, for inherited money is the great preserver of dead cultures.' Inherited money is also a wonderful insulator from reality, which all goes to explain why the historic country house way of life was so long a-dying. The Second World War brought reality into the historic drawing rooms, and when the dust of peace had settled there was no possibility of renewing the old ways.

In the hard world of investment – and it must be remembered that families bought the land in the first place as an investment; the house came second – an asset losing money should go, and so the houses went. Many were demolished; in the five remaining years of the 1940s after the war, 74 historic houses were lost; the 1950s saw the wholesale destruction of 302 – the worst figure was for Suffolk where 21 went in the decade – but in the 1960s the figure dropped to 162. Much of the damage was done by 1969 when 'listed building consent' was required to demolish buildings classified as being of architectural and historic interest.

Nevertheless there are many large historic houses still lived in today. The owners no longer occupy the whole house but have made for themselves comfortable and warm quarters in a corner for winter and use the rest of the house only in summer if they need to – a return to the sixteenth-century plan of having a winter parlour. These owners have stayed because they have held on to the land and the house is not worth opening to the public, either because it is too far from the popular tourist routes or because there is nothing worth showing. Only the very wealthy can afford to live in a house filled with treasures and not share their pleasure with the public. Others, like the Probys at Elton Hall, near Peterborough, have played it several ways by making part of the house comfortable for themselves, converting the rest to flats and opening the best rooms to the public.

It has long been obvious to many who care about historic houses and their contents that a compromise would have to be made if any were to survive. Alternative use has to be found for a house of this kind that is too large for a family to inhabit. The argument for preservation has been given in the preceding chapters and the annual number of visitors to historic properties crushes any opposing view. About seven million visitors go through the gates of National Trust properties annually. Since many of these are members, they are likely to be making far more than one visit. In Britain there are about 1,700 historic houses, sites, ruins and cathedrals to be visited; in total they clocked up between them the astonishing total of nearly 60 million visitors annually – more than the entire population of the country. This is clearly a figure that no government can afford to ignore.

Recent legislation has recognized that the historic house is a huge tourist attraction and cautious steps have been made to preserve the family connection in such properties. Provided that a house is open for a minimum number of days in a year the building, its contents and its immediate surroundings can be passed on to an heir without incurring Capital Transfer Tax. Legislation in the budget of March 1986 abolished the Capital Transfer Tax on gifts provided that the donor survives for seven years after making the gift, thus making it easier to pass property on to an heir. In the introduction to a Treasury publication of 1980, *Capital Taxation and the National Heritage*, there is a significant passage: 'successive Governments . . . have taken the view that where such property [an historic house] remains in private hands, the owners should be encouraged, wherever possible, to retain and care for it and display it to the public.' A similar enlightened attitude to taking items in place of taxation has, for example, enabled the portrait of Henry Howard, Earl of Surrey, of *c.*1550, a copy of a vanished original by William Scrots, to remain in Arundel Castle, Sussex, instead of going to the National Portrait Gallery. It could be argued that the Duke of Norfolk has no right to enjoy a painting that is no longer his and which belongs to the nation, but the fact is that every year nearly 200,000 visitors to Arundel Castle are able to share the Duke's enjoyment of the painting, in its historic surroundings.

Whatever tax privileges are conceded to the owners of historic houses, it is no easy matter to take the decision to open a home to the public. Even if the occupiers are willing to endure the inconvenience of having open days there are other problems. To let the public into a house means that they have to be let out again after a circuit of the principal rooms; there should be no bottlenecks, no crossing paths and no room should be too small to accommodate comfortably the maximum number likely to be in it at any one time. No house manages to meet all of the requirements, for, as we have seen, historic houses were designed for something different.

Blenheim, for example, designed to accommodate the royal court in the state apartments, has an unavoidable bottleneck which occurs in the Churchill rooms soon after the visitor enters the house. If the public could be restricted to the state apartments then all would be well, or if the Churchill rooms could be seen at the end of the circuit there would be no problem. They embody all the bad points of circulation; three small rooms filled with items of interest, of which many visitors will have personal memories. Blenheim is open for approximately 230 days in every year to some 400,000 visitors, which is a daily average of 2,000. Obviously at the height of the season there will be over 5,000 daily visitors and the crush in the Churchill rooms is inevitable; on those days few can enjoy anything of the exhibition of Churchilliana. The tour of Blenheim is not 'open' which means that the public cannot go round on their own; entrance is strictly controlled and guides take groups through the state apartments. The first room seen, the hall, is the biggest, in which a crush of visitors is entertained to a history of the house and family by a guide who opens the door. His is the key job because he controls the numbers entering the house. When the small rooms are full he can let in fewer and entertain them longer. It is doubtful if Blenheim could exceed the number of 400,000 annual visitors.

Blenheim is an extreme example of the problem of pushing large numbers of people through an historic house. It is fortunate in that it is a well-known house, that it is architecturally important, that the contents are equally important, that it is on the tourist route from London to Stratford and the Cotswolds and that its state apartments can contain the number of expected visitors.

Beaulieu, the home of Lord Montagu, is at the other extreme from Blenheim. Palace House, Beaulieu, in Hampshire, originally the abbey gatehouse but altered in 1872, is not of particular architectural interest, although the ruins of the abbey itself are worth a visit; it is not on the tourist route, the contents are not worth a detour and it would be impossible to take sufficient visitors through the house to make the operation economically viable. Before the 1950s it had little to commend it to the visitor. With this sort of problem there is only one answer if the house is going to be open to the public; give the visitor something to see and do outside the house. When Lord Montagu was faced with the necessity of opening his house to the public he was acutely aware of all its drawbacks and of what he had to do. The result today is that Beaulieu has over 400,000 visitors to the best motor museum in the world and the majority of those visitors do not even trouble to see Palace House. Admittedly the environment of the house is completely changed, but from being an expensive liability it has become very profitable. A similar story could be told of Woburn, the home of Lord Tavistock. The pioneer in this initiative was Lord Tavistock's father, the Duke of Bedford. In this case the house and its contents are well worth a detour of many miles but problems of public circulation through the house limit the income from visitors. However, there is enough going on outside the house, including an antiques hypermarket with forty shops in the stables and safari tours of the park, to make Woburn one of the most visited properties in Britain.

It is interesting that in the 1950s when both Beaulieu and Woburn were being developed as tourist attractions, Lord Montagu and the Duke of Bedford faced enormous criticism from established 'house openers' and landowners; it was said that they were debasing the whole aspect of the historic house. Opening a house to coach parties interested only in old cars or exotic animals was felt by some to be a form of prostitution. Undeniably something irreplaceable was destroyed by the enterprise. Yet both owners were doing no more than their founding ancestors had done – turning a liability into an asset. Sometimes the criticism was prompted by envy and it bothered neither owner.

The three cases described are prime examples in which full profit has been made from every possible advantage and, where there was no seeming advantage, it was created. What of the owner of an historic house, the layout of which does not permit public access in sufficient numbers even to pay for the guides, or which is far from centres of population and tourist routes? What of an owner whose house is no architectural or historic gem and has no contents worth showing? It is a very unlucky owner who has to contend with all the disadvantages and even some of these can be turned to good account.

Many disadvantages are currently being developed into profitable advantages. Educational or institutional uses, once thought to be the ultimate fate of the large and remote historic house, are no longer the only answer to the problem of the unwanted historic house; schools are closing and hospitals now demand more modern facilities than can be provided by some of the historic houses they occupy. Thorpe Hall, near Peterborough, built in the 1650s, is an example of an important historic house abandoned as a hospital and standing forlornly empty, notwithstanding promises by the local authority to make it available to the public. One problem faced by anyone finding a new use for a property deserted by an institutional owner is that of the 'hut' syndrome. This occurs where expansion led to the demand for more space than the property contained and the only answer was to erect a sea of wooden or concrete huts. At Pele, a house at Cloven, Borders, that was once a hospital, there is more accommodation provided by huts than is in the house itself.

Fortunately there are now more answers to the question of what use an unwanted historic house can be put to than was the case a few years ago. Conversion to multiple occupancy has been pioneered by the architect Kit Martin; his conversion of Hazells Hall, Bedfordshire (deserted by the family of Francis Pymm, a late member of government, who, however, held on to the land), rescued the building which was converted into twelve elegant self-contained houses, flats and cottages. Martin's first conversion was Dingley

Hall, Northamptonshire, which was in an advanced state of decay and thought to be lost; it is now occupied by eleven families. The Mutual House Owners' Association pioneered the conversion of large historic houses into flats for the elderly: Albury Park, Surrey; Aynho Park, Northamptonshire; Gosfield Hall, Essex; and Swallowfield Park, Berkshire, have all been converted to a new use by this enlightened association.

The Landmark Trust is another organization dedicated to the rescue of buildings; it specializes in smaller, more bizarre properties that can be converted into holiday letting accommodation. These include the Egyptian House of *c.*1812 in Penzance; the Elizabethan gatehouse of Shute Barton, Devon; Luttrell's Tower at Eaglehurst, Hampshire, an eighteenth-century folly; New Inn, Peasenhall in Suffolk, a fifteenth-century small hall house. All are typical of the buildings in the care of the Landmark Trust, many of which would certainly have become derelict had not an alternative use been found. The Vivat Trust, founded some six years ago, restores small historic build-ings for sale or letting and recently completed work on a Tudor banqueting house at Eyton-on-Severn in Shropshire, all that remains of a large house built in 1607 for Sir Francis Newport. The Monument Historic Building Trust, a Sainsbury family charitable trust, has restored many smaller build-ings in Derbyshire, in Bristol and in Much Wenlock, Shropshire, and is currently backing the restoration of Belford Hall, Northumberland. There are also county preservation societies in differing forms, dedicated to raising funds for the restoration of the smaller buildings falling outside the scope of the larger national organizations.

Greywalls, near Edinburgh, a gem by Edwin Lutyens with a garden by Gertrude Jekyll, created in 1901, has been successfully converted by the family into a very pleasant hotel. Gravetye Manor in Sussex – the old home of the gardener William Robinson – has made another successful luxury hotel. Ettington Park, Warwickshire, mentioned in Chapter 1 as the home of the Shirley family, has recently been turned into an hotel, financed with the help of the Business Expansion Scheme; a total of £1.1 million was required for the conversion. In fact the Business Expansion Scheme has been responsible for a number of historic house hotels. The surprising association between the National Trust and Blakeney Hotels, the owners of the Royal Crescent in Bath and Cliveden near Maidenhead, has created at Cliveden a unique hotel which, more than any other hotel in a historic house, caters for an American fantasy vision of British upper-class life. Ston Easton Park, Somerset, built in *c.*1750 by an unknown architect and not by Humphry Repton as the owners claim, was practically derelict twenty-five years ago and is now a renowned nineteen-room hotel. All these houses have been converted to hotels with prestigious restaurants and more than twelve bedrooms – the minimum for economic survival. In this respect it has been said that 'Profit comes from bedrooms, only fame from restaurants'. It remains to be seen where this recent enterprising re-use of historic houses will lead.

When a property is sufficiently near to a large centre of population it can be used as a conference centre. The Marquis of Northampton, who owned two houses both open to the public, Castle Ashby in Northamptonshire and a romantic gem of Tudor architecture, Compton Wynyates in Warwickshire, not surprisingly chose to live in the latter – it is now closed to the public – and Castle Ashby has become a conference centre with public access limited to groups by appointment. Brocket Hall, Hertfordshire, may be hired for 'day or residential senior management meetings'. The splendid reception rooms are backed by twenty twin-bedded rooms – whether the huge capital outlay needed to bring the house into the necessary pristine state for these activities will ever pay off is something that only time will tell. Clarendon Park in Wiltshire is another example of the same type of use and can be hired for 'a wide range of business, social and cultural meetings and events'.

In other cases public-spirited owners, aware that their property should be accessible to the public because of the importance of the building and its contents, have taken advantage of the 1975 Finance Act. This permitted owners to set up charitable trusts by which the house, its contents and its associated land could be willed or transferred free of Capital Transfer Tax to a trust. Leeds Castle in Kent was bequeathed by Lady Baillie as a charitable trust to encourage medical research and to open the house to the public; two activities that are at times opposed to each other, as for example when a medical conference held at the Castle will prevent public access to rooms usually open. Lamport Hall, Northamptonshire, was left by the last of the Isham family with sufficient funds and wide discretion for almost any charitable use the trustees may think fit. Thirlestane Castle, Borders, the home of the Maitland-Carews, was rescued by funding a charitable trust endowed by the National Heritage Memorial Fund and repairs were carried out by means of very large grants. Possibly the best known case is that of Chatsworth; the 11th Duke of Devonshire has always followed a generous and public-spirited policy of making his collection available for research and study, even maintaining a staff of two who spend a great deal of their time coping with the problems of lending items for public exhibitions and answering questions raised by art historians and researchers. Furthermore no public funds have ever been used to repair the fabric of the house. In 1981 the sale of a painting by Poussin for £1,650,000 went a long way towards raising the £2 million needed to provide capital to fund a charitable trust, the Chatsworth House Trust, for the maintenance of the house and collection. A further sale of books brought the fund to £200,000 more than the required figure. The chapel has undergone a much needed restoration and the vast roof is being repaired before work can begin on the painted ceilings of the state rooms. All this is financed out of untaxed income from the Trust, and Chatsworth is safe for a hundred years – the period of the lease the charity holds on the property and part of the contents. The Duke now pays a market rent to the Trust for the very comfortable apartments he and the Duchess have occupied at Chatsworth since they moved back there in 1959 – he is a sub-tenant in his own house. The whole scheme has meant that the Duke has lost the ownership of a masterpiece by Poussin and some very valuable books. Since none of these was seen by the public nothing has been lost to the visitor – the loss has been entirely the Duke's. Technically the house is no longer his but will revert to his descendants in a hundred years.

One automatically thinks of the National Trust and the National Trust for Scotland in connection with the preservation of historic houses, from Chartwell with the highest number of visitors annually (160,000) to the tiny Priest's House at Muchelney in Somerset (viewed by appointment only) with the lowest number, sixty. The Trust owns some 300 major houses and gardens and with half a million acres is the second biggest landowner in Britain after the Crown. Yet the Trust only really got into the historic house business in 1940 following the second National Trust Act of 1937. By this Act the Trust was able to set up the Country House Scheme which allowed an owner to transfer a house and contents, with a sufficient endowment, to the Trust, while the family and heirs could continue to occupy part of the building subject to the house being open to the public.

This arrangement has been successful, for example, at Knole where several members of Lord Sackville's family occupy flats, and at Plas Newydd which is still partly occupied by the Marquis of Anglesey. The arrangement at Hardwick Hall, however, is less successful; the rooms set aside for the use of the Duke of Devonshire, since the house came to the National Trust in 1960, have never been used. It is unlikely that anyone will use them because they offer no privacy from the visiting public and are too small for their purpose. At Shugborough, where the Earl of Lichfield occupies part of the house (the property of the National Trust since 1966), the house is open every day of the week from March to October and 50,000 people a year go through the house and gardens. The peace and privacy expected even in the smallest home is no longer available to Lord Lichfield and he would have to be extremely tolerant of the curious public to endure a summer at Shugborough.

Blickling Hall, Norfolk, the first property acquired under the National Trust Country House Scheme, was given to the Trust in 1940 by Lord Lothian, who had been partly responsible for the Act. By the end of the Second World War the Trust had taken fourteen houses into its care in the same way. The scheme depended on the substantial endowment needed as a gift by the owner and this should have ruled out cases where an endowment was not offered.

In fact the Trust burnt its fingers by accepting at least one property with no endowment and had to maintain the building from funds that should have been used for other purposes. In later cases of houses of exceptional historic or architectural quality accepted with no endowment, any short-fall in the value was made up from the Land Fund established in 1946, involving a book-keeping juggle with the Inland Revenue. Saltram in Devon, for example, was acquired by this method in 1957 with £57,000 and £37,000 for the contents, and Shugborough in 1966 with £64,000 and £99,000 for the contents; these are two typical acquisitions with capital provided by the Land Fund. In both cases the lack of endowment was covered by the Government agreeing to make up any deficit incurred for repairs or running costs out of the Historic Buildings Council's grant money. Hardwick Hall and its park, although taken in lieu of death duties in 1959, still needed nearly £200,000 from the Land Fund, and since then the Historic Buildings Council has continued to support the enormous repair bill for a programme of reroofing, reflooring, reglazing, replastering and the replacement of all perished stonework – none of which could ever have been afforded by any private owner or the Trust alone.

All these complicated schemes were the result of successive governments refusing to tackle the problem of preservation head-on and, through political expediency, concocting byzantine plans to do the job without appearing to be directly involved. It was preservation at arm's length. Today the National Trust is a very large and powerful organization, pioneering many educational programmes, methods of preservation, ways of presenting houses and their contents, and research into the historical arrangement of furniture and correct interior design. Although the Trust is basically an independent organization, responsible neither to the Government nor to the public, it does take its responsibility to the visiting public seriously and is constantly seeking ways of improving access and facilities.

The Historic Houses Association is a very different organization, although superficially it may appear to be similar to the National Trust – visitors to the member-houses are often under the impression that they are visiting National Trust property. The organization is simply a trade union for private owners and it can undertake some very effective lobbying when it feels the need. It now has a thousand members and the visiting public may join as 'friends' to have, in return, free access to any of the participating houses; there are approximately three thousand subscribing friends. However, this is an organization for the historic house owner's benefit and the visiting public is not considered in the same way as is the case with the National Trust. There are some members who take their responsibility seriously; there are others who do not and regard open days as an intrusion on their privacy – rooms advertised as being accessible on one day in the week may be capriciously closed because the family, for example, wishes to watch Wimbledon on television. Many of these owners have taken repair grants from the HBC and in return have undertaken to make the house available to visitors, or have taken advantage of the arrangement whereby by being open for a minimum number of annual days the property and contents can be transferred to an heir without incurring Capital Transfer Tax. In both cases the owners have a responsibility to the visiting public.

Despite all the problems facing the historic houses that we have encountered on these pages, how much poorer we would be without them. New uses for the buildings often have to be found, to which both owners and the visiting public must adapt themselves. Even so, many of them remain with their contents undisturbed in the rooms in which succeeding generations were born, lived, loved, had babies and died.

Notes

Introduction

1. *The Edwardians* by Vita Sackville-West, Viking Press, New York, 1961, p. x.
2. *Guidelines* by Adrian Tinniswood, University of Nottingham Department of Adult Education, 1982, p. 11.

CHAPTER 1: *Evolution*

1. *English Landed Society in the Nineteenth Century* by F. M. L. Thompson, Routledge & Kegan Paul, 1963, p. 104.
2. Ibid.
3. Ibid.
4. Ibid., p. 105.
5. The existing building accounts, deposited at Nottingham University Library, cover these periods: Bk 1: March to March 1582-3; Bk 2: November to November 1584-5; Bk 3: March to March 1586-7; Bk 4: March to March 1587-8; Bk 5: March to November 1588.
6. *The Building of Hardwick Hall*, Part 2, edited by David N. Durant and Philip Riden, Derbyshire Record Society, Vol. IX, 1984, p.lvi.
7. 'Thoresby Hall' by Clive Aslet, *Country Life*, 28 June 1979, p. 2085.
8. The accounts are deposited at Nottingham University Library. The cost of building the house was £171,000; the stables, brewhouse, gas works and church brought the total expenditure to £250,000.
9. *English Landed Society in the Nineteenth Century*, op. cit., p. 89.
10. *The Gentleman's Country House and Its Plan 1835-1914* by Jill Franklin, Routledge & Kegan Paul, 1981, p. 260.
11. *English Landed Society in the Eighteenth Century* by G. E. Mingay, Routledge & Kegan Paul, 1963, p. 76.
12. *Disraeli* by Sarah Bradford, Grafton Books, 1985, p. 275.
13. *Bess of Hardwick* by David N. Durant, Weidenfeld & Nicolson, 1977, p. 229.

14. *Life in a Noble Household* by Gladys Scott Thompson, Jonathan Cape, 1950, pp. 148-9.
15. *English Landed Society in the Eighteenth Century*, op. cit., p. 159.

CHAPTER 2: *Provisioning*

1. *The Cecils of Hatfield* by Hugh Cecil, Constable, 1973, p. 261.
2. *Life in a Noble Household*, op. cit., p. 155.
3. Ibid., p. 160.
4. *Bess of Hardwick*, op. cit., p. 166.
5. Clwyd Record Office, ref: DD/PH216.
6. *Travels in England and Scotland 1784* by B. F. de Saint Fond, Hugh Hopkins, Glasgow, 1907, pp. 240-6.
7. Chatsworth Library, ref: Hardwick MS 7, f. 101.

CHAPTER 3: *Eating*

1. *The Experienced English Housekeeper* by Elizabeth Raffold, R. Baldwin, 1782, pp. iv-v.
2. *The Diary of a Country Parson* by James Woodford, ed. John Beresford, Oxford University Press, 1978, p. 69.
3. *The Babees Book* edited by F. J. Furnivall, The Early English Text Society, 1868, p. 311.
4. *Art and Power: Renaissance Festivities, 1450-1650* by Roy Strong, Boydell Press, 1984, p. 19.
5. British Museum, ref: Harleian 6815, ff. 23-38v.
6. *The Babees Book,* op. cit., Vol. 2, p. 160.
7. Ibid.
8. Ibid., pp. 164-6.
9. *History of the Sackville Family* by Charles T. Phillips, Cassell, 1930, Vol. I, p. 275.
10. *History of Hampton Court* by Ernest Law, 1885-91, p. 146.
11. *Travels in England and Scotland 1784*, op. cit., pp. 240-6.
12. *English Interior Decoration in the Eighteenth Century* by John Fowler and John Cornforth, Barrie & Jenkins, 1974, p. 67.

CHAPTER 4: *Sleeping*

1. *Horace Walpole's Correspondence* edited by W. S. Lewis, Yale Press, 1955, Vol. 28, p. 414.
2. *Evelyn's Diary and Correspondence* edited by William Bray, F. Warne, n. d., p. 450.
3. *A Collection of Ordinances and Regulations for the Government of the Royal Household*, Society of Antiquaries, 1790.
4. The Chatsworth inventory of *c.* 1566 is in Chatsworth Library under ref: Hardwick Drawer 143 (6).

5. *Middleton*, Historical Manuscripts Commission, p. 465.
6. *Carlisle*, Historical Manuscripts Commission, p. 85.
7. *Appollo*, June 1973, pp. 581-3.
8. *Blenheim Palace* by David Green, Country Life, 1951, p. 169.
9. *Country Life Annual*, 1963, p. 37.
10. *Characters by Lord Chesterfield*, 1847, Vol. 1, pp. 165-6.

CHAPTER 5: *The Grand Life*

1. *A Catalogue of Letters and Other Historical Documents Exhibited in the Library at Welbeck* edited by S. A. Strong, John Murray, 1903, p. 210.
2. *Diary of Lady Margaret Hoby* edited by Dorothy M. Meads, George Routledge, 1930, p. 83.
3. *Journal of a Somerset Rector* edited by H. Coombs and A. N. Bax, 1930.
4. *The Greville Diary* edited by P. W. Wilson, Heinemann, 1927, Vol. 1, p. 28.
5. *Disraeli*, op. cit., p. 285.
6. *The Country House Remembered* edited by Merlin Waterson, Routledge & Kegan Paul, 1985, p. 64.

CHAPTER 6: *The Collectors*

1. *Seventeenth Century Interior Decoration in England, France and Holland* by Peter Thornton, Yale University Press, 1978, p.254.
2. *The Torrington Diaries* by John Byng, Methuen, 1970, Vol. 1, p. 231.

CHAPTER 7: *Below Stairs*

1. *History of The Sackville Family* by Charles T. Phillips, Cassell, 1930, Vol. 1, pp. 275-6.
2. *Middleton*, Historical Manuscripts Commission, pp. 538-42.
3. *Elizabethan England* by William Harrison, ed. L. Withington and F. J. Furnival, 1921.
4. *Memoirs of an Eighteenth-Century Footman* by John Macdonald, Century Publishing, 1985.
5. *English Landed Society in the Nineteenth Century*, op. cit., pp. 188-9.
6. Ibid., p. 189.
7. Although the house has gone the board exists in the Berkshire Record Office under ref: D/EMt 24.
8. Clwyd Record Office, Hawarden.
9. Clwyd Record Office, Hawarden, Box 124/6.
10. *The Creevey Papers* edited by Sir H. Maxwell, John Murray, 1903.
11. *The Greville Diary* edited by P. W. Wilson, Heinemann, 1927, Vol. 1, p. 28.
12. *Book of Orders and Rules of Viscount Montague in 1597*, Sussex Archaeological Collection VII, 1854, p. 184.

CHAPTER 8: *Transport*

1. *English Landed Society in the Eighteenth Century*, op. cit., p. 151.
2. *English Landed Society in the Nineteenth Century*, op. cit., p. 97.
3. *The Country House Remembered*, op. cit., p. 85.
4. *Everybody's Pepys* edited by E. H. Shepard, G. Bell, 1926, p. 276.
5. *Rutland*, Historical Manuscripts Commission, Vol. IV, p. 413.
6. Ibid., p. 525
7. *Life in a Noble Household*, op. cit., pp. 208-9.
8. *Rutland*, Historical Manuscripts Commission, Vol. IV, p. 550.
9. Ibid.
10. Ibid., Vol. I, p. 421.
11. Ibid., p. 454.
12. *Townsend*, Historical Manuscripts Commission, pp. 202-3.

CHAPTER 9: *The Setting*

1. *Capability Brown* by Dorothy Stroud, Faber & Faber, 1975, pp. 93-4.
2. *The Journeys of Celia Fiennes* edited by Christopher Morris, The Cresset Press, 1947, p. 98.
3. *Mansfield Park* by Jane Austen, Macmillan, 1950, p. 47.

CHAPTER 10: *Last Things*

1. *Sarah, Duchess of Marlborough* by David Green, Collins, 1967, p. 257.
2. *The Verneys of Claydon* edited by Sir Harry Verney Bt, Pergamon Press, 1968, pp. 247-8.
3. *Evelyn's Diary and Correspondence*, op. cit., p. 468.
4. *Death, Burial and the Individual in Early Modern England* by Clare Gittings, Croom Helm, 1984, p. 190.
5. Ibid., p. 30.

Selective List
of Historic Houses

(NT=National Trust)

Apsley House Museum, London (Victoria and Albert Museum). A surviving example of the row of noblemen's houses which once lined the north side of Piccadilly. Built for Lord Bathurst in 1771–78 by Adam, it was bought by the 1st Duke of Wellington in 1817 and enlarged and refaced in stone by B. Wyatt in 1828. Notwithstanding Wyatt's alterations there is still something of the Adam interior left: the staircase, the Drawing Room and the Portico Room. Wyatt's masterpiece is the Waterloo Gallery. The main rooms of entertainment have been restored to the state in which they were in Wellington's time, but the house remains a museum. Nevertheless, this is the only example of a large London town house interior to survive.

Arundel Castle, West Sussex (Duke of Northumberland). Dating from the twelfth century, the building was heavily restored in the last century and the interior is noteworthy as an example of thirteenth-century design as seen from the nineteenth century. The state apartments have the original electric fittings.

Auckland Castle, County Durham (Church Commissioners). The historic home of the Bishops of Durham from the twelfth century. The fourteenth-century great hall was remodelled by James Wyatt in 1795. In addition, the range of state apartments are a good example of how a wealthy bishopric held court. The medieval chapel is the size of a parish church and the park contains one of the few surviving eighteenth-century deer houses.

Belton House, Lincolnshire (NT). The crowning achievement of Restoration country house architecture. Built from the legal fortune made by Sir John Brownlow in 1684–88, the plan still follows the original baroque layout of saloon and withdrawing rooms, with bed chambers in projecting wings. Genuine Grinling Gibbons wood carving.

Blenheim Palace, Oxfordshire (Duke of Marlborough). Begun in 1705 by Vanbrugh for the 1st Duke of Marlborough, this magnificent baroque building was decidely old fashioned when it was completed in 1725 – the Palladian style was in fashion by that time. The sequence of rooms in the state apartments can still be followed, even though their names have changed. Originally two ranges of apartments radiated from the central saloon, consisting of a withdrawing room, presence chamber, bed chamber and closet, intended for a king and queen. The family lived more comfortably in their own snug wing, which is occasionally open to the public.

Boughton House, Northamptonshire (Duke of Buccleuch and Queensberry). The 1st Duke of Montagu was twice Ambassador to France, which explains the French exterior of this very large house, begun in the 1680s. The interior plan is English with great hall and state apartments on the first floor – there is a fifteenth-century monastic building buried beneath later rebuilding and a small cloister remains as one of seven courtyards. The state apartments have much of their original furniture and state beds from *c*.1700. The contents of Boughton are outstanding; from paintings by El Greco, forty Van Dycks, Mortlake tapestries and ceilings by Cheron, to French furniture of astonishing quality.

Buckland Abbey, Devon (NT). A thirteenth-century Cistercian monastery bought by Sir Richard Grenville in 1541. His conversion of the monastic buildings indicates the compromises necessary in this type of conversion; Grenville made his house out of the monastery church and demolished the cloister buildings. It made as uncomfortable a house as the alternative method used at Newstead Abbey and Lacock.

Burghley House, Northamptonshire (Burghley House Trustees). Begun in the 1550s or 1560s for William Cecil, Chief Secretary of State and Principal Adviser to Elizabeth I, and not completed until *c*.1587. The house has the original great hall and some of the 1550s interior survives on the back stairs. The house's exterior clearly demonstrates the change in taste from the 1560s to the 1580s. The state rooms were extensively altered in the 1680s to make a range of baroque state apartments, with ceilings and walls by Verrio and Laguerre. Unfortunately the public sees these rooms in the reverse order from that in which they would have been used. There is a good collection of Tudor portraits and a fine state bed.

Castle Drogo, Devon (NT). Designed by Lutyens in 1910–13 for Julius Drewe, founder of the Home and Colonial Stores. The Castle provides a romantic look at a past age. The service rooms show how living in the grand style was achieved between the wars, using a smaller staff and labour-saving devices. Drewe's bathroom is a brilliant example of washing luxury. Many of the interior furnishings were bought from a bankrupt Spanish financier.

Castle Howard, North Yorkshire (The Hon. Simon Howard). Designed by Vanbrugh, assisted by Hawksmoor, in 1699–1726 for the 3rd Earl of Carlisle who was building a 'Palace of the Gods' for himself. Naturally everything is on the grand scale, although not so grand as Blenheim. Similar in plan to Blenheim, there is a central saloon behind a grand entrance hall, with apartments radiating from two sides. A serious fire in 1940 gutted one of the wings and destroyed the dome painting; the latter has been restored but the house is now only half what it once was. Nevertheless, this is still a great baroque house.

Charlecote Park, Warwickshire (NT). Although this gives the impression of being an Elizabethan house, only the gatehouse remains from the 1550s. The house was 'restored' in the 1820s and 1850s and the main rooms are now arranged to appear as they might have done in the 1860s. In the brewhouse is all the original equipment for brewing and storing beer. There is also a selection of wheeled vehicles in the coach house.

Chastleton House, Oxfordshire (Mrs Clutton-Brock). A Jacobean building of *c.*1603 attributed to Robert Smythson, which has remained structurally unaltered. The great hall, parlour and great chamber still remain and are furnished in a style that was common at the beginning of the nineteenth century – family pieces, some of quality, and plainer furniture are mixed together in a haphazard fashion.

Chatsworth, Derbyshire (Chatsworth House Trust). The present building dates from 1687, partly built by Talman and Archer for the 1st Duke of Devonshire. Built in a piecemeal fashion, one side at a time, on the foundations of an Elizabethan courtyard house by Bess of Harwick in the 1550s, it must have appeared somewhat bizarre in 1700 when it had three baroque façades and one remaining Elizabethan one. By the time of the Duke's death in 1707 the house was complete, and today has a range of baroque apartments of state, with painted ceilings by Laguerre, Ricci and Verrio, containing the fabulous Chatsworth collection. The park was laid out by 'Capability' Brown in the 1760s. The cascade is all that remains of a huge formal garden, laid out in *c.*1700 for the 1st Duke by London and Wise, altered by the 3rd and 4th Dukes in the eighteenth century and finally reaching its present form under Paxton, who worked for the 6th Duke in the first half of the nineteenth century.

Chiswick House, London (English Heritage). Chiswick, built by the 3rd Earl Burlington in 1723, was not the first example of the Palladian revival; Mereworth Castle and Wanstead preceded this elegant villa, which is modelled loosely on Palladio's Villa Capra. Originally attached to a Jacobean house, it was not intended as a house to be lived in but as a Temple of the Arts. Nevertheless, on the *piano nobile* there was a saloon, withdrawing room and state bed chamber, with services in the basement. The surrounding park and gardens were in part the work of Kent, Burlington's protégé, whom he met on his Grand Tour. Burlington's only child, Charlotte, married the 4th Duke of Devonshire and all the Burlington art treasures, as well as estates, came to the already rich Devonshires.

Clandon Park, Surrey (NT). A Palladian house built for Lord Onslow in *c.*1730 by Leoni, an Italian architect. Although Palladian, the interior is still baroque in plan, with saloon, withdrawing rooms and bed chambers on the ground floor. Nevertheless there are also some outstanding examples of Palladian interiors, redecorated by John Fowler in 'authentic' colours. Dry-scrubbed oak floors add to the authenticity.

Corsham Court, Wiltshire (Lord Methuen). An Elizabethan building (1582) with a magnificent picture gallery by Capability Brown (1760s). The windows, in correct style, have festoon curtains. The art collection, including two vast Van Dycks, is still virtually complete and many of the paintings have hung in the same arrangements for two hundred years. Two pier glasses by Robert Adam, and other good furniture in the state rooms, complete this splendid interior. The park was laid out by Brown and Repton.

Cragside, Northumberland (NT). Built in a haphazard manner, between 1864 and 1895, for Lord Armstrong, an armaments manufacturer. N. Shaw was the architect chiefly responsible, and the interior is a good example of the idealized domesticity of the period. Cragside was one of the first houses to have electric lighting.

Croxteth Hall, Merseyside (Merseyside County Museums). The house was badly affected by a fire in the 1950s. Nevertheles the kitchens of 1874, and the bathrooms of the same date, are well worth seeing. The rooms are furnished in the style of an Edwardian country house. The home farm has been restored and provides a good insight into how this aspect of the estate was managed.

Culzean Castle, Strathclyde (NT for Scotland). Robert Adam's finest Scottish house, completed in 1792. Perched on top of a high cliff above the sea, the site is both dramatic and romantic. The suite of rooms of entertainment shows the different, more relaxed social attitude from that of fifty years before. Much of the furniture, Chippendale and Sheraton, was made for the house.

Dyrham Park, Gloucestershire (NT). A late seventeenth-century rebuilding of a Tudor hall, added to by Talman (1700–4), and left untouched to this day. With furniture of the period 1690–1700, it provides an almost unique insight into the grand social life of *c.*1700. A state bed of considerable magnificence has outer draw curtains – not often seen – and the windows still have festoon curtains. It is a good example of a rich baroque interior. The once vast gardens, with a long canal, are now, unfortunately, a shadow of their former opulence.

Erddig, Clwyd (NT). This house offers a great deal; it is an example of how an eccentric family regarded their servants, and contains one of the finest surviving state beds with matching furnishings. The service rooms have been restored, the estate office looks as though the agent has just left the room, and the farm buildings, coach house, early motor cars and woodyard all give the impression that the Yorke family still lives at Erddig. The baroque gardens have been restored to their original layout.

Floors Castle, Borders (Duke of Roxburghe). This is the largest inhabited house in Britain, designed in 1721 by William Adam, the father of Robert, and altered and added to by Playfair in the 1840s. The suite of rooms of entertainment, dating from the 1840s, gives a clear insight into how the very grand entertained. The contents – tapestries, porcelain, paintings, and English and French furniture – are entirely suited to the taste of that period.

The Georgian House, Bristol (City of Bristol). A Georgian town house of the 1790s, furnished and decorated throughout in the fashionable colours of that period, which demonstrates how the rooms and furniture were used at the time. Smaller tables and chairs have been moved from the sides into the middle of the room, where they were then used, indicating that servants had, by that time, finally been relegated to attics and basements.

The Georgian House, Edinburgh (NT for Scotland). This is a genuine Adam house and the interior has been restored and furnished in the style of the period, even down to the dry-scrubbed wood floors. There is also a successful restoration of the basement kitchen.

Haddon Hall, Derbyshire (Duke of Rutland). A highly attractive medieval house, altered in the sixteenth century and restored in the 1930s. The great hall, parlour and great chamber have retained much of their original decoration. The kitchens contain good examples of sixteenth-century service furnishings. Two garderobes towers still stand in the lodgings of the lower court.

Ham House, Surrey (NT and Victoria and Albert Museum). Originally an H-shaped Jacobean house, built in 1610, with a great hall, parlour and great chamber on the first floor. The building was altered in the 1670s by the 1st Duke of Lauderdale and his wealthy wife, Elizabeth, into a floor plan suitable for a baroque courtier expecting to accommodate his monarch. Miraculously, the house has remained unaltered and much of the baroque furniture has survived; in addition, a surprising number of inventories have survived showing where the furniture used to stand. The interior has been restored to its original baroque colour scheme and the furniture put back in the rooms intended for it. The result is a unique example of baroque apartments on the ground floor, radiating from a central saloon and, on the first floor, of Jacobean rooms, adapted to a suite of royal state apartments.

Hampton Court Palace, London (Department of the Environment). Cardinal Wolsey built a very grand country house around two courtyards. Henry VIII took Hampton Court from his Cardinal and enlarged it; it has been a Royal Palace ever since. So much can be said about Hampton Court, but here only the state apartments need concern us. William III determined to rival Versailles at Hampton Court and created two ranges of apartments, one for himself and one for Queen Mary, who died in 1694 before they were completed. Today, we can see on the first floor of the south wing of the Cloister Court, overlooking the Privy Garden, the range of six rooms, culminating in the King's bed chamber, which made up William's apartments. The names have been changed but it is possible to work out their original purpose; what is now the Audience Chamber was the Withdrawing Room, occupying the prime position in the centre; the Ante-Room followed (now called the Withdrawing Room) and led into the Bed Chamber, with the Royal Closet, or Dressing Room, off it. In the Queen's apartments, the Bed Chamber is off the Withdrawing Room and the Ante-Room is dispensed with. Two canopies of state are preserved in the King's First and Second Presence Chambers. Originally, the first was the only Presence Chamber and the second was the Privy Chamber, used by William for private dining.

Hardwick Hall, Derbyshire (NT). Attributed to Robert Smythson, Hardwick was begun for Bess of Hardwick in 1590 and the interior had still not been completed by the time of her death in 1608. Hardwick Hall is the least altered of all the great Elizabethan houses. The Great Hall, although furnished with later tapestries and furnishings, has not been altered, apart from higher panelling installed by the 6th Duke of Devonshire in the nineteenth century. The family apartments remain in their original progressional order and the state apartments, on the top floor, include a High Great Chamber still with original hangings and amazing plaster frieze. The State Withdrawing Chamber still has some of the original furnishings, although the ceiling was lowered in the eighteenth century, and the State Bed Chamber has its original hangings. The Long Gallery, a magnificent room, also has the original hangings, but is now furnished with late seventeenth-century pieces. Hardwick is an experience not to be missed.

Harlaxton Manor, Lincolnshire (University of Evansville). Not the usual run-of-the-mill house open to the public; the Manor is now the European campus of a mid-West USA university. However, the building is being carefully restored and is the best example of the architect Salvin. It was built in 1835–57 to contain the collection of the eccentric Gregory Gregory. The collection has since been dispersed but part of it still remains in the interior. The main staircase is an astonishing confection of Austrian baroque revival.

Hatfield House, Hertfordshire (Marquis of Salisbury). Built in 1607–12 for Robert Cecil, Earl of Salisbury. Although, inevitably, altered in the nineteenth century, much of the original interior remains intact, and the original plan of state apartments for a member of the court circle is not difficult to discern. There is a good collection of Tudor portraits. Hatfield was lit by electricity in 1881.

Hever Castle, Kent (Broadlands Properties Ltd). Another example of the British heritage being rescued by American money. The thirteenth-century, double-moated Castle, childhood home of Anne Boleyn, was in a sad state when acquired by William Waldorf Astor in 1903. Astor set about its restoration with enthusiasm and the interior represents a splendid example of early twentieth-century wealthy living tempered by an historical awareness. Rather than spoil the Castle by adding to it, Astor had the guest rooms built as a village beyond the moat, so retaining something of the original impression of the Castle.

Holkham Hall, Norfolk (Viscount Coke). This statement of dynastic ambition was built for the 1st Earl of Leicester by what amounted to a committee of three, Leicester himself, Lord Burlington and Kent, between 1734 and 1761. The cost outran Leicester's funds and he died, before the house was completed, in debt. The project was financed and completed out of the profits of improved agriculture. Leicester conceived the plan for the house on his Grand Tour and the inspiration is from Palladio, consisting of a central block with four wings. The interior is much as Kent intended; the entrance hall is a dramatic piece of theatre, and the central saloon is hung with crimson velvet to match Kent's chairs. The rooms of parade conclude with the Green State Bed Chamber, containing Kent's state bed, covered in the original Genoese cut velvet, and *en suite* furniture. Paintings in the Landscape Room (originally the ante-room to the State Bed Chamber), like many others at

Holkham, are from Leicester's extended Grand Tour. The old kitchens have been successfully restored. Brown was responsible for the landscaping and there is an ice-house surviving not far from the house. The terraces are a nineteenth-century intrusion into Brown's original landscape.

Houghton Hall, Norfolk (Marquess of Cholmondeley). The house, begun in 1721, just pre-dates Holkham and was built for Robert Walpole, the Whig Prime Minister. It is an early example of the Whig taste for Palladianism. Campbell was employed as architect, but the four domes were added by Gibbs, and it was left to Kent to complete the interior. The basement was intended for 'hunters, hospitality, noise, dirt and business', while the *piano nobile* (the main floor above) was dedicated to 'taste, expense, state and parade', which explains the extravagant interior provided by Kent. The central saloon, with the state bed, represents one of Kent's finest achievements. The grounds were originally laid out by Bridgman and are an early example of the 'natural' landscape.

Hovingham Hall, North Yorkshire (Sir Marcus and Lady Worsley). For those who forget how important the horse was until this century, a visit to Hovingham will act as a timely reminder. A Palladian house, built in *c.*1745–55 by Thomas Worsley, the rooms of entertainment are directly over the stables and riding school. The ballroom, in the centre of the house, has an observation window into the riding school.

Ickworth, Suffolk (NT). This extraordinary architectural curiosity was never seen by its creator, the eccentric Earl of Bristol and Bishop of Derry, who died in Italy in 1803 and after whom so many Hotels Bristol are named. In its original conception, the Earl-Bishop intended to live in the grand central rotunda, taken from the much smaller rotunda, Belle Isle, in Windermere. His collection of paintings and sculpture was to be displayed in the radiating wings, connected to the main house by curving passages. The collection was unfortunately lost when Napoleon invaded Italy, and only some few fragments ever reached Ickworth. The house, unfinished in 1803, was left to the heirs to complete in the 1930s, and also contains some interiors of the 1870s by Crace. The staircase was never installed as intended and the interior of the dome is still unfinished: the Earl-Bishop's heirs found the cost of completion too high.

Ightham Moat, Kent (NT). One of the best examples of a moated manor house, dating, in parts, from the fourteenth century. It was much restored in the nineteenth century, but the fourteenth-century hall remains more or less as it was, and the chapel, with a heraldic painted ceiling of the 1520s, is typical of the period.

Kedleston Hall, Derbyshire (NT). Built between 1759 and 1765 for Sir Nathaniel Curzon in the true Palladian style by two successive architects, Brettingham and Paine, it was already an outmoded style by 1760 when neo-classicism was in fashion. Robert Adam, lately returned from Italy, finished the house, which has one of the most complete Adam interiors.

Kingston Lacey House, Dorset (NT). A seventeenth-century house, designed by Pratt, a follower of Inigo Jones, and similar in plan to Belton in that it originally had the bedrooms on the ground floor, as in most baroque houses. However, considerable alterations were carried out by Barry in the nineteenth century which changed the building inside and outside. The alterations should not be regretted, because William Bankes (1786–1855) was an inspired collector and we have gained the benefit of a splendid collection of paintings and furniture in a setting of the 1830s.

Knole, Kent (NT). Dating mainly from the fifteenth century, Knole is one of the largest private houses in England. Built by Archbishop Bouchier over a period of thirty years from 1456, and enlarged into a palace by Henry VIII, the estate was given by Queen Elizabeth I to the 1st Earl of Dorset, whose descendants still occupy flats in the house. This vast double courtyard house still has the great hall and range of baroque state apartments, which contain some astounding royal furniture procured by the 6th Earl of Dorset when he was Lord Chamberlain to William III. The house is unrivalled for the rarity and importance of its seventeenth-century furniture and textiles. These include noteworthy royal state beds with *en suite* furniture, one in silver, which is very rare since most others were melted down for their sterling worth.

Lacock Abbey, Wiltshire (NT). A good example of the conversion of a monastic to a domestic dwelling. The thirteenth-century Abbey was granted to William Sharrington in the 1530s. Sharrington demolished the Abbey church and converted the cloisters to make his house. Conversion of such buildings was always difficult, but undoubtedly Sharrington could not have made a better choice than Lacock. A small banqueting house in a roof tower contains an early example of English Renaissance taste: a small stone table supported by Greek gods and goddesses. In the room below, which was originally a muniment, or strong-room, is another stone table of similar design supported by four satyrs.

Lanhydrock House, Cornwall (NT). The house was built between 1630 and 1642 around a courtyard by a rich Truro merchant whose family became Barons Robartes, and Lanhydrock became the Great House of Cornwall. Now the yard is open on one side, giving a wide view from the main part of the house. The difference from the original house does not stop there; a serious fire in 1881 destroyed the entire interior apart from the Long Gallery, with the result that the house now contains a very comfortable interior of the 1880s, even down to shoes, hats and riding crops. The large service wing, added after the fire, is splendidly equipped with everything one could need to cater for a large Cornish household of the 1880s.

Leeds Castle, Kent (Leeds Castle Foundation). Called the 'most beautiful castle in England', Leeds justly deserves this accolade. Rising from two small islands in the middle of a lake, the building dates back to the twelfth century when it became a royal palace for three centuries. In 1926, Leeds was bought by the Hon. Lady Baillie, who restored and modernized the Castle. Lady Baillie's mother was one of the wealthy Whitneys; in her will the Castle was bequeathed to the Leeds Castle Foundation, the purpose of which is to preserve the Castle in perpetuity and provide a centre for medical research and the arts. A unique presentation of two rooms, with furnishings of *c.*1420, as they would have been for Catherine de Valois, Queen of Henry V, deserves applause.

Little Morton Hall, Cheshire (NT). A picturesque example of the Cheshire half-timber construction. The original unseasoned timber has warped under the strain of the weight, giving the impression that the building is about to fall apart. The great hall, the parlour of *c.*1480 and the long gallery of *c.*1580 have survived. Garderobe turrets discharge water into the surrounding moat.

Longleat, Wiltshire (Marquis of Bath). The building began life as a small medieval priory and was bought by Sir John Thynne in 1541. Thynne was in the process of enlarging the house when it was burnt down in 1567. He rebuilt it on a grander scale, which is what we see today, employing a Frenchman, Allen Maynard, and Robert Smythson as chief masons – Maynard was also probably the architect. The exterior of Longleat remains virtually unchanged from the 1580s and was the first Renaissance house in England. The interior was drastically altered in the nineteenth century, and of the original Tudor rooms only the great hall remains. J. Wyatville rearranged the interior in 1801–11, and the state apartments were redecorated by Crace in the 1870s. Why it was felt appropriate to have Venetian ceilings, copied from the Doge's Palace, in a large Wiltshire house is inexplicable, although, admittedly, it was in the best taste of the 1870s. There is much good French furniture in the state apartments, again in accordance with contemporary taste of the 1870s. There is also a good restoration of a large kitchen of the period.

Lower Brockhampton Hall, Herefordshire (NT). A small half-timbered manor house of *c.*1400, with its open hall intact.

Montacute House, Somerset (NT). Built in 1598 for Sir Edward Phelips, a West Country lawyer, the house is an example of provincial Elizabethan architecture at its best. The garden has two banqueting houses and the great hall and long gallery are unaltered. The house's original layout was turned back to front when the façade from Clifton Milbank, of the 1540s, was added.

Newby Hall, North Yorkshire (R. E. J. Compton Esq). Originally paid for by profits from coal, the house was built in the 1690s for Sir Edward Blackett. It had the familiar baroque floor plan of entrance hall, saloon, withdrawing rooms and bed chambers in the wings. William Weddell bought the Hall in 1748, and his descendants have lived here ever since. Between 1770 and 1780 Weddell employed Adam to redesign the interior and to add two wings to the rectangular house. Although there has been some inevitable moving of furniture and additions to the contents, and although the dining room was altered into a library, it still remains a complete Adam interior on the ground floor. The Adam Sculpture Gallery contains sculpture brought back by William Weddell from Italy on his Grand Tour.

Newstead Abbey, Nottinghamshire (Nottingham City Council). The thirteenth-century Priory of Newstead was bought in 1540 by Sir John Byron, who followed the example of Lacock – he demolished the Priory church and converted the cloisters into his living quarters. By a stroke of genius Byron left the façade of the church standing, which gives an unrivalled panorama of the building. Lord Byron, the poet, sold the estate in 1818 and the building and interior were restored; it was restored again later in the century, creating an interior that has little to do with the medieval priory it once was. Appropriately, Newstead contains the finest museum of Byronia.

Obsorne House, Isle of Wight (English Heritage). Built for Queen Victoria and Prince Albert as their summer home, Osborne has remained unaltered inside since Prince Albert's death in 1861. Furnishings, decoration and fittings are of the highest quality, and Prince Albert's bathroom alone is worth a visit.

Osterley Park, London (NT and Victoria and Albert Museum). Little remains of the original building, built round three sides of a courtyard in the late 1570s, because it was completely altered in the late 1750s for a wealthy banker, Robert Child. The interior and grand portico of the late 1570s are by Adam. The interior has been very successfully restored to the original Adam decorative scheme and the furniture of the Great Apartment in the south wing is in its original setting.

Penshurst Place, Kent (Lord De L'Isle). One of the best surviving examples of a large medieval house. The great hall, with central hearth, screen passage, minstrels' gallery, buttery and pantry – the kitchen has gone – dates from the 1340s. The Great Chamber is now the state dining room. The panelled Long Gallery dates from 1599 and was restored some fifty years ago, when a fake Jacobean ceiling was inserted. The house contains a collection of Elizabethan portraits and fine furniture from the sixteenth, seventeenth and eighteenth centuries. Penshurst provides a good example of the compromises necessary when a private house, which is still occupied by the family, is opened to the public.

Polesdon Lacey, Surrey (NT). The earlier history of this house, which began as a Regency villa built in the 1820s, was totally eclipsed in 1906 when it was bought by the Hon. Ronnie Greville and his wife, who is best known as an Edwardian hostess and friend of the King. The house was added to and the interior completely modernized and furnished by Mrs Greville, and today presents a good picture of Edwardian society. Wide passages prevented loaded servants meeting head-on; they could circulate discreetly by alternative routes without encountering guests. Edward VII was entertained in this house and King George VI and Queen Elizabeth, then Duke and Duchess of York, spent part of their honeymoon here in 1923.

Powis Castle, Powys (NT). This medieval stronghold of Welsh princes became the home of the Herberts in 1547; they have lived there ever since. The interior has been adapted to changing social demands. However, the late seventeenth-century state bed remains as it was installed, situated behind a balustered rail – a lone survivor of what was once a useful feature. The eighteenth-century ballroom is also a rare survivor. Clive of India married into the Herbert family and there is a Clive of India Museum here. The interior was altered in the eighteenth century and again in the late nineteenth century. The steep gardens, made on terraces, provide an example of the late seventeenth-century fashion for Italian gardens.

Rousham House, Oxfordshire (C. Cottrell-Dormer Esq). The grey stone house was built in *c.*1635 in the common E-shaped plan. In 1738, W. Kent added to the house and decorated the interior. The painted parlour has a Kent ceiling, decorated in an early use of the 'grotesques' style. The garden, laid out by Kent, is justly the best known of Rousham's attractions: it is an early example of the 'natural' garden, using curves in place of the geometric shapes nature had been made to conform to previously. The garden is surprisingly small when compared with the vast spaces Brown contended with later.

Stokesay Castle, Shropshire (Sir Philip and Lady Magnus-Allcroft). Not a castle but a fortified manor house. The great hall, of 1270–80, with unglazed windows providing access for birds and an earth floor, offers a good example of medieval living standards.

Sudbury Hall, Shropshire (NT). Built in 1662–1700, the interior has the richest Charles II decoration in England. Grinling Gibbons contributed much of the carving. The National Trust has restored the decoration to its 'authentic' pastel colours. The park has a 'gothick' deercote.

Syon House, London (Duke of Northumberland). Built as a large court-yard house, incorporating a fifteenth-century nunnery, by the Duke of Somerset in 1547, the whole building was remodelled inside and out by Adam for the 1st Duke of Northumberland in 1769. The result is a splendid succession of rooms of entertainment with contrasting decorative schemes. Today we can walk through the rooms along the route intended by Adam, and experience the changing shapes and contrasting colours that his contemporaries would have appreciated. Syon is classed as one of Adam's best works.

Tattershall Castle, Lincolnshire (NT). The first castle was built in 1231 and acquired by Ralph Cromwell, Lord Treasurer of England, who built the high brick great tower and constructed an outer moat between 1430 and 1450. Here is an example of apartments of state placed one above the other, rather than horizontally as at Haddon Hall. The buildings were restored by Lord Curzon in 1911.

Traquair House, Borders (P. Maxwell Stuart Esq). The oldest inhabited house in Scotland, originally a royal hunting lodge, it dates mainly from the sixteenth and seventeenth century. Traquair contains a good collection of seventeenth-century needlework, an early eighteenth-century state bed, letters written by Mary Queen of Scots and a working brewery.

Waddesdon Manor, Buckinghamshire (NT). Baron Ferdinand de Rothschild bought the hillside in 1874 and waved a magic wand. The result was a French château by Destailleur, a mature park, and a luxurious interior filled with treasures, mainly French. Apart from the contents, which take many visits to appreciate, the rooms provide a background to the way in which a very rich banker and his leisured family lived. It requires little imagination to fill in the picture. The present-day tea room is in the old kitchens and servants' hall.

Wightwick Manor, West Midlands (NT). An example of 'new money' used with taste. Built in the 1890s for Theodore Mander, a paint manufacturer, the interior is one of the best examples of the work of Morris & Co. and of the 'advanced' taste of the 1890s.

Wilton House, Wiltshire (Earl of Pembroke). Of the Tudor house built by the 1st Earl of Pembroke, only the gatehouse is visible on the east front. The south front was designed in *c.*1636 by de Caux, advised by the Royal Architect, Jones, and in this wing are the deservedly famous state rooms which, after a serious fire in 1647, were restored by J. Webb, one of Jones's pupils. They are the most splendid pre-Restoration interiors in England; particularly notable are the single and double cube rooms. The Van Dyck portraits are mounted in the wall panelling, where they have been since the 1650s, and are a unique example of the taste of the time. J. Wyatt 'gothicized' some of the interiors in 1801 and changed the north and west wings.

Wimpole Hall, Cambridgeshire (NT). The main block was built by 1670 and 'improved' for Lord Hardwicke in the 1790s; the wings were added in the 1720s. The park is a case history of English landscaping from 1590 up to 1830 and includes work by Brown and Repton. The home farm provides a good example of how food was provided for the household of a grand family.

Picture Credits

Index